JEFFREY J. SCHOTT
assisted by JOHANNA W. BUURMAN

THE URUGUAY ROUND
An Assessment

Institute for International Economics
Washington, DC
November 1994

Jeffrey J. Schott, *Senior Fellow*, was a Senior Associate at the Carnegie Endowment for International Peace (1982–83) and an International Economist at the US Treasury (1974–82). He is coauthor of *Western Hemisphere Economic Integration* (1994), *NAFTA: An Assessment* (rev. 1993), *North American Free Trade: Issues and Recommendations* (1992), *Completing the Uruguay Round* (1990), *Economic Sanctions Reconsidered* (Second edition 1990), *Free Trade Areas and US Trade Policy* (1989), *The Canada–United States Free Trade Agreement: The Global Impact* (1988), *Auction Quotas and US Trade Policy* (1987), and *Trading for Growth: The Next Round of Trade Negotiations* (1985).

Johanna W. Buurman, Research Assistant at the Institute, is a graduate of the Georgetown University Graduate School of Foreign Service and of Nijenrode Business School in the Netherlands.

INSTITUTE FOR INTERNATIONAL
ECONOMICS
11 Dupont Circle, NW
Washington, DC 20036-1207
(202) 328-9000   FAX: (202) 328-0900

Cover design by Michelle M. Fleitz
Typesetting by Automated Graphic Systems
Printing by Automated Graphic Systems

Printed in the United States of America
97 96 95 94   5 4 3 2 1

Library of Congress Cataloging-in-Publication Data

Schott, Jeffrey J., 1949–
    The Uruguay round : an assessment / Jeffrey J. Schott.
    p. cm
    Includes bibliographical references and index.
    1. General Agreement on Tariffs and Trade (Organization)   2. Uruguay Round (1987–   )   3. Foreign trade regulation.   4. Dispute resolution (Law)   5. Commercial policy.
    I. Title.
HF1713.S38   1994   94-5627
382'.92—dc20   CIP

ISBN 0-88132-206-7

Marketed and Distributed outside the USA and Canada by Longman Group UK Limited, London

The views expressed in this publication are those of the authors. This publication is part of the overall program of the Institute, as endorsed by its Board of Directors, but does not necessarily reflect the views of individual members of the Board or the Advisory Committee.

Contents

List of Figures

Box

Preface

The Institute for International Economics has devoted extensive attention to the global trading system throughout the history of its research program. The second conference that we held, and second set of publications that we released, addressed *Trade Policy in the 1980s* at a time when there was considerable disarray in the system (1982–83). At the request of USTR William Brock, we prepared one of the initial blueprints for the Uruguay Round in *Trading for Growth: The Next Round of Trade Negotiations* (1985). We analyzed three of the key issues in the talks in *Subsidies in International Trade* (1984), *Agriculture and the GATT: Rewriting the Rules* (1987), and *The Future of World Trade in Textiles and Apparel* (1987, 2nd ed. 1990). Jeffrey Schott offered a midcourse assessment and recommendations for closing the deal in *Completing the Uruguay Round: A Results-Oriented Approach to the GATT Trade Negotiations* (1990).

This volume seeks to complete the process by appraising both the individual components of the final Uruguay Round package and the aggregate impact of the overall bargain. It follows the model that the Institute has developed in analyzing the results of other recent trade negotiations involving the United States: *United States–Canada Free Trade: An Evaluation of the Agreement* (Jeffrey J. Schott, 1988) and *NAFTA: An Assessment* (by Gary C. Hufbauer and Jeffrey J. Schott, 1993). We hope that this study, like its predecessors, will help inform both Congressional approval of the agreement and understanding of it by the broader public.

The Institute for International Economics is a private nonprofit institution for the study and discussion of international economic policy. Its purpose is to analyze important issues in that area and to develop and communicate practical new approaches for dealing with them. The Institute is completely nonpartisan.

The Institute is funded largely by philanthropic foundations. Major institutional grants are now being received from the German Marshall Fund of the United States, which created the Institute with a generous commitment of funds in 1981, and from the Ford Foundation, the William and Flora Hewlett Foundation, the William M. Keck, Jr. Foundation, the Andrew Mellon Foundation, the C. V. Starr Foundation, and the United States–Japan Foundation. A number of other foundations and private corporations also contribute to the highly diversified financial resources of the Institute. The Dayton Hudson Foundation provides support for the Institute's program of studies on trade policy. Cargill Inc. provided partial support for this project. About 12 percent of the Institute's resources in our latest fiscal year were provided by contributors outside the United States, including about 5 percent from Japan.

The Board of Directors bears overall responsibility for the Institute and gives general guidance and approval to its research program—including identification of topics that are likely to become important to international economic policymakers over the medium run (generally, one to three years), and which thus should be addressed by the Institute. The Director, working closely with the staff and outside Advisory Committee, is responsible for the development of particular projects and makes the final decision to publish an individual study.

The Institute hopes that its studies and other activities will contribute to building a stronger foundation for international economic policy around the world. We invite readers of these publications to let us know how they think we can best accomplish this objective.

C. FRED BERGSTEN
Director
October 1994

Acknowledgments

The authors would like to thank Robert Baldwin, C. Fred Bergsten, Julius Katz, Patrick Messerlin, and Soogil Young for their insightful comments on earlier drafts of the entire manuscript. The authors also benefitted from extremely useful comments on specific sections of the manuscript by Robert Hudec, Gary Clyde Hufbauer, John Jackson, Marcus Noland, J. David Richardson, David Robertson, and David Walters. Thanks are also due to Carol Gabyzon, Albert Kim, and Marie-Helene Le Manchec for their valuable research assistance. We especially appreciate the work of Michael Treadway, who carefully edited the text, as well as Faith Hunter, Brigitte Coulton, Valerie Norville, and Christine Flint Lowry for their tireless efforts in publishing the book.

Overview

The Uruguay Round was the eighth in a series of multilateral trade negotiations held under the auspices of the General Agreement on Tariffs and Trade (GATT). The negotiations were launched by a ministerial declaration issued at Punta del Este, Uruguay, in September 1986 (hence the "Uruguay Round.") In late 1993, after seven years of hard bargaining, the negotiators produced more than 400 pages of detailed trade agreements, supplemented by more than 22,000 pages containing schedules of commitments by member nations regarding access to their markets for specific goods and service sectors. The agreements were signed in Marrakesh, Morocco, in April 1994 and are expected to enter into force on 1 January 1995.[1]

This book is designed as a user-friendly guide through the dense maze of trading rules and market access commitments concluded in the Uruguay Round. The Uruguay Round agenda was comprehensive and encompassed both familiar areas, some of which have long been resistant to reform (e.g., agriculture and textiles), and new issues such as trade in services and trade-related intellectual property and investment measures. Not surprisingly, the negotiations turned out to be more complex and convoluted than those in previous rounds. The objective of this study is to translate the complex legal texts into plain English, to highlight the results that have the most significant economic implications for world trade and the world trading system, and to assess the success of the round as a whole.

---

1. The Marrakesh Declaration adopted on 15 April 1994 notes that signatories "commit themselves to seek to complete all steps necessary to ratify the WTO [World Trade Organization] Agreement so that it can enter into force by 1 January 1995 or as early as possible thereafter." The final decision on the start date for the WTO is expected to be made in December 1994.

The analysis is divided into three parts. This first part provides an overview of the negotiations, summarizes the principal results and their broad economic effects, and reviews the extensive agenda of issues for which negotiations are ongoing or will be initiated by the year 2000.

The second part of the book provides a detailed assessment of the main components of the Uruguay Round package. It analyzes the agreements concluded in 13 major areas of the negotiations, examines their implications for the United States and for the world trading system, and assesses their overall impact.

The third part summarizes in tabular form the key provisions of each agreement and compares the results with those recommended in the Institute's earlier study, *Completing the Uruguay Round* (Schott 1990), which was prepared in anticipation of the projected conclusion of the negotiations in December 1990. This part is designed to be a quick reference guide to the Uruguay Round results discussed in more detail in the second part of the book.

The book also includes two appendices: appendix A summarizes key aspects of the US implementing legislation, and appendix B summarizes the findings of computable general equilibrium models by other authors that project the economic effects of the Uruguay Round reforms.

A Brief Negotiating History

The Uruguay Round was conceived at a time when global recession and the subsequent debt crisis in developing countries were threatening to unravel the results of the just-completed Tokyo Round (1973–79). World trade declined in both value and volume terms in 1981–82 and only slowly recovered in the remainder of the first half of the decade.

In 1982 the United States proposed the initiation of a new round of GATT talks to blunt protectionist pressures generated by the strengthening dollar and mounting US job losses; to reinforce domestic efforts to cut agricultural and other subsidies; and to enhance access to foreign markets for US suppliers. In addition, the proposal for new GATT talks sought to reverse the erosion of support for the multilateral trading system and to bring the GATT up to date by extending its coverage to areas of international trade of growing importance that were not yet subject to existing provisions. The harvest of the Tokyo Round had been bountiful, but incomplete. Agriculture and textiles had been essentially exempted from liberalization, safeguards negotiations had broken down, and participation in the new codes governing nontariff barriers, particularly by developing countries, was very limited.

Finally, the United States regarded a new round as a means to integrate the developing countries more effectively into the world trading system. Special exemptions or preferences designed to protect their nascent industries meant that little was demanded of developing countries in the way of trade reform. This "special and differential treatment" often proved counterproductive to the growth of their trade and investment, however, and seemed distinctly inappropriate for the newly industrializing countries, which had become increasingly competitive in a broad range of traditional and high-technology products. The fact that the GATT ministerial meeting that eventually launched the new round was held in Uruguay underscored the importance of this goal and the focus of what was then thought to be principally a North-South negotiation.

The US proposal to launch a new GATT round met scant support at the 1982 GATT ministerial. As a result, US negotiators turned instead to bilateral arrangements with Israel and Canada to leverage international support for the new GATT talks, to provide building blocks for future GATT accords (especially in new areas such as services), and to maintain domestic support for an open trade policy in the face of growing protectionist pressures in Congress (Destler 1994).

Developing countries initially resisted the US-led initiative because they feared that reforms of longstanding merchandise trade barriers to their exports would be deferred if the GATT took on a new agenda. By the time of the Punta del Este meeting, however, a broad coalition of developed and developing countries had recognized the need to pursue multilateral trade liberalization, both to complement domestic economic policy reforms and to counter the growing trend in the United States and Europe toward unilateral actions and the negotiation of preferential trading arrangements.

The expected North-South focus never really emerged in the talks, in large part because of the dramatic economic policy reforms undertaken in Latin America and other developing countries during the 1980s. Many of the trade reforms that were initially the objective of the GATT negotiations were implemented unilaterally by developing countries in the context of their domestic economic programs and well before the conclusion of the Geneva talks. Although these reforms facilitated acceptance of the Uruguay Round accords, they were designed primarily to improve the efficiency and productivity of domestic industries so that they could better compete both abroad for new export markets and at home against foreign suppliers. In other words, the ongoing GATT negotiations were not the driving force behind the domestic reforms, but they did reinforce the reforms' basic goals.

As a result, a broad coalition of developed and developing countries evolved in support of new global trade talks. At the Punta del Este meeting, hard-core opposition by Brazil, India, and a few other developing countries gave way to a compromise that approved an extensive agenda for new GATT negotiations comprising both traditional and "new" trade issues. Fifteen working groups were established, and trade officials were charged with completing the negotiations by the end of 1990.

During the period 1986–90, the progress of the GATT negotiations reflected the maxim that "the best is the enemy of the good." Efforts to seek drastic reforms in current policies promoted a dialogue of the deaf, especially in agriculture where US demands for zero subsidies were met by equally intransigent demands by the European Community that its Common Agricultural Policy (CAP) remain essentially intact. The resulting impasse hampered the ability to agree on meaningful, if incomplete, reforms across the range of issues on the Uruguay Round agenda.

Unlike in previous GATT rounds, however, other countries refused to let US-EC farm trade disputes scuttle the agricultural negotiations. A strong coalition of 14 agricultural exporting countries, the Cairns Group,[2] insisted that the Uruguay Round achieve substantial reduction in farm subsidies, and linked their support for reforms in other areas such as services with progress on agriculture.

Evidence of the debilitating influence of the agriculture dispute became clear during the midterm review of the Uruguay Round negotiations in Montreal in December 1988. The Montreal meeting was designed to take stock of the progress to date and to achieve an "early harvest" of accords to give momentum to the ongoing negotiations. Disputes over agriculture, textiles, intellectual property, and safeguards blocked progress in Montreal and forced the review to be suspended until April 1989, when the United States and the European Community agreed to a procedural arrangement for continuing negotiations on agricultural reforms. Nonetheless, the midterm review did achieve several notable results, including interim reforms of GATT dispute settlement procedures, the provisional introduction of a new trade policy review mechanism, and commitments to reduce tariffs on average by about one-third.

The April 1989 understanding on agriculture soon dissipated. New proposals put forward in 1990 by Aart de Zeeuw and Mats Hellström failed to bridge the gap.[3] The stalemate over agriculture ultimately provoked the collapse of the GATT ministerial meeting in Brussels in December 1990 and prevented the scheduled conclusion of the Uruguay Round.

In December 1991 GATT Director General Arthur Dunkel compiled a comprehensive draft agreement consisting of the texts of existing agreements reached ad referendum during the first five years of the talks and proposed compromises for those areas, including agriculture, where agreement had not yet been reached. However, the so-called Dunkel text suffered from a crucial omission: it did not include most of the market access commitments in areas such as tariffs, services, and government

---

2. The Cairns Group was founded in 1986 by Argentina, Australia, Brazil, Canada, Chile, Colombia, Fiji, Hungary, Indonesia, Malaysia, New Zealand, the Philippines, Thailand, and Uruguay.

3. De Zeeuw, a former Dutch government official, chaired the GATT negotiating group on agriculture in Geneva. Hellström, the Swedish agriculture minister, headed up the farm talks at the Brussels ministerial.

procurement, which by their nature had to be scheduled in specific terms by each country. Nonetheless, the Dunkel text established a draft framework for the final stage of negotiations in 1992–93. In the end, a large part of the Dunkel text survived with surprisingly few changes.

The final two years of the Uruguay Round were marked by numerous lapses in the negotiations, due primarily to EC problems in forging an internal consensus on CAP reform but also in part to election campaigns in North America, Europe, and Japan. Apart from the Blair House accord (November 1992), which narrowed important differences between the US and European positions on agriculture, scant progress was made on substantive issues. Despite frequent meetings of trade ministers from the so-called Quad group (the United States, the European Community, Japan, and Canada), which sought to produce a consensus among the major players, and despite hortatory declarations by heads of government at the Group of Seven (G-7) summits extolling the importance of a GATT deal, it took another US initiative to spur the final efforts needed to conclude the talks.

US President Bill Clinton essentially set the final deadline for the Uruguay Round by requesting in the spring of 1993 that Congress renew US "fast-track" negotiating authority only for a limited period, until 15 December 1993. This action heightened the risk that the United States would actually walk away from the talks if this deadline were passed without an agreement, since it seemed unlikely that the Clinton administration could go back to the Congress for yet another extension of fast-track authority for the Uruguay Round.

Meanwhile, Clinton's initiatives in a different forum, that of the Asia Pacific Economic Cooperation (APEC), also provoked concerns in Europe that the United States would pursue regional alternatives to the GATT. APEC members (essentially all the countries of the Pacific Rim) represent a large subset of the global trade community, accounting for about half of world GDP and 40 percent of world exports. The success of the APEC ministerial meeting in Seattle in November 1993 demonstrated to European trade officials that the United States and its Asian partners had an attractive alternative they could pursue if the GATT talks continued to drift.

Prodded by a demanding new GATT director general, Peter Sutherland, the United States and the European Union engaged in intensive negotiations in the first half of December 1993. These efforts culminated in compromises on agriculture and antidumping issues that received tepid support from other countries, left the agreement on textiles in the Dunkel text essentially intact, and provided the basis for acceptance in April 1994 of the overall package of Uruguay Round agreements.

A Uruguay Round Scorecard

Table 1 summarizes the results of the negotiations in the key areas of the Uruguay Round agenda. The table groups thirteen subjects of the talks

Table 1   Scorecard: Uruguay Round results[a]

Area	Grade
Trade liberalization (25 percent)	
Agriculture	B+
Textiles and apparel	B+
Tariffs	A−
Government procurement	A−
Trade rules (25 percent)	
Antidumping	C+
Subsidies and countervailing measures	A−
Safeguards (including balance of payments safeguards)	B
New issues (25 percent)	
Services	B+
Investment	B−
Intellectual property	B+
Institutional issues (25 percent)	
Dispute settlement	A
World Trade Organization	B+
Trade policy review mechanism	B+
Final Grade	**B+**

a. Grades are based on the standard of how well the negotiators met the recommendations prescribed by the author in *Completing the Uruguay Round* (Schott 1990) for the most feasible and desirable outcome in each area.

under four main headings: trade liberalization, trade rules, new issues, and institutional issues. Some areas overlap—in particular, trade liberalization in the "new issues" of trade in services—but overall these four categories capture the essence of the negotiated results. Each category is accorded equal weight in the assessment, and each subject is accorded equal weight within its category.[4] The outcome in each area is graded on a scale from A (excellent) to F (failure); scores of B and C indicate results that contain worthwhile provisions but notable flaws as well.

Overall, the Uruguay Round agreements earn a respectable grade of B+. This final grade recognizes a job well done, but acknowledges that additional work needs to be done in many areas to strengthen world trade rules and to promote trade and investment in goods and services.

All of the grades are subjective and depend importantly on the standard or baseline against which the negotiated outcome is judged. The standard adopted here is conformity of the results with the recommendations prescribed by the author in mid-1990 (Schott 1990) in anticipation of the round's originally scheduled conclusion by December of that year. Those recommendations took stock of the first four years of negotiations and proposed compromises that would produce the most economically desir-

---

4. This scheme somewhat overstates the importance of the trade policy review mechanism and government procurement results but does not bias the overall grade.

able result possible, given the political demands on the key negotiators and the constraints imposed by the negotiating history.

Of course, other standards could have been used. For example, one could gauge whether the results in each area represent net improvements from the status quo ante, both in economic terms and in terms of strengthening the world trading system. In almost all respects, the Uruguay Round strengthened the multilateral trading rules and advanced the process of trade liberalization. By this standard the new accords would receive very high marks. Even higher grades would be awarded if one took into consideration what might have happened if the round had failed (see below). The only area where a positive result would be open to question is antidumping (on which more will be said shortly).

Another approach to standard-setting would examine how well the results of the round met the objectives put forward in the Punta del Este Declaration, or in the US Omnibus Trade and Competitiveness Act of 1988. However, unlike the comprehensive recommendations used as the standard in this assessment, both these sources set forth broad-based objectives that are generally qualitative in nature and lack much detail.

Finally, one could judge the Uruguay Round results against the most rigorous academic standard, that of pure, unfettered free trade. On this basis the negotiated outcome falls well short. But the pure free trade standard is too harsh for a global trade deal—eliminating trade barriers among two or three countries is hard enough; among 125 countries it is an Olympian task! Suffice it to say that the GATT negotiators made a great deal of progress in the Uruguay Round, but much remains to be done to open markets and strengthen world trading rules.

The Uruguay Round Results

Overall, the Uruguay Round produced a rich array of accords that should open substantial new trading opportunities, strengthen world trading rules, and reinforce the institutional foundation of the world trading system. The Uruguay Round agreements are not perfect: all countries, including the United States, resisted lowering their most politically sensitive trade barriers. But the accords do break down many longstanding restrictions that had impeded trade for decades.

The success of the GATT talks is important both for what it achieves *and* for what it forestalls. Failure or continued drift of the Uruguay Round would have resulted in undesirable changes in the trade policies of major industrial countries.

First, the conclusion of the Uruguay Round halts the erosion in confidence in the multilateral trading rules and removes uncertainty about the future course of trade policy by the major trading countries. In particular, it lays to rest the concern that a breakdown in the GATT talks could have led to a sharp growth in unilateralism on the part of both the United States and the European Union.

A second, related point is that the Uruguay Round accords restore credibility to the multilateral negotiating process. Here again, if the Uruguay Round had failed, or merely continued to drift without resolution, countries would have turned to other means to work out trade problems. Besides unilateral actions, attention would have refocused on bilateral and regional trade talks as substitutes, not complements, for the multilateral negotiations—just as it did on several occasions in the past few years when the GATT talks seemed on the verge of collapse. Instead, the success of the Uruguay Round revitalizes the multilateral process and reinforces efforts to ensure that ongoing regional initiatives complement rather than conflict with the multilateral system.

Third, the agreement will help control protectionist pressures in the United States (and elsewhere) by opening up new export opportunities around the globe. Given the sharp increase in the US merchandise trade deficit, which reached about $130 billion in 1993 and is likely to soar to a record level of $160 billion in 1994, protectionist pressures in the Congress could have bubbled to the boiling point and threatened the introduction of new import restrictions if the Uruguay Round had failed.

The following sections summarize under four broad categories the results for the main agreements concluded in the Uruguay Round. Each accord is analyzed in more detail in the second part of the study.

Trade Liberalization

In the category of trade liberalization, the Uruguay Round accords achieved significant success in such "traditional" areas as agriculture and textiles that had long been resistant to reform, cut tariffs on average by almost 40 percent, and expanded access to the government procurement markets of selected countries.[5] Although many saw the negotiations as focusing more on trade rules than on trade liberalization, the results in the four areas within the latter category were surprisingly strong and deserve grades of B+ and A−.

The agreements on agriculture and textiles both merit a grade of B+ for reversing decades of hard-core sectoral protection. The agreement on agriculture requires significant reductions in export subsidies and modest cuts in domestic subsidies over a six-year period, and transforms nontariff barriers into equally restrictive but more transparent tariffs, which are then subject to an average cut of 36 percent. In addition, tariff-rate quotas

---

5. Although formally separate from the Uruguay Round negotiations, the revision of the existing government procurement code proceeded in tandem with the round, and the new agreement will be one of four plurilateral pacts under the World Trade Organization and subject to its dispute settlement process.

are established to provide minimum access for imports that have up to now been all but excluded from certain markets (e.g., Japanese and Korean imports of rice), and new guidelines are set out regarding the trade effects of sanitary and phytosanitary measures that will prevent these regulations from serving protectionist objectives. The new obligations exempt some important income support programs of the United States and the European Union, but nonetheless establish for the first time significant multilateral disciplines on trade-distorting farm programs.

In textiles the Uruguay Round reforms signal the death knell for the Multi-Fiber Arrangement (MFA) by setting a 10-year phaseout of bilateral quotas negotiated under the MFA umbrella. However, many countries will retain substantial tariff protection, and the most restrictive quotas will not be removed until the very end of the transition period, in 2005. Moreover, during the transition period countries will be able to invoke special safeguards to blunt import surges and to constrain the growth of remaining quotas already subject to strict limits under existing bilateral agreements.

The tariff package receives a grade of A- for achieving cuts larger (in percentage terms) than those agreed in the Kennedy and Tokyo rounds, for binding maximum rates for about 60 percent of developing country products and almost all industrial country tariffs, and for expanding the scope of duty-free trade. Overall, tariffs will be cut by a trade-weighted average of almost 40 percent, and major trading countries will eliminate them altogether for a number of product sectors (e.g., pharmaceuticals) as a result of the so-called zero-for-zero sectoral negotiations.

The new Government Procurement Agreement also receives an A- for opening access to a broad range of government contracts worth hundreds of billions of dollars, and for extending the coverage of its obligations to certain specified services and to subnational entities. Most of these commitments have been extended on a reciprocal basis and do not necessarily apply to all signatories. The agreement is one of the few WTO accords that does not require universal membership, and the number of countries participating in the pact remains quite limited. However, the agreement provides a strong foundation for extending the reforms to new sectors (including those recently the subject of US-Japan disputes) and new members.

Trade Rules

In the area of trade rules, which comprises accords relating to unfair trade practices (antidumping and subsidies) and import safeguards, the results are mixed. The Uruguay Round produced useful results in the areas of subsidies and import safeguards but did little to assuage concern about the abuse of unfair trade laws such as antidumping. Overall, the agreements in this area receive an average grade of B.

The antidumping agreement contains some procedural improvements (such as the sunset clause and de minimis provisions) but also adds some arbitrary methodological rules, relating to the calculation of dumping margins and the determination of injury, that only reinforce concerns about "process protectionism."[6] Despite the political clamor provoked by this accord, it mitigates neither exporters' and consumers' concerns about the overzealous use of antidumping statutes, nor the concerns of import-competing industries about dumped imports and circumvention of dumping duties.

In brief, the accord adds new layers of arbitrary rules to the administration of antidumping laws. Some industries will find it somewhat easier, and others somewhat more difficult, to obtain import relief against unfair foreign trade practices, but overall the impact of the changes on existing practices should be small. On economic criteria alone, the accord deserves low marks; on the political economy criteria adopted by this study, the antidumping accord receives a grade of C +, the lowest given any agreement in the Uruguay Round.

In contrast, the Agreement on Subsidies and Countervailing Measures improves upon the existing Tokyo Round accord. The new accord strengthens the GATT's antisubsidy rules, expands the list of proscribed practices, and creates a safe haven for certain "desirable" subsidies that support research and development, pollution control investments, and regional development programs not targeted on specific industries. In addition, the agreement establishes for the first time strong disciplines on the export subsidies of developing countries after a short transition period. Although concerns have been raised about the potential for expanding subsidies in the "nonactionable" categories, the new accord allows countermeasures against these practices if the subsidies cause serious adverse trade effects. Overall, the accord strengthens multilateral disciplines in this important area and merits a grade of A −.

The agreement on import safeguards, or escape clause actions, deserves high praise for its ban on the use of voluntary export restraints, the most pernicious form of import protection applied over the past two decades. Nonetheless, countries maintain a limited right to impose other selective safeguards. The new accord provides new incentives for the use of safeguard measures (e.g., by waiving retaliation rights for the first three years), but these provisions do not appear to overcome the incentives to resort to other GATT rules to seek import relief—by simply raising tariffs up to levels bound in the GATT, or by invoking balance of payments safeguards, or by resorting to unilateral action under unfair trade laws. On balance, the safeguards accord improves the body of GATT rules but is

---

6. Not surprisingly, US legislation implementing the Uruguay Round focuses heavily on amending US antidumping law to incorporate the changes required by this agreement. See appendix A.

likely to have little impact on the actual use of safeguards; accordingly, it receives a grade of B.

New Issues

The Uruguay Round broke new ground by broadening the coverage of world trade rules to important areas never before subject to effective multilateral discipline: notably trade in services, trade-related aspects of intellectual property rights, and trade-related investment measures. Agreements in these areas were more successful in developing trading rules than in enhancing market access opportunities, but in all three cases a firm foundation was laid for future negotiations. Accordingly, this category receives a strong B as the average grade.

The new General Agreement on Trade in Services (GATS) establishes pathbreaking rules to govern the almost $1 trillion in world services trade; these rules are in many respects comparable to the GATT rules for trade in goods. However, national treatment is afforded only when countries undertake specific market access commitments. The GATS is comprised of three interrelated parts: a framework of principles to guide the formulation of national laws, policies, and regulations and to ensure that foreign suppliers can access markets and receive national treatment; annexes that describe how those principles apply to specific sectors; and commitments to liberalize existing barriers to trade.

Efforts to liberalize barriers to services trade in particular sectors achieved only mixed results. More than 80 countries put forward offers regarding market access in specified service sectors, and bilateral negotiations continue to try to improve offers, particularly in the financial services, maritime, and telecommunications sectors. On balance, the GATS deserves a grade of B +: the framework of rules developed in the GATS, coupled with market access commitments that in some sectors (e.g., professional services) are quite extensive, provides a solid foundation for the future evolution of world trade disciplines in this area.

The agreement on trade-related aspects of intellectual property rights (TRIPs) establishes new trade disciplines with regard to patents, trademarks, copyrights, and trade secrets that supplement existing intellectual property conventions administered primarily by the World Intellectual Property Organization. In contrast to those conventions, however, the TRIPs accord sets out extensive obligations for the enforcement of property rights both at the border and within the domestic market. The Uruguay Round accord also covers newer forms of intellectual property such as semiconductor layout designs and biotechnology patents, and sets standard terms for protection of patents, copyrights, and trademarks. Although the accord allows a relatively long transition period for implementation by developing countries, and excessively long delays in requiring protection for certain products, the TRIPs agreement is on balance an important achievement and merits a grade of B+.

Negotiations on trade-related investment measures (TRIMs) were handicapped from the start by limitations on the terms of reference (which excluded, for example, establishment issues and investment incentives) and never received significant attention. Nonetheless, the TRIMs accord achieved a few notable results. All TRIMs maintained by national and subnational governments must be notified, and local-content and trade-balancing requirements must be eliminated within a short transition period.

Ironically, the countries most responsible for limiting the scope of the TRIMs negotiations subsequently implemented unilaterally investment reforms that go much further than those contemplated by the original proponents of investment talks in the GATT. Although these reforms are not bound in Uruguay Round commitments, they should facilitate future negotiations on investment matters, including the nexus of investment and competition policies, which members will consider at their five-year review of the operations of the TRIMs accord. For these reasons, and given the optimistic prospects for the future evolution of multilateral rules in this area, the limited TRIMs accord still earns a grade of B−.

Institutional Reforms

In the area of institutional reforms the Uruguay Round produced three notable results. It strengthened the multilateral dispute settlement mechanism so that countries will be more likely to comply with GATT rulings and not act unilaterally in contravention of GATT obligations; it fortified the institutional charter of the GATT by establishing a new World Trade Organization (WTO) to consolidate the results of previous trade negotiations under a common framework; and it reinforced the trade policy review mechanism (TPRM) that had been applied on a provisional basis since the Montreal midterm review. Accordingly, these agreements earned grades of A and B+, comparable to the scores for trade liberalization.

The Dispute Settlement Understanding (DSU) receives the highest grade of any Uruguay Round accord, a solid A. The DSU integrates the dispute settlement mechanisms of the various agreements, past and present, under the umbrella of the new WTO. The Uruguay Round reforms expedite decision making, institute a new appeal procedure for panel rulings, and establish procedures that should encourage compliance with GATT decisions, including acceptance of cross-sector retaliation.

Interestingly, the DSU does not require the renunciation of, or even major modifications in, US section 301. The United States can continue to use section 301 to defend its trading interests. Indeed, the use of section 301 against foreign unfair practices is likely to be more GATT-consistent than in the past, since authority to retaliate will be almost automatically granted by the WTO, after a panel ruling in the United States' favor. However, since the expanded coverage of the WTO obligations reduces the range of policies and practices that can be contested without first obtaining a WTO review, the incidence of "unilateral" US action should be sharply reduced.

The Uruguay Round Final Act transforms the GATT into a permanent international institution, the World Trade Organization, responsible for governing the conduct of trade relations among its members. The WTO ties together in an integrated legal framework the various trade pacts that have been negotiated under GATT auspices: the original GATT from 1947 as amended in subsequent negotiations through the Uruguay Round (called GATT 1994), the GATS, the TRIPs and TRIMs accords, the four plurilateral agreements (government procurement, civil aviation, meat, and dairy), the DSU, and the trade policy review mechanism (see below). In essence, the WTO Agreement is a "mini-charter"; it merely consolidates the various trade pacts that have accumulated in the series of postwar trade negotiations. It does not create an unwieldy new international organization. In most respects, the WTO will operate just as the GATT has operated, with decisions usually made by consensus on matters such as amendments, waivers, or interpretations of WTO obligations.

The most significant aspect of the WTO Agreement is the "single undertaking": member countries must adhere not only to GATT rules but (with a few exceptions) to the broad range of trade pacts that have been negotiated under GATT auspices during the past two decades. As a result, many countries, especially developing countries, will immediately have to undertake substantial new obligations in areas (such as the Tokyo Round codes) where they formerly enjoyed a free ride. If there is a legitimate concern about the transfer of national sovereignty to the WTO, it relates to the single undertaking.

In contrast, the more frequently espoused concern that the WTO will usurp the sovereignty of the US government is grossly exaggerated. Concerns about US sovereignty primarily involve two issues: whether the United States will be forced to change its laws at the behest of WTO decisions, and whether majority voting by WTO members will rewrite the trade rules to the disadvantage of major trading powers. The answer to both questions is no.

First, WTO decisions are not self-executing in US law. If a US practice is found to violate US international obligations, the Congress must decide whether to amend US law. If the United States does not comply with its obligations, affected WTO members have the right to demand compensation (which would most likely require congressional action) or to retaliate. Contrary to the claims of WTO critics, there is little risk that economic pressure will be brought to bear on the United States to conform to WTO rulings if the Congress does not believe it to be in the US interest to do so. Few countries ever retaliate against the United States, because such action imposes costs on their own producers and consumers and sours relations with the world's largest trading nation.

Second, there is no evidence of block voting in the GATT, even though it has operated under an unweighted voting rule since its inception, as will the WTO. In large part the threat that blocs of small countries will wield influence beyond their importance in world trade is exaggerated, because the WTO, like the GATT, will act in most instances by consensus. When votes are taken, concerns about unweighted voting are substantially mitigated by checks and balances that preclude majority votes from undercutting the rights of other participants.

By itself, the WTO "mini-charter" would merit an A grade for strengthening the institutional framework of the world trading system. However, the overall grade is reduced to B+ because of flaws in the WTO's organizational structure, particularly the failure to establish a management committee comparable to the executive boards of the IMF and the World Bank. WTO operations will in effect be managed inefficiently by a committee of the whole. Until the WTO follows more closely the management model of its sister Bretton Woods institutions, informal groups such as the Quad countries will have free rein to continue their work as the de facto GATT steering committee.

The final piece of the institutional reforms, the formal establishment of the trade policy review mechanism, seems (and is) minor in comparison with the WTO and the DSU. Yet the TPRM is an important component of the institutional procedures that reinforce the multilateral rules established by the Uruguay Round accords and thus strengthen the trading system. In essence, TPRM reviews cast a spotlight on the trade policies of member countries, examine how countries are meeting their trade obligations, and document the barriers that obstruct trade in goods and services. They do not, however, attempt to judge the conformity of national practices with multilateral obligations.

The TPRM reviews provide an important survey of national trade policies, but they have notable shortcomings. For example, the TPRM reports do little to analyze the costs of protection (which would be useful in promoting domestic policy debates on such measures), nor do they propose alternative approaches or adjustment measures that could be deployed instead of trade restraints. Furthermore, they should be allowed to inform WTO members on whether national laws and policies are consistent with the country's obligations. In short, the TPRM is a valuable exercise that could yield even more important dividends in terms of promoting domestic and international policy reforms, if the scope of the analysis were expanded. As presently constituted, however, the agreement establishing the TPRM still merits a grade of B+.

Global Economic Implications

The Uruguay Round reforms contribute to economic growth in several ways. Most important, trade reforms promote the more efficient and

Table 2 Estimates of computable general equilibrium models of the impact of the Uruguay Round agreements on income and trade[a]

Model	Increases in GDP (billions of dollars)		Increases in trade (percentages)	
	Global	United States	Global	United States
Francois et al.				
(1994)[b]	122–512	33–126	15.4	17.3
	100–477	31–121	14.8	17.1
Yang (1994)[c]	60–116	17–27[d]	n.a.	n.a.
GATT (1993)	230	67[d]	12.4[e]	8.0[d]
OECD (1993a)	274	28	n.a.	n.a.
Goldin et al. (1993)	213	14.8	n.a.	n.a.
Nguyen et al. (1993)	212[f]	36	20	n.a.

n.a. = not available (not calculated or not reported)

a. Whereas most models use the Dunkel draft or other "Uruguay Round-like" scenarios, Francois et al. (1994), Yang (1994), and GATT (1993) base their liberalization scenarios as closely as possible on the actual concessions in the Final Act, albeit at rather aggregate levels. Francois et al. (1994), Yang (1994), and GATT (1993) report results for 2005 in 1992 dollars; OECD (1993a) and Goldin et al. (1993) estimate the effects by 2002 in 1992 dollars; Nguyen et al. (1993) for 1986 in 1986 dollars.
b. Upper-bound income estimates and all trade estimates assume scale economies and imperfect competition as well as certain investment-income dynamics.
c. Upper-bound estimates incorporate export externalities.
d. United States and Canada combined.
e. Equivalent to an increase of $745 billion.
f. Equivalent to an increase of 1.1 percent.

productive use of resources. Efficient exporters will benefit as trade reforms increase their access to foreign markets and allow them to exploit economies of scale in production. Consumers of both final and intermediate goods will benefit as increased imports dampen inflationary pressures and expand the range of goods from which to choose. Governments will lose some revenue because of reduced tariff rates, but gain some back as the volume of imports increases and as domestic economic activity expands. However, producers that have been sheltered from competition by trade barriers, or have received subsidies, will lose part of these windfall gains. To abbreviate a complicated story, the long-run efficiency gains from trade liberalization make more resources available for additional consumption and/or investment, promote increased productivity and innovation, and thus propel a virtuous cycle of economic growth.

Describing these effects is far easier than calculating them for a particular economy or for the world as a whole. Economists have developed complex computable general equilibrium (CGE) models to estimate the impact on the world economy of a reduction in trade protection broadly comparable to that achieved in the Uruguay Round. The results of these models are summarized in table 2.

Overall, the models forecast that the Uruguay Round agreements will generate a modest increase in the size of the world economy after a 10-year transition period. In other words, the Uruguay Round reforms will create a permanently larger global economic pie. The expected gains vary significantly in magnitude from study to study, reflecting the different assumptions used in each.[7] The most widely quoted estimates are from studies by the GATT (1993) and the Organization for Economic Cooperation and Development (OECD 1993a), which forecast a gradual increase in world income and trade over a 10-year period.

The GATT study estimates that world GDP will be $230 billion higher in 2005 (in 1992 dollars) than it would be in the absence of the Uruguay Round reforms, while global trade is forecast to increase by $745 billion (or by 12.4 percent over baseline projections). The GATT model is heavily skewed toward natural resource sectors, which may understate the absolute and relative gains from liberalization for those countries whose economies are not strongly dependent on natural resources.

The OECD study predicts a permanent increase in world GDP of $274 billion by the year 2002 (in 1992 dollars). However, the OECD model focuses primarily on the liberalization of agricultural protection, and the reforms actually achieved in this area fall well short of what the OECD modelers assumed. On the other hand, the model does not attempt to calculate tariff equivalents for nontariff barriers, which means that, inter alia, the effect of eliminating quantitative restrictions on textiles and apparel is not counted.

Nonetheless, the CGE results should be considered a lower-bound estimate of the economic effects of the Uruguay Round, for several reasons (see box 1). First, they omit important results in key areas of the negotiations. In particular, the models do not reflect the impacts of improved trade rules, commitments on government procurement, and new disciplines on services and intellectual property regimes, which are inherently hard to quantify. Second, these models typically assume constant returns to scale, and most do not take into account the long-run dynamic effects of trade reforms. Furthermore, their estimates of welfare benefits are subject to a downward bias because the analysis focuses on highly aggregated product sectors. Finally, the models calculate gains from a baseline that assumes that the status quo would be sustained in the absence of the negotiated results. A strong argument could be made that the relevant counterfactual, namely, failure of the Uruguay Round, would have been a significant reversal of trade reforms already achieved, and thus that the economic gains from the successful conclusion of the Round should be calculated from that lower baseline, not the status quo ante.

---

7. The results range from a modest $60 billion increase in world GDP as a result of Uruguay Round trade liberalization (Yang 1994) to estimates (which factor in quasi-dynamic effects) of a permanent increase in global GDP of more than $500 billion by the year 2005 (Francois et al. 1994). See appendix B for a more detailed discussion of the CGE studies.

Box 1   Economic modeling of the impact of the Uruguay Round

In recent years a number of computable general equilibrium models have been used to forecast the Uruguay Round's effects on world output. All of these models predict an increase in output, but they differ on how large it will be, over what time period the benefits will be felt, and how the gains will be distributed, both within and among countries (see table 2).

There is no single best estimate of the likely effects of the Uruguay Round on the world economy, for a number of reasons:

- Much of the analytical work to date was begun while the Uruguay Round was still in progress, and therefore had to make certain assumptions about the eventual negotiated results. Differences in these assumptions about the extent to which trade barriers would be lowered have produced differences among the forecasts about the round's economic effects, and differences between the assumptions of any one model and the actual outcome of the round obviously bias the model's forecasts.

- The Uruguay Round includes changes to the international rules governing trade in services, investment, and intellectual property. Many of the round's effects will operate through these improved trade rules. But most economic models disregard these changes and only estimate the effects of cuts in merchandise tariffs (and sometimes also selected nontariff barriers); several focus primarily on the agricultural sector (and generally assume more profound agricultural trade reforms than were actually achieved).

- Most models simulate the effects of tariff reductions in terms of comparative statics, ignoring the dynamic gains from trade liberalization (the additional spurt in economic growth caused by, for example, additional investment generated by households and businesses saving a portion of their welfare gains). Those studies that tried to include dynamic gains failed to capture them in a comprehensive manner.

- The models calculate gains from a baseline that assumes that the status quo would be sustained in the absence of a negotiated agreement. This tends to understate the gains from the round if one believes that the global trading system would have deteriorated, and trade itself diminished, had the talks failed.

- Most of the modeling studies analyze trade at the level of very broad economic sectors. The high level of aggregation precludes any meaningful sector-specific analysis.

In sum, the models used to forecast the economic effects of the Uruguay Round accords exaggerate the results in the limited sectors covered by their calculations, but probably underestimate by a substantial amount the aggregate growth and productivity gains resulting from the market access reforms and improved trading rules.

Implications for the United States

The Uruguay Round agreements present important new trading opportunities for a broad range of US industrial and agricultural producers, and should result in modest but positive gains for the US economy as it enters the 21st century. Compared with other trade policy initiatives, the Uruguay Round provides the biggest bang for the buck. Simply put, US trade reforms "buy" comparable commitments from the more than 120 countries participating in the Uruguay Round. Bilateral or regional free trade pacts may complement the GATT results and indeed achieve deeper cuts in trade barriers in a single market, but few can match the range of new trade opportunities provided on a global basis by the GATT talks.

Trade and Welfare Effects

Given data limitations, the analysis in this study focuses primarily on the first-round trade and welfare impacts of the Uruguay Round tariff cuts on individual US manufacturing sectors.[8] However, we also incorporate analysis of the welfare effects of the elimination of US textile and apparel quotas based on work by Cline (1993) and Hufbauer and Elliott (1994).

The results reported here are modest because they measure only the effects of the tariff cuts. They do not take account of the impact of farm trade and MFA reforms or the prospective gains that should accrue from reform in services and intellectual property regimes and, more broadly, from interactions between the various sectors (e.g., the more efficient provision of intermediate inputs) and other dynamic effects of trade liberalization. Because they do not reflect the potential expansion of the volume of US trade arising from Uruguay Round–induced increases in domestic and foreign income, or the macroeconomic and cross-sectoral effects of the liberalization of many sectors simultaneously, these estimates provide a very conservative projection of the minimum gains that could be derived from the Uruguay Round accords.

We start by assuming that tariff cuts will be applied to the same composition of trade as in 1989 for US imports, and 1988 for US exports—the years on which the United States based its Uruguay Round industrial tariff concessions. We then project the base levels of US imports and exports for most chapters of the Harmonized Tariff Schedule (HS) for 1995, the first year of implementation of Uruguay Round–mandated tariff cuts, from trade data provided by the Office of the US Trade Representative.[9]

Table 3 shows US imports from all countries in 1995 for 78 industrial commodity groups, and the pre–Uruguay Round level of duties collected

---

8. Compared with the CGE models cited above, our partial equilibrium (PE) analysis offers more sectoral detail and has the advantage of being both relatively simple and transparent. However, like all PE analysis it ignores the interaction between different sectors and markets, thereby missing critical economywide aspects of the Uruguay Round.

9. The USTR base-year data accounted for only 72 percent of total US merchandise imports in 1989, and 67 percent of total US merchandise exports in 1988. To simplify the calculation, we assumed that trade with other countries had the same commodity mix, and then scaled up the USTR data to generate an estimate for all merchandise trade.

Table 3 Projected trade and welfare effects of Uruguay Round liberalization on US merchandise imports, 1995 (millions of dollars except where noted otherwise)

HS chapter	US demand for imports before UR cuts[a]	Duties collected[a]		Calculated average tariff (%)		Average tariff cut (%)	Tariff revenue loss based on pre-UR import levels	Decrease in price of US imports due to cuts (%)[b]	Increase in US demand for imports[c]	US demand for imports after UR cuts[d]	Increase in US demand for imports (%)	Tariff gains on increased US imports[e]	Gain to US consumers[f]
		Before UR cuts	After UR cuts	Before UR cuts	After UR cuts								
All commodities	671,020	27,751	18,244	4.14	2.72	34.26	9,507	1.36	18,018	689,037	2.69	482	9,253
US imports affected by Uruguay Round cuts:													
All affected commodities	602,847	27,751	18,244	4.60	3.03	34.28	9,507	1.51	18,018	620,864	2.99	482	9,253
03—Fish, crustaceans & aquatic invertebrates	6,683	10	5	0.15	0.07	51.67	5	0.08	10	6,693	0.15	0	5
05—Products of animal origin, NESOI	31	1	1	3.01	3.01	0.00	0	0.00	0	31	0.00	0	0
15—Animal or vegetable fats, oils etc. & waxes	139	7	7	4.77	4.77	0.00	0	0.00	0	139	0.00	0	0
16—Edible preparations of meat, fish, crustaceans etc	926	86	76	9.34	8.23	11.84	10	1.01	19	944	2.02	2	9
25—Salt; sulfur; earth & stone; lime & cement plaster	1,862	13	4	0.70	0.23	67.69	9	0.47	18	1,879	0.94	0	9
26—Ores, slag and ash	2,356	15	11	0.63	0.46	26.81	4	0.17	8	2,364	0.33	0	4
27—Mineral fuel, oil etc.; bitumin subst; mineral wax	72,317	510	509	0.71	0.70	0.19	1	0.00	2	72,318	0.00	0	1
28—Inorg chem; prec & rare-earth met & radioact compo	6,434	58	47	0.91	0.74	18.70	11	0.17	22	6,455	0.34	0	11
29—Organic chemicals	10,085	724	395	7.18	3.92	45.37	328	3.04	613	10,698	6.08	24	316
30—Pharmaceutical products	1,741	70	0	4.04	0.00	100.00	70	3.88	135	1,876	7.76	0	70
31—Fertilizers	1,429	0	0	0.00	0.00	0.00	0	0.00	0	1,429	0.00	0	0
32—Tanning & dye ext etc; dye, paint, putty etc; inks	1,642	163	86	9.95	5.21	47.69	78	4.32	142	1,784	8.63	7	74
33—Essential oils etc; perfumery, cosmetic etc preps	980	49	4	5.01	0.42	91.58	45	4.37	86	1,066	8.75	0	45
34—Soap etc; waxes, polish etc; candles; dental preps	390	19	8	4.90	2.06	57.91	11	2.71	21	411	5.41	0	11
35—Albuminoidal subst; modified starch; glue; enzymes	302	12	2	3.84	0.66	82.74	10	3.06	18	320	6.12	0	10
36—Explosives; pyrotechnics; matches; pyro alloys etc	211	9	9	4.13	4.08	1.13	0	0.04	0	211	0.09	0	0
37—Photographic or cinematographic goods	2,536	98	92	3.88	3.62	6.60	6	0.25	12	2,548	0.49	0	6
38—Miscellaneous chemical products	1,201	52	37	4.34	3.07	29.31	15	1.22	29	1,230	2.44	1	15
39—Plastics and articles thereof	9,050	434	396	4.80	4.38	8.84	38	0.41	73	9,123	0.81	3	37
40—Rubber and articles thereof	7,452	212	102	2.84	1.37	51.82	110	1.43	213	7,666	2.88	3	108
41—Raw hides and skins (no furskins) and leather	1,158	45	34	3.85	2.92	24.25	11	0.90	21	1,178	1.80	1	11

continued next page

Table 3 Projected trade and welfare effects of Uruguay Round liberalization on US merchandise imports, 1995 (millions of dollars except where noted otherwise) (continued)

HS chapter	US demand for imports before UR cuts[a]	Duties collected[a]		Calculated average tariff (%)		Average tariff cut (%)	Tariff revenue loss based on pre-UR import levels[b]	Decrease in price of US imports due to cuts (%)[b]	Increase in US demand for imports[c]	US demand for imports after UR cuts[d]	Increase in US demand for imports (%)	Tariff gains on increased US imports[e]	Gain to US consumers[f]
		Before UR cuts	After UR cuts	Before UR cuts	After UR cuts								
42—Leather art; saddlery etc; handbags etc; gut art	5,510	606	553	11.00	10.04	8.68	53	0.86	95	5,605	1.72	10	48
43—Furskins and artificial fur; manufactures thereof	625	34	22	5.44	3.59	34.11	12	1.76	22	647	3.52	1	11
44—Wood and articles of wood; wood charcoal	7,938	377	256	4.75	3.22	32.17	121	1.46	232	8,170	2.92	7	118
45—Cork and articles of cork	108	2	0	1.80	0.18	89.94	2	1.59	3	111	3.18	0	2
46—Mfr of straw, esparto etc.; basketware & wickerwirk	346	24	19	7.07	5.56	21.45	5	1.42	10	358	2.83	1	5
47—Pulp of wood etc; waste etc of paper & paperboard	4,425	0	0	0.00	0.00	0.00	0	0.00	0	4,425	0.00	0	0
48—Paper & paperboard & articles (inc papr pulp artl)	12,318	280	0	2.27	0.00	100.00	280	2.22	548	12,865	4.45	0	280
49—Printed books, newspapers etc; manuscripts etc	2,235	9	0	0.41	0.00	100.00	9	0.41	18	2,253	0.81	0	9
50—Silk including yarns and woven fabric thereof	411	21	1	5.13	0.28	94.63	20	4.62	38	449	9.24	0	20
51—Wool & animal hair, including yarn & woven fabric	249	50	25	19.98	10.10	49.43	25	8.23	41	289	16.46	4	22
52—Cotton, including yarn and woven fabric thereof	1,688	149	136	8.85	8.08	8.63	13	0.70	24	1,712	1.40	2	12
53—Veg text fib NESOI; veg fib & paper yns & wov fab	235	5	0	2.00	0.08	96.05	5	1.89	9	244	3.77	0	5
54—Manmade filaments, including yarns & woven fabrics	1,240	176	148	14.18	11.97	15.62	27	1.94	48	1,288	3.88	6	25
55—Manmade staple fibers, incl yarns & woven fabrics	1,085	144	112	13.29	10.29	22.62	33	2.65	58	1,142	5.31	6	30
56—Wadding, felt etc; sp yarn; twine, ropes etc.	444	41	9	9.14	1.97	78.41	32	6.56	58	503	13.13	1	31
57—Carpets and other textile floor coverings	885	57	23	6.43	2.63	59.11	34	3.57	63	948	7.14	2	33
58—Spec wov fabrics; tufted fab; lace; tapestries etc	425	47	34	11.07	8.07	27.13	13	2.70	23	448	5.41	2	12
59—Impregnated etc text fabrics; tex art for industry	476	29	14	6.01	2.85	52.54	15	2.98	28	504	5.96	1	15
60—Knitted or crocheted fabrics	178	25	19	14.27	10.77	24.54	6	3.08	11	189	6.13	1	6
61—Apparel articles and accessories, knit or crochet	10,731	2,565	2,315	23.90	21.57	9.74	250	1.88	403	11,135	3.76	87	205

continued next page

Product												
62—Apparel articles and accessories, not knit etc.	18,662	3,296	3,005	17.66	16.10	8.84	291	1.33	495	19,158	2.65	80	251
63—Textile art NESOI; needlecraft sets; worn text art	1,606	146	115	9.12	7.19	21.21	31	1.77	57	1,662	3.55	4	29
64—Footwear, gaiters etc. and parts thereof	12,019	1,287	1,201	10.71	9.99	6.73	87	0.65	157	12,175	1.30	16	79
65—Headgear and parts thereof	439	33	26	7.53	5.82	22.63	7	1.58	14	452	3.17	1	7
66—Umbrellas, walking-sticks, riding-crops etc. parts	196	16	12	8.31	5.87	29.32	5	2.25	9	205	4.50	1	5
67—Prep feathers, down etc; artif flowers; h hair art	2,874	225	209	7.82	7.28	6.91	16	0.50	29	2,903	1.00	2	14
68—Art of stone, plaster, cement, asbestos, mica etc.	1,467	60	32	4.07	2.20	45.92	27	1.80	53	1,519	3.60	1	27
69—Ceramic products	2,933	312	189	10.63	6.48	39.26	122	3.77	221	3,155	7.55	14	115
70—Glass and glassware	2,472	204	153	8.27	6.18	25.26	52	1.93	95	2,567	3.86	6	49
71—Nat etc pearls, prec etc stones, pr met etc; coin	15,379	352	289	2.29	1.68	18.05	64	0.40	124	15,504	0.81	2	62
72—Iron and steel	12,212	573	37	4.70	0.30	93.62	537	4.20	1,026	13,237	8.40	3	534
73—Article of iron or steel	9,606	385	134	4.01	1.39	65.25	251	2.51	483	10,088	5.03	7	247
74—Copper and articles thereof	3,650	75	47	2.06	1.30	36.97	28	0.75	54	3,704	1.49	1	27
75—Nickel and articles thereof	2,338	12	8	0.50	0.33	34.63	4	0.17	8	2,346	0.35	0	4
76—Aluminum and articles thereof	5,732	188	162	3.28	2.83	13.68	26	0.43	50	5,782	0.87	1	25
78—Lead and articles thereof	153	5	3	3.58	2.16	39.74	2	1.37	4	157	2.75	0	2
79—Zinc and articles thereof	2,163	37	35	1.73	1.60	7.62	3	0.13	6	2,189	0.26	0	3
80—Tin and articles thereof	1,088	3	2	0.24	0.16	32.71	1	0.08	2	1,090	0.16	0	1
81—Base metals NESOI; cermets; articles thereof	678	32	23	4.86	3.44	26.13	8	1.16	16	694	2.33	1	8
82—Tools, cutlery etc. of base metal & parts thereof	2,798	179	129	6.39	4.62	27.75	50	1.67	93	2,891	3.34	4	47
83—Miscellaneous articles of base metal	2,506	123	60	4.91	2.39	51.24	63	2.40	120	2,628	4.80	3	62
84—Machinery and mechanical appliances, and parts thereof	85,111	3,027	947	3.56	1.11	68.71	2,080	2.36	4,017	89,128	4.72	45	2,056
85—Electrical machinery and equipment, and parts thereof	80,038	3,611	1,199	4.51	1.50	66.80	2,412	2.88	4,616	84,654	5.77	69	2,375
86—Railway or tramway stock etc; traffic signal equip	1,134	39	29	3.40	2.56	24.75	10	0.81	18	1,152	1.63	0	9
87—Vehicles, except railway or tramway, and parts etc	108,055	4,159	3,988	3.85	3.69	4.10	171	0.15	329	108,384	0.30	12	165
88—Aircraft, spacecraft, and parts thereof	5,044	26	0	0.52	0.00	99.34	26	0.51	52	5,096	1.02	0	26
89—Ships, boats and floating structures	845	11	9	1.25	1.01	19.30	2	0.24	4	849	0.48	0	2
90—Optical, photographic, measuring, and medical instruments	17,492	820	279	4.69	1.60	65.93	540	2.95	1,032	18,524	5.90	16	531
91—Clocks and watches and parts thereof	1,230	75	69	6.06	5.62	7.22	5	0.41	10	1,240	0.83	1	5
92—Musical instruments; parts and accessories thereof	1,165	65	50	5.61	4.32	23.07	15	1.23	29	1,193	2.45	1	14
93—Arms and ammunition; parts and accessories thereof	680	32	12	4.66	1.69	63.69	20	2.84	39	719	5.68	1	20
94—Furniture; bedding etc; lamps NESOI etc; prefab bd	7,675	345	120	4.50	1.56	65.30	225	2.81	432	8,107	5.62	7	222

Table 3 Projected trade and welfare effects of Uruguay Round liberalization on US merchandise imports, 1995 (millions of dollars except where noted otherwise) (continued)

HS chapter	US demand for imports before UR cuts[a]	Duties collected[a] Before UR cuts	Duties collected[a] After UR cuts	Calculated average tariff (%) Before UR cuts	Calculated average tariff (%) After UR cuts	Average tariff cut (%)	Tariff revenue loss based on pre-UR import levels	Decrease in price of US imports due to cuts (%)[b]	Increase in US demand for imports[c]	US demand for imports after UR cuts[d]	Increase in US demand for imports (%)	Tariff gains on increased US imports[e]	Gain to US consumers[f]
95—Toys, games & sport equipment; parts & accessories	11,185	656	85	5.87	0.76	87.08	572	4.83	1,080	12,265	9.65	8	566
96—Miscellaneous manufactured articles	1,748	114	75	6.50	4.32	33.62	38	2.05	72	1,820	4.11	3	37
US imports not affected by Uruguay Round cuts:													
97—Works of art, collectors' pieces and antiques	3,087	n.a.	n.a.	n.a.	n.a.	n.a.	n.a.	n.a.	n.a.	3,087	n.a.	n.a.	n.a.
98—Special classification provisions, NESOI	14,059	n.a.	n.a.	n.a.	n.a.	n.a.	n.a.	n.a.	n.a.	14,059	n.a.	n.a.	n.a.
99—Special import provisions, NESOI Not elsewhere classified	3,969	n.a.	n.a.	n.a.	n.a.	n.a.	n.a.	n.a.	n.a.	3,969	n.a.	n.a.	n.a.
	14,320	n.a.	n.a.	n.a.	n.a.	n.a.	n.a.	n.a.	n.a.	14,320	n.a.	n.a.	n.a.
Agricultural products and chemicals	32,737	n.a.	n.a.	n.a.	n.a.	n.a.	n.a.	n.a.	n.a.	32,737	n.a.	n.a.	n.a.

n.a. = not available

a. Estimated by multiplying 1989 values adjusted from USTR by a factor of 1.43 (US merchandise imports in 1995 as projected by the OECD divided by actual US merchandise imports in 1989). The data provided by USTR accounted for only 72 percent of total US merchandise imports in 1989, and excluded, for example, imports from Canada (18.6 percent) and Mexico (5.8 percent). Assuming the same commodity mix, the USTR data were scaled up to generate an estimate for all US merchandise imports.

b. The decrease in price of US imports due to the tariff cuts is calculated as: $\partial P_M = 1 - (T_{M1}/T_{M0})$ where T_{M1} is the post-Uruguay Round calculated average tariff on US imports, and T_{M0} is the pre-Uruguay Round calculated average tariff on US imports.

c. The increase in US demand for imports due to the Uruguay Round-mandated cuts is based on an assumed US price elasticity of demand for imports of −2, and calculated as: $\partial D_M = \partial P_M \cdot D_{M0} \cdot \mu_M$ where ∂D_M is the increase in US demand for imports, ∂P_M is the decrease in price of US imports due to the tariff cuts, D_{M0} is the pre-Uruguay Round level of imports, and μ_M is the US price elasticity of demand for imports.

d. US demand for imports after Uruguay Round cuts (D_{M1}) is calculated as: $D_{M1} = D_{M0} + \partial D_M$

e. Tariff gains on increased US imports (∂TR) are calculated as: $\partial TR = \partial D_M \cdot T_{M1}$ where T_{M1} is the post-Uruguay Round calculated average tariff on US imports.

f. US consumer surplus gains include transfers from domestic producers of import-competing products. The gain to US consumers (CG) is calculated as: $CG = (D_{M0} \cdot \partial P_M) + (0.5 \cdot \partial P_M \cdot \partial D_M)$

Source: Data from the Office of the US Trade Representative and authors' calculations.

on those imports, in value as well as in percentage terms. On the assumption that the US industrial tariff concessions are implemented immediately, table 3 then shows the post–Uruguay Round level of duties collected on US imports and the average tariff cut. According to these data, US tariff cuts (excluding those in agriculture) will average 34.3 percent and lower the average tariff applied to nonagricultural imports to 3 percent. Note, however, that the data in table 3 exaggerate the total duties collected, and thus somewhat inflate the average tariff cut, because reductions are calculated from most-favored nation (MFN) tariff rates and thus do not take account of trade that already receives preferential treatment under the Generalized System of Preferences (GSP), other tariff preference programs, or free trade agreements.[10]

Based on the average tariff cut per imported commodity group, and a conservative estimate of how sensitive US consumers are to lower prices for these imports (i.e., the US price elasticity of demand for imports), we calculate the expected increase in US demand for imports, assuming immediate implementation of the tariff cuts.[11] In addition, we calculate the gain to US consumers due to the resulting lower prices for US imports.[12] Overall, reductions in tariffs on US imports of industrial goods should result in an increase in US imports of about 2.7 percent, or $18.0 billion.

Table 4 shows US exports to all countries in 1995 for 77 commodity groups, and the average pre– and post–Uruguay Round foreign tariffs on these commodities. According to these data, the duty that foreign governments collect on US exports will be cut by 43.2 percent—from a trade-weighted average tariff of 9.2 percent to 5.2 percent. Again, assuming that the foreign tariff concessions are implemented immediately, table 4 presents the likely increase in world demand for US exports and the resulting gain to US producers.[13]

---

10. In 1993 the GSP program provided duty-free entry for about 3.4 percent of US merchandise imports, and free trade agreements with Canada and Israel affected about 20 percent of US merchandise imports. In 1992, 10.8 percent of US merchandise imports entered under HS subchapter 9802 (formerly TSUS 806/807), of which about one-quarter entered duty-free.

11. To give our calculations a conservative bias, we assume a rather high US price elasticity of demand for imports of -2, thereby overstating the increase in US demand for merchandise imports due to tariff cuts, and inflating somewhat the related gains to US consumers.

12. The increase in US import levels partly replaces US domestic production and partly reflects an increase in total US consumption. Hence, US consumer gains consist of some loss to US producers *and* increased consumption. However, one should note that other US producers gain significantly from greater export opportunities created by foreign tariff cuts (see below).

13. In the absence of reliable commodity-specific estimates for the foreign price elasticity of demand for US goods—given the high level of disaggregation and the long-run effects of tariff liberalization—it is assumed that, for identical tariff cuts and levels of trade, the percentage changes in imports and exports are the same. The welfare gain to US producers is calculated using a low estimate for the supply elasticity of US exports, which has been estimated in other studies at between 4 and 20 (see, e.g., US Treasury, Office of Tax Analysis 1983, table B-1).

Table 4 Projected trade and welfare effects of Uruguay Round liberalization on US merchandise exports, 1995
(millions of dollars except where noted otherwise)

HS chapter	World demand for US exports before UR cuts[a]	Duties collected[a]		Calculated average tariff (%)		Average tariff cut		Change in price of US exports due to cuts (%)[b]	Increase in world demand for US exports[c]	World demand for US exports after UR cuts[d]	Increase in world demand for US exports (%)	Short-term net US producer surplus gain from foreign liberalization[e]
		Before UR cuts	After UR cuts	Before UR cuts	After UR cuts	Percent	Millions of dollars					
All commodities	507,534	42,321	24,035	8.34	4.74	43.21	18,286	3.33	33,153	540,687	6.53	8,626
US exports affected by Uruguay Round cuts:												
All affected commodities	461,131	42,321	24,035	9.18	5.21	43.21	18,286	3.63	33,153	494,285	7.19	8,628
Agricultural commodities	54,467	7,751	4,809	14.23	8.83	37.96	2,942	4.73	5,151	59,618	9.45	1,349
03—Fish, crustaceans & aquatic invertebrates	4,517	351	208	7.77	4.61	40.65	143	2.93	265	4,781	5.86	68
05—Products of animal origin, NESOI	460	15	12	3.22	2.61	18.81	3	0.59	5	465	1.17	1
15—Animal or vegetable fats, oils etc. & waxes	2,521	644	558	25.54	22.14	13.34	86	2.72	137	2,658	5.43	35
16—Edible preparations of meat, fish, crustaceans etc	862	82	68	9.54	7.92	16.99	14	1.48	26	888	2.96	6
25—Salt; sulfur; earth & stone; lime & cement plaster	1,994	90	64	4.50	3.21	28.71	26	1.24	49	2,043	2.47	12
26—Ores, slag and ash	2,438	31	19	1.28	0.77	38.68	12	0.48	23	2,462	0.96	6
27—Mineral fuel, oil etc.; bitumin subst; mineral wax	13,365	622	395	4.65	2.95	36.55	227	1.63	435	13,799	3.25	110
28—Inorg chem; prec & rare-earth met & radioact compo	7,124	551	314	7.73	4.41	42.92	236	3.08	439	7,563	6.16	113
29—Organic chemicals	17,179	2,039	1,126	11.67	6.56	44.77	913	4.75	1,632	18,811	9.50	427
30—Pharmaceutical products	3,260	215	33	6.58	1.02	84.56	181	5.22	340	3,601	10.44	90
31—Fertilizers	2,097	118	70	5.62	3.33	40.85	48	2.17	91	2,189	4.35	23
32—Tanning & dye ext etc; dye, paint, putty etc; inks	1,666	202	120	12.10	7.20	40.51	82	4.37	146	1,811	8.74	38
33—Essential oils etc; perfumery, cosmetic etc preps	1,254	156	69	12.47	5.50	55.90	87	6.20	155	1,409	12.40	41
34—Soap etc; waxes, polish etc; candles; dental preps	871	102	60	11.75	6.85	41.69	43	4.38	76	948	8.77	20
35—Albuminoidal subst; modified starch; glue; enzymes	517	59	38	11.45	7.63	33.36	20	3.43	35	552	6.85	9
36—Explosives; pyrotechnics; matches; pyro alloys etc	461	66	44	14.39	9.47	34.21	23	4.30	40	501	8.61	10
37—Photographic or cinematographic goods	2,578	230	135	8.92	5.23	41.36	95	3.39	175	2,752	6.77	45
38—Miscellaneous chemical products	5,087	483	275	9.49	5.41	43.00	208	3.73	379	5,466	7.45	98
39—Plastics and articles thereof	13,731	2,045	1,179	14.89	8.59	42.34	886	5.49	1,507	15,237	10.97	397
40—Rubber and articles thereof	3,923	435	288	11.10	7.34	33.92	148	3.39	266	4,188	6.78	69

Category											
41—Raw hides and skins (no furskins) and leather	3,393	243	138	7.16	4.06	43.29	105	2.89	196	3,589	5.78	50
42—Leather art; saddlery etc; handbags etc; gut art	630	87	60	13.87	9.48	31.62	28	3.85	49	678	7.70	13
43—Furskins and artificial fur; manufactures thereof	602	62	50	10.25	8.34	18.80	11	1.73	21	623	3.46	5
44—Wood and articles of wood; wood charcoal	8,640	176	122	2.04	1.42	30.47	54	0.61	105	8,745	1.22	26
45—Cork and articles of cork	17	1	1	5.53	3.67	33.61	0	1.76	1	18	3.52	0
46—Mfr of straw, esparto etc.; basketware & wickerwirk	9	1	1	12.15	7.77	38.05	0	3.91	1	10	7.81	0
47—Pulp of wood etc; waste etc of paper & paperboard	5,885	315	160	5.35	2.71	49.25	155	2.50	294	6,180	5.00	75
48—Paper & paperboard & articles (inc papr pulp artl)	6,107	598	140	9.76	2.30	76.48	456	6.80	830	6,937	13.60	222
49—Printed books, newspapers etc; manuscripts etc	3,392	96	13	2.83	0.39	86.25	83	2.37	161	3,553	4.74	41
50—Silk including yarns and woven fabric thereof	19	2	1	8.09	7.24	10.46	0	0.78	0	20	1.57	0
51—Wool & animal hair, including yarn & woven fabric	207	18	11	8.81	5.53	37.16	7	3.01	12	219	6.02	3
52—Cotton, including yarn and woven fabric thereof	3,609	148	110	4.10	3.04	25.86	38	1.02	74	3,682	2.04	19
53—Veg text fib NESOI; veg fib & paper yns & wov fab	48	13	8	26.36	16.52	37.35	5	7.79	7	56	15.59	2
54—Manmade filaments, including yarns & woven fabrics	1,950	327	194	16.79	9.92	40.88	134	5.88	228	2,179	11.75	61
55—Manmade staple fibers, incl yarns & woven fabrics	1,135	173	104	15.21	9.13	39.96	69	5.28	120	1,255	10.55	32
56—Wadding, felt etc; sp yarn; twine; ropes etc.	565	73	50	12.84	8.85	31.10	23	3.54	40	605	7.08	10
57—Carpets and other textile floor coverings	525	93	62	17.73	11.71	33.92	32	5.11	54	579	10.21	14
58—Spec wov fabrics; tufted fab; lace; tapestries etc	292	60	38	20.66	12.96	37.28	22	6.38	37	329	12.77	10
59—Impregnated etc text fabrics; tex art for industry	804	130	84	16.15	10.42	35.50	48	4.94	79	883	9.87	21
60—Knitted or crocheted fabrics	218	50	30	22.81	13.60	40.40	20	7.50	33	251	15.01	9
61—Apparel articles and accessories, knit or crochet	694	132	101	19.07	14.47	24.08	32	3.86	54	748	7.71	14
62—Apparel articles and accessories, not knit etc.	1,353	317	229	23.42	16.90	27.86	88	5.29	143	1,496	10.57	38
63—Textile art NESOI; needlecraft sets; worn text art	741	126	95	17.06	12.85	24.66	31	3.59	53	794	7.19	14
64—Footwear, gaiters etc. and parts thereof	546	105	82	19.17	14.98	21.85	23	3.51	38	585	7.03	10
65—Headgear and parts thereof	100	11	7	11.09	6.54	41.04	5	4.10	8	109	8.19	2
66—Umbrellas, walking-sticks, riding-crops etc. parts	12	3	2	27.46	17.88	34.89	1	7.52	2	14	15.03	0
67—Prep feathers, down etc; artif flowers; h hair art	17	5	3	31.02	20.91	32.59	2	7.71	3	19	15.43	1

continued next page

Table 4 Projected trade and welfare effects of Uruguay Round liberalization on US merchandise exports, 1995 (millions of dollars except where noted otherwise) (continued)

HS chapter	World demand for US exports before UR cuts[a]	Duties collected[a] Before UR cuts	Duties collected[a] After UR cuts	Calculated average tariff (%) Before UR cuts	Calculated average tariff (%) After UR cuts	Average tariff cut Percent	Average tariff cut Millions of dollars	Change in price of US exports due to cuts (%)[b]	Increase in world demand for US exports[c]	World demand for US exports after UR cuts[d]	Increase in world demand for US exports (%)	Short-term net US producer surplus gain from foreign liberalization[e]
68—Art of stone, plaster, cement, asbestos, mica etc.	628	65	40	10.41	6.43	38.23	25	3.60	45	673	7.21	12
69—Ceramic products	592	58	38	9.84	6.48	34.17	20	3.06	38	628	6.12	9
70—Glass and glassware	1,825	193	81	10.55	4.45	57.83	111	5.52	201	2,026	11.04	53
71—Nat etc pearls, prec etc stones, pr met etc; coin	10,917	210	122	1.92	1.12	41.69	88	0.79	172	11,089	1.57	43
72—Iron and steel	4,350	412	227	9.46	5.21	44.88	185	3.68	337	4,687	7.76	103
73—Article of iron or steel	3,908	520	298	13.31	7.62	42.76	222	5.02	393	4,300	10.05	103
74—Copper and articles thereof	2,387	230	125	9.64	5.24	45.59	105	4.01	191	2,578	8.02	50
75—Nickel and articles thereof	525	26	14	5.01	2.69	46.32	12	2.21	23	549	4.42	6
76—Aluminum and articles thereof	5,348	306	186	5.72	3.47	39.30	120	2.13	228	5,575	4.25	58
78—Lead and articles thereof	112	7	4	5.79	3.27	43.57	3	2.38	5	118	4.77	1
79—Zinc and articles thereof	246	32	17	13.02	7.02	46.10	15	5.31	28	273	10.62	7
80—Tin and articles thereof	135	10	6	7.63	4.31	43.53	4	3.09	8	143	6.17	2
81—Base metals NESOI; cermets; articles thereof	963	66	38	6.88	4.00	41.92	28	2.70	52	1,015	5.40	13
82—Tools, cutlery etc. of base metal & parts thereof	1,614	182	127	11.25	7.87	30.03	55	3.04	98	1,712	6.07	25
83—Miscellaneous articles of base metal	1,378	161	105	11.71	7.61	35.01	56	3.67	101	1,479	7.34	26
84—Machinery and mechanical appliances, and parts thereof	91,399	7,198	3,571	7.88	3.91	50.39	3,627	3.68	6,724	98,123	7.36	1,743
85—Electrical machinery and equipment, and parts thereof	46,071	4,876	2,635	10.58	5.72	45.97	2,242	4.40	4,054	50,125	8.80	1,058
86—Railway or tramway stock etc; traffic signal equip	545	98	65	17.90	11.97	33.12	32	5.03	55	600	10.06	14
87—Vehicles, except railway or tramway, and parts etc	42,646	4,353	2,862	10.21	6.71	34.25	1,491	3.17	2,706	45,351	6.34	698
88—Aircraft, spacecraft, and parts thereof	31,714	1,015	448	3.20	1.41	56.04	569	1.74	1,102	32,816	3.48	280
89—Ships, boats and floating structures	1,146	103	75	9.02	6.54	27.48	28	2.27	52	1,198	4.55	13
90—Optical, photographic, measuring, and medical instruments	20,913	1,478	614	7.07	2.94	58.45	884	3.86	1,614	22,527	7.72	419
91—Clocks and watches and parts thereof	213	36	22	16.93	10.47	38.15	14	5.52	24	237	11.05	6
92—Musical instruments; parts and accessories thereof	380	28	15	7.41	4.06	45.20	13	3.12	24	403	6.24	6
93—Arms and ammunition; parts and accessories thereof	2,722	372	194	13.66	7.12	47.88	178	5.75	313	3,035	11.51	83

94—Furniture; bedding etc; lamps NESOI etc; prefab bd	1,843	235	105	12.73	5.69	55.28	130	6.24	230	2,073	12.48	61
95—Toys, games & sport equipment; parts & accessories	1,913	205	94	10.70	4.94	53.87	110	5.21	199	2,112	10.41	52
96—Miscellaneous manufactured articles	1,374	183	119	13.31	8.63	35.14	64	4.13	113	1,488	8.25	30
97—Works of art, collectors' pieces and antiques	1,444	14	10	1.00	0.67	32.29	5	0.32	9	1,453	0.64	2
US exports not affected by Uruguay Round outs:												
98—Special classification provisions, NESOI	35,435	n.a.	n.a.	n.a.	n.a.	n.a.	n.a.	n.a.	n.a.	35,435	n.a.	n.a.
Not elsewhere classified	10,968	n.a.	n.a.	n.a.	n.a.	n.a.	n.a.	n.a.	n.a.	10,968	n.a.	n.a.

n.a. = not available

a. Estimated by multiplying 1988 values adjusted from USTR by a factor of 1.58 (US merchandise exports in 1995 as projected by the OECD divided by actual US merchandise exports in 1989). The data provided by USTR accounted for only 67 percent of total US merchandise exports in 1988, which included exports to Austria, Australia, Canada, the European Union, Finland, Iceland, India, Japan, Korea, Malaysia, Mexico, South Africa, Sweden, Switzerland, and Thailand. Assuming trade with other countries had the same commodity mix, the USTR data were scaled up to generate an estimate for all US merchandise exports.

b. The change in price of US exports due to cuts (∂P_x) is calculated as: $\partial P_x = 1 - (T_{x1}/T_{x0})$ where T_{x1} is the post-Uruguay Round calculated average tariff collected on US exports abroad, and T_{x0} is the pre-Uruguay Round calculated average tariff collected on US exports abroad.

c. The increase in world demand for US exports is based on an assumed foreign price elasticity of demand for US exports of -2, and calculated as: $\partial D_x = \partial P_x \cdot D_{x0} \cdot \mu_x$, where ∂D_x is the increase in demand for US exports, ∂P_x is the change in price of US exports due to the foreign tariff cuts, D_{x0} is the pre-Uruguay Round level of world demand for US exports, and μ_x is the foreign price elasticity of demand for US exports.

d. World demand for US export after the Uruguay Round-mandated cuts (D_{x1}) is calculated as: $D_{x1} = D_{x0} + \partial D_x$

e. The short-term net US producer surplus gain from foreign liberalization (PG) is based on an assumed price elasticity of supply of US exports of 4, and calculated as: $PG = [(\partial D_x/\mu_S) \cdot D_{x0}] + [0.5 \cdot (\partial D_x/\mu_S) \cdot \partial D_x]$ where μ_S is the price elasticity of supply of US exports.

Source: Data from the Office of the US Trade Representative and authors' calculations.

On the basis of these assumptions, the United States could expect to increase its exports by 6.5 percent, or $33.2 billion, from what otherwise would have occurred, as a result of Uruguay Round cuts in foreign tariffs affecting US exports.[14] Product sectors that should benefit from the tariff liberalization include machinery and mechanical appliances, and parts thereof ($6.7 billion in increased exports); electrical machinery and equipment, and parts thereof ($4.1 billion); automobiles and auto parts ($2.7 billion); organic chemicals ($1.6 billion); optical, photographic, measuring, and medical instruments ($1.6 billion); and plastics ($1.5 billion).

Interestingly, major increases in US imports are expected in many of the same product sectors that benefit from increased export opportunities. This conclusion merely confirms the general point that trade liberalization does not result in wholesale destruction of industries, but rather promotes rationalization by which some segments within the industry expand and others contract, depending on their global competitiveness. In other words, the Uruguay Round reforms should promote intraindustry trade.

The above calculations assumed immediate implementation of the total tariff cuts. Since most tariff cuts will be phased in over five years in equal annual increments, it is assumed in table 5 that the increase in the levels of trade due to the Uruguay Round–mandated tariff cuts, as well as the associated US welfare gains, will accrue in equal annual increments over five years starting in 1995. These calculations assume that baseline exports and imports both grow at an annual rate of 6 percent, roughly equal to the real annual growth in US exports and imports from 1982 to 1992.

Table 5 shows that US exports will be $41.9 billion higher, and US imports $22.7 billion higher, by the year 2000 than they would have been in the absence of the Uruguay Round tariff cuts. Net US exports increase by $19.1 billion because foreign tariff cuts are larger than US tariff cuts by a sizable amount.[15] This result seems heavily skewed in the United States' favor, but it is only one part of the overall deal. As part of the reciprocal negotiations, the United States offered improved market access to its markets in apparel and various services and agriculture sectors, in return for, inter alia, larger tariff concessions by other countries, especially developing countries.

Table 5 projects that US consumers could gain an annual $11.7 billion by the year 2000 because the tariff cuts lower the prices they pay for

---

14. The 6.5 percent increase in US exports is somewhat lower than the figure calculated by the GATT (1993); see table 2.

15. Net exports are slightly overstated because table 4 includes cuts in foreign tariffs on US agricultural exports, whereas table 3 excludes tariff cuts affecting US agricultural imports and thus assumes no increase in US imports of agricultural commodities. Although correcting this bias would reduce the estimated gains, this would be more than offset if the effects of reductions in the level of nontariff protection (e.g., MFA quota elimination) and the dynamic effects of trade liberalization were incorporated.

Table 5 Projected US gains from Uruguay Round tariff liberalization over five years (millions of dollars except where noted otherwise)

Year	US GDP (billions of dollars)[a]	US demand for imports before UR cuts[b]	World demand for US exports before UR cuts[b]	Increase in US imports due to UR[c]	Increase in US exports due to UR[c]	Net US exports due to UR — Millions of dollars	Net US exports due to UR — As % of GDP	Welfare gains[c] — To US consumer from US import liberalization[d]	Welfare gains[c] — To US producers from foreign import liberalization	Welfare gains[c] — Government net tariff revenue loss[e]	Welfare gains[c] — Total welfare gains
Base		671,020	507,534	18,018	33,153	15,135		9,253	8,626	9,025	8,853
1995	6,753	671,020	507,534	3,604	6,631	3,027	0.04	1,851	1,726	1,805	1,771
1996	6,888	711,281	537,988	7,640	14,057	6,417	0.09	3,923	3,657	3,827	3,754
1997	7,028	753,958	570,265	12,147	22,351	10,204	0.15	6,238	5,815	6,084	5,969
1998	7,166	799,195	604,481	17,168	31,589	14,421	0.20	8,816	8,219	8,599	8,438
1999	7,310	847,147	640,750	22,747	41,855	19,108	0.26	11,681	10,890	11,394	11,177
				63,304	116,482	53,178		32,508	30,306	31,708	31,106

a. US GDP for 1995 is estimated by adjusting actual 1993 GDP for growth in 1994 and 1995 as projected by the OECD (OECD Economic Outlook 54, December 1993); for 1996 through 1999 an annual growth rate of 2 percent is assumed.

b. In the absence of Uruguay Round liberalization, imports and exports are both assumed to grow at an annual rate of 6 percent.

c. The increase in the levels of imports and exports due to Uruguay Round cuts, and the corresponding welfare gains, are assumed to accrue in equal annual increments over five years, subject to an annual growth rate of 6 percent, starting in 1995.

d. Increases in US import levels due to import liberalization partly replace US domestic production and partly reflect a net increase in total consumption. The US consumer surplus gains therefore include some loss from liberalization to US producers of import-competing products.

e. These figures are not comparable to those reported by government agencies for a variety of methodological reasons. Generally, they base their calculations for total government revenue effects on actual duties collected, not duties collected on an MFN basis; they exclude imports that benefit from preferential treatment under the GSP, free trade agreements, or other arrangements, because the tariff revenues lost are already accounted for in the budget; also, they provide for offsets—roughly 25 percent—in gross tariff revenue losses for ensuing changes in the US tax base (in other words, they calculate total government revenue loss, not government tariff revenue loss).

Source: Base values are from tables 3 and 4.

31

imported goods; part of these gains stem from lower prices for import-competing domestic products, and are offset by losses suffered by domestic producers of these goods. US producers of exported goods are expected to gain about $10.9 billion from increased export opportunities due to foreign tariff cuts; and US tariff revenue will decline by $11.4 billion.[16] In sum, the total annual US welfare gain is projected to be $11.2 billion by 2000, equal to about 0.15 percent of US GDP. The *cumulative* national welfare gain over five years is forecast at $31.1 billion.

In comparison, the OECD (1993a) projects that annual gains in US GDP will amount to about $28 billion after 10 years, while the GATT (1994) anticipates an annual increase of $67 billion in the combined GDPs of the United States and Canada at the end of a 10-year period. If our results are projected out over 10 years as is done in the OECD and GATT studies, the annual welfare gains grow to $15.0 billion, or 0.19 percent of US GDP, still much lower than the other estimates.

Cline (1993) and Hufbauer and Elliott (1994) have estimated the specific impact of MFA reform. According to Hufbauer and Elliott, immediate elimination of US quotas on textile and apparel imports could result in gains to US consumers of almost $16 billion (in 1990 dollars). However, most of the impact of the removal of MFA quotas will not be felt until the end of the 10-year transition period. Quota liberalization will, of course, adversely affect some US producers, whose losses will offset to some extent the consumer welfare gains.[17]

Employment Effects

Trade liberalization has a more pronounced effect on the *composition* of employment in an economy than on its level. Total employment in the United States is essentially determined by macroeconomic conditions and

---

16. Note that our estimates of the expected *cumulative* net tariff revenue loss to the US government ($31.7 billion over five years in table 5) is not comparable with the totals reported by government agencies (e.g., the Congressional Budget Office's estimate of $11.5 billion over five years), for a variety of methodological reasons. Our estimates overestimate the tariff revenue loss and thus underestimate the US welfare gain, because they are based on duties collected on an MFN basis, not on actual duties collected. In 1995 actual duties collected (based on pre–Uruguay Round tariff levels) are projected to amount to $19.2 billion—in table 3, base duties collected ($27.8 billion) are calculated at the MFN rate. In addition, government agencies calculate total government revenue loss, not gross tariff revenue loss. Hence, they exclude imports that benefit from preferential treatment (e.g., through free trade agreements and the GSP), because the resulting tariff revenue losses are already accounted for in the budget. In addition, they provide for offsets—of roughly 25 percent—in the gross tariff revenue loss for ensuing changes in the US tax base.

17. The model developed by Cline (1993), and adjusted to reflect the actual outcome of the round, projects that by 2005 US imports of apparel would increase by about $20 billion (in 1989 dollars) or 31 percent more than would occur in the absence of reform. The model also projects that US job losses will increase by 77,000 by 2005, lowering the level of employment in the apparel sector by about 10 percent compared with continued protection.

policies. Whether the total number of US jobs increases over time will depend on how much of the welfare gain resulting from the trade reforms is due to increased productivity (i.e., more output per worker) rather than more workers employed. As the US economy approaches full employment, more people may decide to enter the work force for the first time, induced by higher wages.

Microeconomic events such as trade liberalization have a minimal impact on total employment over time. Given the nature of the Uruguay Round reductions in trade protection, one should not expect any sudden surge or fall in levels of employment in the United States over a period of 10 years or longer. However, over the next decade, increased export opportunities arising from the round should support rather than undermine the growth-led increases in higher-value-added employment now apparent in the economy.

Based solely on our estimate of the economic effects of the Uruguay Round tariff cuts, which we estimate will generate a $19.1 billion increase in *net* US exports by the year 2000, we can project that, as a first-round effect, the Uruguay Round may support an additional 265,000 jobs in the United States by the year 2000.[18] This figure represents only a partial equilibrium assessment of one category of Uruguay Round reforms. Our analysis ignores any intersectoral effects. It also needs to be supplemented by the net effects of trade reforms in services, agriculture, and government procurement, as well as the prospective job losses due to the MFA reforms noted above. Even then, the aggregate total is likely to be small in comparison with the job gains and losses that normally occur in the US economy each year. As in the debate over the North American Free Trade Agreement, the impact on jobs tends to be grossly exaggerated by both proponents and opponents of the trade deal.

The WTO Agenda

The Uruguay Round achieved historic results, yet in many respects it is not yet over. Negotiations on financial services and a long list of other

---

18. This figure is calculated on the basis of 14,000 jobs for every $1.0 billion change in the US trade balance. The US Department of Commerce (1994) estimates that, in 1992, every $1.0 billion in US exports supported 16,500 jobs, but does not track a similar relation between US imports and jobs. The ratio is hard to calculate because imports are generally more labor intensive, but not all imports are substitutes for domestically produced goods. Our calculation assumes a similar relation between US imports and jobs—thus overstating the potential job losses as a result of increased imports—as well as a 2 percent annual improvement in US labor productivity. Hence, $16,500 \times 0.98^8 = 14,000$ jobs per $1.0 billion of change in US trade balance by the year 2000. Other analyses of US employment effects include US Department of the Treasury (1994), which estimates that, as a result of the Uruguay Round–induced boost in real US GDP, 300,000 to 700,000 additional Americans will be at work in 2004; and DRI/McGraw-Hill (1993), which projects that the Uruguay Round trade reforms will support an additional 764,000 jobs by the year 2000.

issues are continuing, and new talks on agriculture and services will be launched within five years (see table 6). In addition, new issues are likely to be added to the negotiating agenda, including environmental issues and investment and competition policies. Discussion of these issues will be facilitated by the institutional reforms incorporated in the WTO Agreement that establish a permanent forum for negotiations.

The multilateral agenda is composed of three types of activities. First, WTO members need to complete the unfinished business of the Uruguay Round. For example, negotiations were extended for up to 18 months in an attempt to resolve problems relating to financial services, basic telecommunications, and maritime services. In addition, the GATS provides for continuing negotiation of emergency safeguards and provisions relating to the movement of people.

Second, the Uruguay Round accords themselves require regular review of the operations of specific provisions of particular agreements and of the entire agreement itself. For example, the Committee on Subsidies and Countervailing Measures is charged with examining, by July 1996, the operation of the provisions regarding nonactionable research and development subsidies, and, by 1 January 2000, all the provisions on nonactionable subsidies and serious prejudice; the TRIPs Committee is required to examine the effectiveness of the provisions on geographical indications (e.g., for wines and spirits) by 1 January 1997; and WTO members must revisit, by 1 January 1998, the provisions regarding the standard of review for panels judging disputes in the antidumping area, and consider whether comparable rules should apply in disputes involving countervailing duties. In addition, WTO members are scheduled to review the operation of the agreement on sanitary and phytosanitary standards by 1 January 1998, and to review the MFN exemptions invoked for specific sectors under Article II of the GATS by 1 January 2000.

Third, several WTO accords contain commitments to launch new negotiations after a set period of time, to build on the results achieved in the Uruguay Round. These new negotiations must start as early as 1 January 1997 for the inclusion of government procurement contracts in the GATS, and 1 January 1999 for new talks to update the Government Procurement Agreement. More important, new negotiations must be initiated by 1 January 2000 in two critical areas: agriculture, to continue the reform process begun in the Uruguay Round, and services, to promote additional liberalization of trade.

Finally, the WTO agenda will continue to expand to address issues that have not been the subject of previous trade negotiations. At the top of this list is the issue of trade and the environment, on which the GATT has already issued some preliminary reports and held rudimentary discussions over the years. However, the Marrakesh ministerial declaration mandated the establishment of a new WTO Committee on Trade and the

Table 6   Timetable for further WTO negotiations

Date		Item	Source
1995	January 1	WTO enters into force[a]	Marrakesh Declaration, to be confirmed at GATT meeting in late 1994
	June 30	Deadline for negotiations on financial services and on movement of natural persons	GATS Annex; ministerial decision
1996	January 1	Government Procurement Agreement enters into force	GPA Article XXIV.1
	April 30	Deadline for negotiations on basic telecommunications services	GATS Annex; ministerial decision
	June 30	Review of operation of provisions regarding R&D subsidies	Article 8.2, footnote 25 of subsidies agreement
	June 30	Deadline for negotiations on maritime services	GATS Annex; ministerial decision
1997	January 1	Start negotiations on government procurement of services	GATS Article XIII
	January 1	First review of provisions on preshipment inspection (reviews every three years thereafter)	Article 6 of preshipment inspection agreement
	January 1	First review of TRIPs section on geographical indications	TRIPs Article 24.2
	December 31	Deadline for negotiations on emergency safeguards for services	GATS Article X
1998	January 1	Examine standard of review for antidumping disputes, and consider its application to countervail cases	Ministerial agreement
	January 1	First review of operation and implementation of technical barriers to trade provisions (reviews are to be held every three years thereafter)	Article 15.4 of agreement on technical barriers to trade
	January 1	Deadline for report with recommendation from Working Party on Trade in Services and the Environment on modifications of GATS Article XIV (general exceptions)	Ministerial decision
	January 1	Review of operation and implementation of sanitary and phytosanitary provisions (further reviews to be held as need arises)	Article 12.7 of sanitary and phytosanitary agreement
1999	January 1	Start negotiations on further improvement of the GPA (extension of coverage)	GPA Article XXIV.7

(continued on next page)

Table 6 Timetable for further WTO negotiations, (continued)

Date		Item	Source
1999	January 1	Deadline for review of provision on patent or sui generis protection of plant varieties	TRIPs agreement Article 27.3.b
	January 1	Deadline for review of dispute settlement rules and procedures	Ministerial decision
	June 30	Start review of provisions on serious prejudice and nonactionable subsidies	Article 31 of subsidies agreement
2000	January 1	Start first round of negotiations on progressive liberalization of services (new negotiations to increase the general level of specific commitments)	GATS Article XIX
	January 1	Review of Article II (MFN) exemptions	GATS Annex
	January 1	Launch new negotiations to continue reform process in agriculture	Article 20 of agriculture agreement
	January 1	First review of TRIPs agreement; reviews to be held every two years thereafter	TRIPs agreement Article 71.1
	January 1	Deadline for review of TRIMs agreement and consideration of whether to complement it with provisions on investment and competition policy	TRIMs agreement Article 9
	January 1	Review of interpretation of the rules on modification and withdrawal of concessions	Understanding on Interpretation of GATT Article XXVIII
	January 1	First review of grandfathering of US Jones Act (and like provisions); reviews to be held every two years thereafter	Paragraph 2 of GATT 1994
	January 1	Deadline for appraisal of TPRM	TPRM agreement section F
	Unspecified	Negotiations on increased protection for geographical indications for wines and spirits	TRIPs agreement Articles 23 and 24.1
	Unspecified	Subsidies in services	GATS Article XV

a. Most deadlines are specified in terms of months or years after the WTO enters into force, which we assume for purposes of this table to be 1 January 1995.

Environment and commissioned a group to immediately prepare for the WTO's work in this area by examining:

- the transparency of the present international system;

- export of domestically prohibited goods;

- the relationship between the GATT dispute settlement system and that of international environmental agreements;

- environmental measures with an effect on trade, such as packaging, labeling, and marking requirements, product standards, and environmental taxes or charges;

- the relationship between market access and the environment (including tariff escalation).

In addition to trade and environment, the link between trade and labor issues has also been proposed as an item on the work program of the WTO. The United States tried but failed at the Marrakesh ministerial to attain agreement on the establishment of a committee on worker rights under the WTO, analogous to the Committee on Trade and Environment, which would "explore the possible relationship between internationally recognized labor standards and trade."[19] The US proposal received only tepid support from the European Union and faced strong opposition from developing countries, which feared that developed countries could use alleged abuses of worker rights as a rationale for protectionist measures.

This rich agenda means that ongoing negotiations will be a central activity of the WTO. Although each issue has a separate mandate, the talks in each area will necessarily have a bearing on progress in the others. The WTO will need to organize this process to maximize the potential results. The next section discusses how to do so.

The Round to End All Rounds?

The Uruguay Round was an ordeal: from start to finish, the talks consumed almost eight years. At the end, officials threw up their hands and swore, "Never again!" Multilateral rounds of negotiations, they complained, had become too complex and took too long to complete. Such protestations echo identical statements made after both the Kennedy and the Tokyo rounds in the 1960s and 1970s, and seem to reflect negotiating fatigue more than anything else.

Criticisms of the practice of achieving multilateral trade liberalization through negotiating rounds do not stand up to careful analysis. The long duration of the GATT talks, which actually lasted about 12 years from the original proposal to the end of the negotiations, can be better explained by extraordinary economic factors rather than flaws in the GATT process.

---

19. However, both the United States and the European Union stressed that the issue of "social dumping" (offsetting other countries' comparative advantage of low labor costs with trade measures) should be delinked from other worker rights issues (e.g., child labor, prison labor, and other basic worker rights).

The difficulty in engaging countries to begin the negotiations resulted from a combination of unfavorable economic conditions in the first half of the 1980s and overanxious diplomacy on the part of the United States. The initial US initiative for new world trade talks was tabled in the midst of a global recession and at the advent of the developing country debt crisis (and the subsequent US recovery outpaced that of Europe and much of the developing world). Moreover, the trade initiative occurred just as the United States was engaged in fractious disputes with Europe over trade in steel and agricultural products, and over economic sanctions designed to blunt the construction of natural gas pipelines from the Soviet Union to Europe. No wonder the US proposals received an icy reception!

Second, the Uruguay Round, once launched, lasted for more than seven years primarily because of rancorous US-EC disputes over agriculture. Negotiators spent much of the time sitting on their hands, awaiting a breakthrough in the big-power impasse that had seized up talks across the GATT agenda. The fact that so much of the 1991 Dunkel text made its way into the final agreement indicates just how much time was spent idle during the round.

In contrast, negotiating rounds can help sustain commitments to trade liberalization and promote the achievement of additional reforms. In the flush of victory (and the ache of fatigue), negotiators often forget an important lesson of history: after each GATT round, protectionist pressures, which have been held in abeyance lest they threaten to disrupt ongoing trade talks, rapidly surface to challenge and attempt to roll back the reforms just negotiated. To preempt a protectionist backlash, and to keep the "bicycle" of trade liberalization upright and moving forward, countries need to rededicate themselves to the remaining problems and to undertake new trade initiatives promptly.

What needs to be done this time to prevent a relapse? First, WTO members need to move quickly to implement the agreements concluded in the Uruguay Round, and to continue talks in areas mandated by the new accords. Second, WTO members should establish a new eminent persons' group, much like the one that was commissioned in the mid-1980s (Leutwiler, et al. 1985) to recommend terms of reference for the Uruguay Round negotiations, to cover new issues such as trade and the environment, to lay the foundation for discussions of competition policy, to supplement the initial negotiations on investment issues (which to date have yielded rather meager results), and to deal with other items left unresolved in the Uruguay Round. The group should submit their report within a year of its establishment, with the aim of launching a new round of negotiations in 1997.

The reductions in trade barriers negotiated in the Uruguay Round create new opportunities to expand trade, but they do not guarantee increased sales. Companies have to be able to succeed in increasingly sharp global competition both to win new markets abroad and to maintain or increase their own domestic market share. To that end, the Uruguay Round reforms must be complemented by domestic economic policies that promote greater efficiency in the production of goods and services, and higher labor productivity. Just as important as the removal of foreign trade barriers and unfair trade practices is the removal of *domestic* disincentives that constrain productivity growth, discourage efficiency, and thus undercut the global competitiveness of domestic firms.

In sum, the successful conclusion of the Uruguay Round should reinforce the market-oriented reforms that have been instituted in most GATT member countries over the past decade. The estimated welfare gains from the trade reforms represent only a small share of global output, but when these results are introduced in conjunction with continuing domestic economic reforms, the impact should be multiplied and yield significant increases in trade and growth.

At the same time, the Uruguay Round results should restore confidence in the multilateral trading rules and credibility in the multilateral negotiating process, and significantly mitigate concerns about the spread of unilateralism and discriminatory regional trading pacts. If indeed "nothing succeeds like success," the new WTO should be able to build on the positive results of the Uruguay Round to reinforce and augment the important trade reforms already achieved.

However, success should not breed complacency, as has happened too often after previous GATT rounds. The trading system needs to keep pace with the changing nature and expanding scope of global trade in goods and services, not to mention the evolving national trade laws and regulations and the often innovative interpretations of those rules by trade bureaucrats. Fortunately, the Uruguay Round results already lay the groundwork for new negotiations, since the just-completed agreements mandate a host of new negotiations to be launched by the end of the decade. It is not too soon to start!

II

Assessment of the Major Components of the Uruguay Round Package

Trade Liberalization

Agriculture

Agriculture provided the glue, not the guts, of the Uruguay Round package of agreements.[1] Agriculture accounts for only about 13 percent of world trade. However, without substantial reforms in agricultural policies, a broad range of countries would neither have agreed to significant liberalization of other trade barriers nor accepted extensive new rights and obligations in the new areas of the negotiations.

The Uruguay Round marked the first GATT negotiation in which farm trade policies were covered in a comprehensive manner. After a great deal of agony and much rancor, the talks yielded significant reforms, even though the results paled in comparison with the ambitious initial proposals put forward by US negotiators and were less demanding even than the compromise proposals of the later stages of the round. Nonetheless, the Uruguay Round Agreement on Agriculture produced several notable achievements:[2]

- The agreement caps farm export subsidies and requires substantial reductions in both the value of subsidies (36 percent) and the volume of subsidized exports (21 percent) over six years.

---

1. This section benefited substantially from comments by Dale Hathaway, Tim E. Josling, Julius L. Katz, and Fred Sanderson, although they do not necessarily agree with its conclusions in all respects.

2. This section focuses primarily on temperate agricultural products and does not review commitments related to tropical products.

- It requires modest reductions (20 percent) in the aggregate domestic support provided to farmers.[3]

- It converts nontariff barriers into tariff equivalents, binds all tariffs, and opens minimum access quotas for products whose trade was largely blocked by past protection.

Most important, the accord halts the escalation of farm export subsidies (particularly in the grains sector) that have distorted world agricultural trade for decades, and begins to reduce, albeit modestly, domestic farm support programs. The agreement makes agricultural protection more transparent, reinforces reforms instituted by the major producing countries during the course of the seven-year negotiations (including the 1990 US farm bill and the European reform of the Common Agricultural Policy, or CAP), and sets a ceiling for *aggregate* domestic support that imposes GATT discipline on many farm subsidy programs for the first time. However, the exclusion of income support subsidies from the GATT disciplines may soften somewhat the impact of the new rules on national farm policies.

Negotiating History

Because of the extensive attention given to the agricultural negotiations, and to better understand the final results, it is worth examining the negotiating history. In the Punta del Este Declaration countries sought "to achieve greater liberalization of trade in agriculture and bring all measures affecting import access and export competition under strengthened and more operationally effective GATT rules and disciplines," including "by increasing discipline on the use of all direct and indirect subsidies and other measures affecting directly or indirectly agricultural trade."

US negotiators initially demanded the removal of all trade-distorting subsidies, but then moderated this position in 1990 to a 75 percent cut in domestic support programs and a 90 percent cut in export subsidies. US negotiating demands mirrored the similarly strident position of the European Community, which essentially sought to limit reform only to modest cuts in domestic price supports.

The US approach on agriculture was sensible, albeit confrontational, since the European Community gave no indication that it was prepared to pursue significant farm reform in the absence of strong external pressure. EC farm negotiators (and their counterparts in Japan and Korea) evidently assumed that, as in past GATT rounds, agriculture would be taken off the table before the end of the negotiations. EC reticence to talk

---

3. Subsidy programs such as direct income payments are exempted from the cuts. To the extent that these subsidies are trade distorting, their exclusion will weaken somewhat the new GATT discipline.

about significant reductions in agricultural protection only reinforced US intransigence to compromise on its proposal, since it made no sense to "negotiate with yourself."

Not surprisingly, these extreme positions resulted in a dialogue of the deaf for the first four years of the round. Discussions of agricultural issues were not seriously engaged until the runup to the Brussels ministerial meeting in December 1990. At the Brussels meeting the United States and most other participating countries agreed to use a compromise proposal drafted by Swedish Agriculture Minister Mats Hellström as the basis for negotiations. The Hellström text called for a 30 percent cut in export subsidies, import restrictions, and domestic supports from 1990 levels, to be phased in over five years. When the EC negotiators refused to discuss the proposal because it exceeded their negotiating mandate, the developing countries in the Cairns Group of agricultural exporting countries walked out of the talks and the Brussels meeting collapsed.

The Brussels fiasco proved helpful in two respects. It demonstrated that the Uruguay Round would not succeed without an agreement on agriculture, and it underscored the importance of accelerated action by the European Community to reform its domestic farm policies so that it could take a more flexible position in the GATT talks. After the Brussels meeting EC Commissioner Ray MacSharry proposed CAP reforms that would inter alia reduce some high price supports in return for direct payments to compensate farmers for the lower prices. The proposal provoked an intense and protracted debate within the Community.

In December 1991 GATT Director General Arthur Dunkel spurred further debate by revising the terms of the prospective GATT farm accord in his Draft Final Act (the so-called Dunkel draft). Despite extensive criticism, the Dunkel proposals defined to a large extent the parameters of the eventual agreement:

- In the export subsidy area the Dunkel text called for a 36 percent reduction in the *value* of subsidies and a 24 percent reduction in the *volume* of subsidized exports (from a 1986–90 base) in six annual installments.

- For domestic subsidies the Dunkel text called for a cut of 20 percent over six years (from a 1986–88 base) in the product-specific support provided domestic farmers.

- On import restrictions the Dunkel text required all nontariff barriers to be converted into tariffs and added to existing tariffs; the resulting tariffs were then to be reduced by an unweighted average of 36 percent (from a 1986–88 base) over a six-year period. However, even for sensitive products the reduction had to be at least 15 percent. In addition, countries had to maintain or improve current market access opportunities[4] and to open up a minimum import quota equal to 3 percent of domestic consumption (increasing to 5 percent by 1999) in product sectors where foreign suppliers have been effectively precluded.

The Dunkel text was summarily rejected by the French before it was even issued, but many other countries stated in January 1992 that they could accept it "as is." European objections to the Dunkel text included Dunkel's refusal to put the Community's proposed new compensation payments (designed to offset the cutbacks in support prices mandated by the CAP reform proposal) in the "green box" of practices exempt from new GATT disciplines,[5] the requirement to reduce the volume of subsidized exports by 24 percent and the value of export subsidies by 36 percent over a six-year period, and the absence of a "rebalancing" provision to allow the raising of barriers on some products while reducing protection overall by the negotiated amount.

Negotiations accelerated after bilateral meetings between US President George Bush and EC President Jacques Delors in April 1992 and the formal adoption of the CAP reform in May. The threat of US retaliation in a long-standing bilateral dispute with the Community over oilseeds added urgency to the talks. However, a US-EC compromise was not reached until after the US election in November 1992.

The Blair House accord of November 1992 broke the deadlock between the United States and the Community on agricultural supports. The agreement substantially modified key elements of the Dunkel text. First, domestic farm subsidies would still be reduced by 20 percent over six years (from a 1986–88 base), but US deficiency payments and EU compensation payments were exempted from the cuts. In addition, the cuts could be spread across all domestic subsidy programs rather than applied on a product-by-product basis. Second, the required cut in the volume of subsidized exports was reduced to 21 percent. Like the Dunkel text, the Blair House accord required equal annual cuts in farm subsidies from the base year, effectively mandating disproportionately larger cuts in the early years if subsidized exports in 1993 exceeded those in the base period. This front-loading of the liberalization affected key exports of both the United States and the Community.

Because of the front-loading requirement and for other reasons, the French refused to ratify the pact, forcing the Community to demand further modifications in continuing GATT talks. In December 1993 the Blair House accord was revamped: US and EU negotiators agreed to

---

4. This provision also served to protect exporters who received preferential treatment under various bilateral arrangements.

5. The intellectual rationale for a "green box" is that support payments that are decoupled from production levels or movements in farm prices need not be disciplined. Neither the US deficiency payments nor EU compensation payments fully meet those conditions.

modify, inter alia, requirements for immediate sharp cuts in export subsidies. This cleared the way for agreement on the final GATT accord.

The Uruguay Round Agreement on Agriculture

The Uruguay Round negotiations achieved the first significant GATT disciplines on both export and domestic subsidies, as well as modest reductions in import barriers and new guidelines for sanitary and phytosanitary measures. The reforms are most extensive with regard to export subsidy programs, and more modest concerning domestic support programs and market access commitments. However, countries committed themselves to a continuing process of policy reform and agreed to relaunch trade negotiations by the year 2000 to build on the reforms implemented to that point.

Export Subsidies

The agreement establishes the first-ever ceiling on both the value and the volume of subsidized exports of farm products. The final negotiated cuts in subsidies are quite close to those proposed in the Dunkel draft. Export subsidy expenditures must be reduced by 36 percent over six years, in equal annual installments, from 1986–90 levels. The volume of subsidized exports must be cut by 21 percent over six years, in equal annual installments, from the same base period.[6] For developing countries the percentage cuts are 24 and 14 percent, respectively, in equal annual installments over 10 years.

Obviously, countries will still be able to extend substantial export subsidies to their farmers, but the accord puts an end to the escalating subsidy wars that have erupted in recent years, particularly between the United States and the European Union. Moreover, the accord limits the spread of subsidy wars to new products by prohibiting export subsidies on products not previously subsidized in the base period.

Reductions will be generally applied to specific products or product groups at the four-digit HS (Harmonized Tariff System) level. However, in some important sectors such as coarse grains and fruits and vegetables, the commitments in some national schedules cover a broader range of goods and thus afford some flexibility to shift subsidies between different products. Nonetheless, countries will have to cap and reduce the overall amount of their subsidies and the quantity of goods that can be subsidized,

---

6. Minor adjustments in annual reductions are permitted in years 2 through 5, so long as the cumulative cuts to that point are within 3 percent of the value and 1.75 percent of the volume commitments specified in the country's liberalization schedule (Article 9.2b).

and the absence of an inflation adjustment means that the real value of support will be reduced further over time.

Special provisions were added at the end of the negotiations to reduce the immediate impact of the subsidy reforms on US and European producers of wheat and on EU producers of beef. Because exports of these subsidized commodities in 1991–92 were higher than in the base period, the agreement would have required large cutbacks in subsidies in these sectors in the first years of the agreement. Instead, the accord adjusts the base period to smooth out the schedule of subsidy cutbacks, so that equal annual reductions can be taken starting from levels achieved in 1991–92 (1986–92 for EU beef). Each country is still required to reduce the volume of its subsidized shipments by 21 percent from 1986–90 levels, but the changes reduce the cuts required in the first few years of the transition period.

For example, the final agreement establishes a ceiling of 19.1 million metric tons (MT) for subsidized exports of EU wheat and wheat flour, even though the base quantity from which the total reductions are calculated is 17 million MT. After six years the European Union must still limit the volume of its subsidized exports to 13.4 million MT (or 79 percent of the base level), but during the six-year transition period the European Union is allowed to subsidize more exports each year than under the terms of the Blair House accord.[7]

Cumulated over the six-year transition period, these changes will allow the European Union to subsidize exports of an additional 8 million MT of wheat and flour, 362,000 MT of beef, and 250,000 MT of poultry above that which would have been possible under the original base-period requirement. Similarly, the United States will be able to subsidize exports of a total of 7.5 million MT of wheat and flour, 1.2 million MT of vegetable oil, and about 700,000 MT of rice more than would have been permitted under the terms of the Blair House accord (Sanderson 1994, 7).

The agreement expressly excludes several types of export subsidy programs from the new disciplines. Export credits, credit guarantees, and insurance programs are not covered, but governments commit themselves to develop and adhere to internationally agreed disciplines in these areas. In addition, privately financed export aid is not covered as long as it is not mandated or arranged by the government or extended to products receiving other governmental support. This provision ensures that those producer-financed export subsidy schemes that provide benefits comparable to those under similar government programs are subject to GATT disciplines.

---

7. The United States receives similar treatment for its subsidized wheat exports. The US commitment sets a ceiling of 20.2 million MT in 1995, dropping to 14.5 million MT in 2000 (see Josling et al. 1994).

Domestic Subsidies

The agreement establishes a ceiling for the *total* domestic support (calculated as the Aggregate Measure of Support, or AMS) that a government may provide to its producers, and requires that the AMS be reduced by 20 percent over six years from the average level in the base period of 1986–88.[8] The commitments encompass both national and subnational subsidies. Because the cuts are applied at an aggregate level, countries maintain flexibility to shift support between products as long as they stay under the overall ceiling.

In calculating the AMS, however, countries may exclude several types of subsidies, thus reducing the range of programs subject to the required subsidy cutbacks. Important programs such as US deficiency payments and EU compensation payments under the 1992 CAP reform are exempted from the AMS calculation,[9] along with a long list of other nonactionable subsidy programs that "have no, or at most minimal, trade distorting effects or effects on production" (Annex 2, paragraph 1).[10]

The carveout for income support programs creates a precedent that can be exploited not only by the United States and the European Union, but also by other countries willing to restructure their farm support programs away from direct production subsidies to income supplements. Japan seems to be considering such changes to compensate its small-scale rice farmers for the limited breach of its import ban agreed to in the Uruguay Round (*Financial Times*, 13 July 1994, 6).

In addition, a de minimis provision allows countries to exclude from the calculation of the AMS product-specific support if it does not exceed 5 percent of the value of production of that commodity, and non-product-specific support where it does not exceed 5 percent of the value of the country's total agricultural production. For developing countries the de minimis level is 10 percent, and specified agricultural input subsidies are excluded from the AMS (Articles 6.2 and 6.4).

Import Liberalization

In the area of market access commitments, the Uruguay Round agreement requires countries to convert all existing nontariff measures into tariffs

---

8. However, if high inflation makes it hard for a country to live up to its commitments, the Committee on Agriculture established to administer this accord may consider requests for modifications of national schedules during its review of the implementation of the agreement (Article 18:4).

9. Direct payments to farmers are not subject to reductions if they are made under production-limiting programs and based on a fixed area and yield or number of livestock, or cover less than 85 percent of base-level production.

10. Other nonactionable subsidies include research and extension services, pest and disease control, inspection services, environmental and conservation programs, resource and producer retirement programs, stockholding for food security, domestic food aid, crop insurance, disaster relief, regional aids, and structural investment aid.

(which are then combined with existing tariffs), to bind all their agricultural tariffs,[11] and then to cut the combined tariffs by an *unweighted* average of 36 percent in equal installments over six years from their 1986–88 levels. Countries have flexibility in structuring the cuts for individual products: tariffs may be cut by much more than the average for some products and by much less for others, as long as each tariff is reduced by at least 15 percent over the six-year implementation period. For developing countries the reductions must average 24 percent, with a minimum cut of 10 percent, and be implemented over 10 years. The least developed countries must bind their tariffs but are exempt from all liberalization commitments.

The trade impact of the tariffication and liberalization commitments probably will be limited because of the ambiguous rules set out to govern the tariffication process. Countries are required to compute the tariff-rate equivalent (TRE) of their nontariff measures as applied in the 1988–90 base period and to notify the GATT of their new tariff bindings, which will then be subject to the 36 percent average reductions.[12] However, the agreement does not establish a procedure for verifying the new tariff levels, almost inviting officials to inflate the TREs to offset the required tariff liberalization. Such "dirty tariffication" has already provoked disputes between the United States and Canada.

In brief, the tariffication requirement will not necessarily create immediate trade opportunities, since the resulting tariffs could be highly inflated. But the tariffs do make the cost of protection to consumers, and the extent of protection against foreign suppliers, more transparent and thus more likely to generate pressure for further liberalization in future negotiations.

Special Safeguards

Under certain narrowly defined circumstances, a country may impose temporary duties (special safeguards) for up to one year on products subject to tariffication commitments. This protection is available "for the duration of the reform process" (Article 5:9), that is, for the six-year liberalization period (10 years for developing countries) as well as to reforms agreed in future trade negotiations.

The safeguard measures may be triggered by sudden movements in either volume (i.e., an import surge) or prices (i.e., a sharp drop in world prices). If the volume of imports rises above a certain trigger level, the importing country may impose temporary duties of up to one-third the

---

11. There are a few minor exceptions to this requirement, notably for Japanese and Korean rice.

12. The commitment to reduce tariffs by 36 percent was contained in a "modalities" paper that served as a negotiating guideline for scheduling commitments on individual products, not in the Agreement on Agriculture itself. The actual obligations are those specified in the national schedules.

normal applicable tariff for the duration of the marketing year. If the price of imports "falls below a trigger price equal to the average 1986 to 1988 reference price," the importing country may impose an additional duty equal to a prescribed ratio of the difference between the import and the trigger price.[13] Countries may impose either volume or price safeguard measures, but both may not be imposed concurrently.

Minimum Access Commitments

Countries also agree to establish "minimum access" import quotas, equal initially to 3 percent of domestic consumption and rising to 5 percent at the end of the sixth year, for products or product groups (e.g., meat and dairy products) where imports have faced prohibitive trade barriers. The commitments generally establish tariff-rate quotas for the specified products, with the in-quota tariff set at a "low or minimal" rate (these rates are detailed in national schedules and generally are no greater than 32 percent of the bound tariff). Although this tariff may still be quite high (e.g., in the triple digits for Japanese rice), it should provide some room for imports to compete against high-cost domestic products.

As a result of the minimum access commitments, countries will have to import modest amounts of their most protected products. More important, the commitments will expose domestic consumers to new sources of supply, which may increase demand for those products and consequently build support for further liberalization.

Perhaps the most significant import embargo that has been breached by the Uruguay Round agreement is the Japanese (and to a lesser extent Korean) ban on rice imports. Under the special provisions of Annex 5 of the agriculture agreement, Japan will establish a minimum access quota equal to 4 percent of domestic consumption, rising to 8 percent by the year 2000 (i.e., slightly higher levels than generally required under minimum access commitments). Korea establishes a 1 percent quota, which increases by 0.25 percent annually for four years, then by 0.4 percent annually for five years, to a level of 4 percent in 2004. At the end of these transition periods the countries must comply with the tariffication requirement, unless the tariffication obligation is otherwise waived in the context of negotiations regarding "continuation of the reform process" (Article 20).

Both these commitments involved wrenching political decisions by the Japanese and Korean governments (and cost the jobs of several sitting ministers) but will have little impact on the farm economy in either country. In Japan, for example, the cumulative volume of rice that Japan commits to import during the entire six-year period (about 3.5 million

---

13. In some respects, this price safeguard acts like a variable levy, except that it is shipment specific.

MT) is about the same volume that Japan imported in the 1993–94 season because of poor domestic rice harvests in the past few years!

Impact on US Programs

The market access reforms will have minimal impact on US imports of sugar and beef, which already exceed the minimum access requirements. However, the United States will have to establish minimum access quotas for certain products covered by Section 22 of the Agricultural Adjustment Act of 1933.

For sugar, the agreement requires little change in existing US programs: the United States will maintain a tariff-rate quota of 1.25 million MT, allocated by country (although the country shares will not be bound in the US national schedule). Thus, if Mexico increases its exports to the United States under the NAFTA, that quantity would likely be taken out of the shares of other countries unless the overall quota is expanded. For beef, restrictions that could be applied under the Meat Import Law will be transformed into a tariff-rate quota of 656,621 MT (slightly larger than the current trigger level for import quotas under the Meat Import Law), with the tariff set at 31.1 percent and reduced by the minimum 15 percent over six years to 26.4 percent.

Minimum access quotas will be established for cheese and for other dairy products (e.g., skim milk powder). The cheese quota will be increased by 31,000 tons during the period 1995–2000 (from 111,000 MT to 142,000 MT), with allocations by country bound in the US schedule, and the tariff dropping from $1.443 per kilogram to $1.227 per kilogram over six years. Section 22 quotas for peanuts will be converted into their tariff-rate equivalents, calculated as 155 percent for shelled peanuts and 193 percent for in-shell peanuts, and then reduced by 15 percent over six years. For cotton, tariff-rate quotas will rise from 51,927 MT to 86,545 MT over six years, with the in-quota tariff dropping from 37 cents to 31 cents per kilogram (Josling et al. 1994, table 4.3).

Sanitary and Phytosanitary (SPS) Measures

The SPS agreement allows countries to impose trade controls "to protect human, animal or plant life or health," if the measure is based on scientific principles and is applied on a nondiscriminatory basis. In essence, these provisions establish an agreed interpretation and elaboration of the exceptions to GATT obligations listed in GATT Article XX.

The agreement encourages the use of international SPS standards and supports efforts to promote the harmonization of SPS standards, where appropriate. The SPS accord also encourages countries to accept different SPS methods applied by other countries (under the "equivalence" principle), if such practices afford the requisite sanitary and phytosanitary protection.

However, the accord does not require that a country maintain international SPS standards. The use of stricter national standards is specifically allowed "if there is a scientific justification" for the higher standard *or* if the country deems that the risk to human, animal, or plant life or health requires additional protection. In such cases, the country is allowed to set its own risk levels but must undertake an assessment of the risk that takes into account both environmental and economic factors.

Policies that are consistent with international SPS standards will presumably be considered consistent with the GATT rules and not open to challenge by other countries. Concerns have been raised that stricter national standards could be subject to challenge under the dispute settlement procedures of the newly established World Trade Organization (WTO). However, the risk of such actions threatening national policies has been greatly exaggerated. Although both scientific tests and risk assessments underpinning national standards will be open to varying interpretations and potential WTO challenge (as already evidenced in the US dispute over the EU ban on hormone-fed beef), the basis for expert panels to condemn such practices is very limited, given the substantial discretion accorded national authorities under the SPS agreement. However, these cases should help clarify issues that require further negotiation in this area.

The "Peace Clause"

Finally, the agreement stipulates that if countries abide by the obligations to reduce their subsidies and trade barriers, they will be immune from GATT complaints for a period of nine years. This "peace clause" (Article 13) does not preclude the imposition of countervailing duties if subsidized imports are found to injure or threaten to injure domestic producers. However, nonactionable subsidies are exempted from countervailing duties, as well as from nullification and impairment and serious prejudice cases under the GATT for a period of nine years.[14]

In essence, the peace clause is designed to reduce the threat of new trade disputes during the period in which the farm trade reforms are being implemented. Some observers have criticized this provision for removing the "stick" to prod Europe and others to the negotiating table, but such leverage has not been very effective in the past. In most instances trade disputes have provoked competitive subsidy wars rather than discouraged subsidized production and trade.

---

14. However, this immunity is lost if domestic support under US and EU programs exempted from the AMS exceeds levels provided in 1992.

Assessment

The agreement on agriculture contains historic, albeit modest, commitments to cap and reduce export subsidies and most domestic subsidy programs. For the United States and the European Union, the accord requires significant reductions in current levels of export subsidies and reinforces reductions in domestic supports implemented since 1986. More important, the liberalization commitments are fixed in nominal terms without inflation adjustments, so that subsidy reductions in real terms will continue even after the 6- or 10-year transition period.

The export subsidy reductions are the most significant results of the agreement and should produce important benefits, particularly in the grains sector. Disciplines on domestic subsidies are softened somewhat by the exemption of the main subsidy programs benefiting farmers in the United States and the European Union. However, concerns that this loophole will lead to sharp increases in the exempted income support subsidies, and thus gut the GATT discipline, are exaggerated. The political prospects, in an era of budget stringency, of transferring large sums of money directly into the pockets of farmers (instead of through the more opaque process of price support payments) seem decidedly remote. In short, the greater transparency of farm subsidy programs should act as a brake on attempts to exploit the GATT loophole.

With regard to import liberalization, the accord requires comprehensive tariffication of nontariff barriers and 36 percent cuts in the unweighted average import protection. However, the most import-sensitive products face only a 15 percent tariff cut over six years. In short, the cost of protection becomes much more transparent, but the level of protection remains high for products currently subject to nontariff measures. For products currently blocked by comprehensive import barriers, such as Japanese and Korean rice, the minimum access quotas will open only a small segment of domestic markets to import competition, but nonetheless start the process of reform of long-standing trade barriers.

Textiles and Apparel

World trade in textiles and apparel has been subject to an increasing array of bilateral quota arrangements over the past three decades. Protection targeted at one market encouraged production to shift to another, although quotas never quite kept up with the expanding number of producing nations. The range of products subject to restraints expanded as well, from cotton textiles under the Short-Term and Long-Term arrangements of the 1960s and early 1970s, to an ever-increasing list of natural and man-made fibers under four iterations of the Multi-Fiber Arrangement (MFA). These restrictions proved highly resistant to reform in both the Kennedy and Tokyo rounds of GATT negotiations.

Despite the increasing severity of the restrictions under these managed trade regimes, and despite high tariffs in major industrial markets, protection has been porous and trade has expanded significantly (Cline 1990). World exports of textiles and apparel increased from $96 billion in 1980 to $248 billion in 1992, and now account for about 7 percent of global merchandise trade. In short, the MFA mismanaged trade to the detriment of producers in many developing countries and consumers everywhere, but without providing the secure import relief sought by producers in industrial countries.

The Uruguay Round Agreement on Textiles and Clothing unravels the web of quotas that has evolved under MFA auspices. After a 10-year transition period, trade in this sector will again be governed solely by the general rules of the GATT. However, the agreement does little to reduce the high tariffs that protect the apparel industry in developed countries and the textile industry in some developing countries.

Phaseout of MFA Quotas

The Uruguay Round accord signals the death knell for the MFA by setting a 10-year phaseout of bilateral quotas negotiated under the MFA umbrella. However, the impact of these reforms on trade flows will be muted for much of the transition period, since the least trade-restrictive measures will be phased out first, and the most restrictive measures will survive for most of the 10-year period.

The agreement calls for the immediate removal of quotas on products that accounted for at least 16 percent of the total volume of imports in 1990.[1] Remaining MFA quotas will be phased out over 10 years, in three stages: after 3 years, quotas will be removed on products that accounted for 17 percent of the total volume of 1990 imports; after 7 years, quotas on an additional 18 percent of 1990 imports will be removed; and after

---

1. The products covered by this commitment are listed in the annex to the agreement.

10 years, all remaining quota restrictions will be eliminated. In short, almost half of the trade covered by quotas will not be liberalized until the end of the transition period in the year 2004.

However, during the transition period, remaining quotas will be enlarged according to a three-stage formula. In the first stage (1995–97) individual country quotas will be increased by at least 16 percent more than the growth rate prescribed in the bilateral agreement concluded under MFA auspices in the year preceding the entry into force of the WTO. In stage 2 (1998–2001) quota growth rates will be 25 percent higher than in stage 1. In stage 3 (2002–04) quota growth rates will be 27 percent higher than the stage 2 rates.

Small producers and the least developed countries are accorded modest preferential treatment. MFA countries whose exports account for not more than 1.2 percent of the volume of a country's imports covered by the MFA as of 31 December 1991 will be granted higher quota growth rates during the transition period (25 percent in stage 1 and 27 percent in stage 2).

If one assumes the average growth rate of 6 percent mandated by the MFA, the annual growth in quotas would be 6.96 percent in 1995–97; 8.70 percent in 1998–2001; and 11.05 percent in 2002–04. As a result, many quotas that are not completely eliminated until the end of the 10-year transition period would, in the meantime, have increased by 134 percent. However, if the base growth rate for bilateral quotas were only 1 percent, then the annual quota growth rate during the transition period would initially be only 1.16 percent, and would never exceed 2 percent. Those quotas would expand by only 16 percent over 10 years.

Since the most sensitive items will be the last to be liberalized, one can expect tremendous political pressure for an extension of the quotas, and/or for the imposition of import safeguards, as the transition period draws to an end. Moreover, the slow rate of expansion of quotas that remain in place during the transition period for some highly competitive developing countries could well increase the overall restrictiveness of many of the surviving trade barriers (measured in tariff-equivalent terms). In that event, a substantial level of protection would remain until the final year of the transition period. The obligation to dismantle the remaining quotas in 2004 would probably generate strong political opposition and demands for negotiations to extend the transition period.

The initial liberalization and subsequent reforms must include some products from each of the following categories: tops and yarns, fabrics, made-up textile products, and clothing. However, the pact does not specify how much from each category must be liberalized at each stage of the transition period, so countries maintain substantial discretion in structuring their quota liberalization. Swing, carryover, and carryforward provisions in force during the base period will be maintained during the transition period.

Within 60 days of entry into force of the WTO, countries must notify all their MFA quotas to a new Textiles Monitoring Body that will be established by the Council for Trade in Goods. These quotas will then be subject to the liberalization schedule outlined above. Non-MFA restrictions not justified under the GATT must be brought into conformity within one year after the entry into force of the agreement, or phased out progressively over 10 years according to a schedule notified to the Textiles Monitoring Body.

In essence, the Uruguay Round agreement thus establishes a freeze on new restrictions in this sector, with two important exceptions. First, countries may impose Article XIX safeguard measures in cases where quotas have been liberalized and trade is again subject to the rules of the GATT 1994.[2] Second, countries may continue to deploy antidumping actions against unfairly traded goods, whether quotas remain in force or not. The prospect of such action has elicited concern in several developing countries that protection of the textiles and apparel sector could shift from quotas to antidumping measures.

Transitional Safeguards

The Uruguay Round agreement on textiles and clothing provides an elaborate selective safeguards mechanism during the transition period. This mechanism is designed to blunt import surges and undoubtedly will be used to coerce developing countries to moderate their export growth.

Safeguard measures may be applied selectively (i.e., on a non-most-favored nation basis) against imports from a country that are still subject to MFA quotas and that cause or threaten serious damage to the domestic industry. However, such safeguard measures are subject to certain conditions.

First, the safeguard action may not reduce the volume of trade below the actual level of exports or imports from the country concerned during the previous 12-month period. Second, the safeguard measure may only remain in place for up to three years, with no provision for extension, or until quotas on the product are liberalized (i.e., integrated into GATT 1994), whichever comes first. Multiyear safeguards must provide for quota growth of at least 6 percent annually. Third, safeguard measures may not be applied against developing country exports of handloom fabrics or products of cottage industries, or traditional folklore handicrafts; textiles that are historically traded in significant quantities; and products made of pure silk.

---

2. Article XIX safeguards may not be imposed on those products still subject to MFA quotas during the transition period.

Implications for the United States

The United States has bilateral quota agreements with 41 countries, whose shipments accounted for about 70 percent of total US apparel imports in 1993 (USITC Publication 2790, June 1994, IV-15). Of that total, China and Taiwan supply 25 percent but are not currently subject to the Uruguay Round reforms because they are not members of the GATT. Once those countries, and any other textile-producing countries, accede to the WTO, they will be eligible for the full quota liberalization by 2004—unless other arrangements are agreed upon in their respective protocols of accession.

The textile and apparel industries receive higher levels of protection than any other US manufacturing sector. The estimated tariff-rate equivalent of all US protection of textiles (tariffs and quotas combined) is 23.4 percent, and 48 percent for apparel. Elimination of all US import barriers would provide a $24 billion windfall to US consumers (Hufbauer and Elliott 1994, 88–89), but the Uruguay Round reforms fall well short of that result in two important respects.

First, substantial tariffs will exist even after the Uruguay Round reforms are fully implemented, including numerous peak tariffs (i.e., those above 15 percent ad valorem). For textiles, US tariff cuts will average about 24 percent. However, more than 50 items will be left with tariffs above 15 percent, particularly wool and wool-blended fabrics.[3] In comparison, textile tariffs will be cut by an average of 31 percent by the European Union, and 39 percent by Japan.

US apparel tariffs will be cut by only 9.2 percent and will still average about 18 percent after the Uruguay Round cuts are fully implemented. These reductions compare with average cuts in apparel tariffs of 12 percent and 34 percent by the European Union and Japan, respectively. About one-quarter of US tariff lines for apparel items will remain above 15 percent. Because developing countries generally offered smaller cuts in their textiles and apparel tariffs,[4] and because they typically ship large-volume items, US tariffs on their exports were in most instances subject to small cuts. Where peak US apparel tariffs were reduced by more than the average cut, the reductions generally benefited suppliers in Europe (USITC Publication 2790, June 1994, IV-15).

Second, during the transition period many US quotas may become more restrictive, and thus more costly to US consumers, until they are

---

3. Despite sizable cuts in tariffs on wool and wool-blended fabrics from an average of about 40 percent, US duties will still average about 25 percent on a trade-weighted basis (USITC Publication 2790, June 1994, IV-11).

4. Some developing countries did commit to significant tariff cuts on products of interest to the United States; for example, Korea and Brazil agreed to average tariff cuts of 29 percent and 53 percent, respectively (US Department of Commerce, International Trade Administration 1994).

finally eliminated. This situation is particularly significant for several East Asian suppliers. In recent renegotiations of MFA bilateral agreements with these countries, the United States sharply curtailed the quota growth rates for many products to only 1 percent.[5] In those instances the Uruguay Round agreement requires that quotas expand by only 1.16 percent annually in the first stage, 1.45 percent in stage 2, and 1.84 percent in stage 3, or by a total of about 16 percent during the transition period.

Assuming a modest increase in US demand during the transition period, Cline (1990) estimated that apparel quotas would have to expand by at least 7 percent annually in real terms to avoid an increase in the level of protection. Consequently, for those countries, access to the US apparel market is likely to get worse before quota liberalization makes it better.

Finally, the Uruguay Round reforms would not apply to China, since that country is not yet a GATT member. However, if China joins the WTO in the near future, it would be entitled to the MFA liberalization included in the Uruguay Round agreement. A major effort of the US and European textile lobbies and (if more quietly) the textile interests of developing countries will be to ensure that China remains subject to a far more restrictive regime.[6]

Assessment

The elimination of MFA quotas over a 10-year transition period is a notable achievement of the Uruguay Round, even if the liberalization schedule is heavily back-loaded. About half of existing quotas are not required to be removed until 2004, but most of these quotas will expand substantially during the transition period.

However, textiles and apparel will remain one of the most heavily protected sectors, even after the phaseout of the MFA quotas, because the agreement does little to reduce the relatively high textile tariffs in developing countries and high tariffs on clothing in developed countries. In addition, recourse to transitional safeguards could constrain annual import growth of the most import-sensitive products during the transition period.

---

5. As a result, the trade-weighted growth rates for all US textile and apparel imports covered by bilateral MFA agreements was 3.9 percent in 1992, substantially lower than the target 6 percent annual quota growth rate set by the MFA.

6. China has already agreed to significant export constraints in its bilateral agreement with the United States signed in early 1994. The pact covers more than $7 billion in Chinese shipments (including for the first time silk products), freezes quotas at 1993 levels, and limits annual quota growth to 1 percent in 1995 and 1996.

Tariff Liberalization

Tariff liberalization in recent GATT rounds was based on a set formula, with exceptions negotiated for specific products or sectors. The Kennedy Round (1963–67) applied a single tariff-cutting formula, with any exceptions specifically negotiated on a negative list, and achieved an overall 35 percent reduction in the average level of industrial tariffs. Negotiators in the Tokyo Round (1973–79) based tariff cuts on a variant of the formula used in the Kennedy Round in an attempt to harmonize peak tariffs, but the negotiated exceptions limited the end result to an average cut of about 34 percent. Overall, the historical approach dramatically reduced the average tariffs of most industrial countries to well below 10 percent but left intact peak tariffs in import-sensitive sectors.

In the Uruguay Round, however, the United States insisted on negotiating tariff cuts on a sector-by-sector basis rather than committing to a general tariff-cutting formula applicable to all products with negotiated exceptions. The ad hoc US approach to tariff liberalization sought to promote four specific objectives: the elimination of tariffs in selected sectors, the harmonization of tariffs at low levels in other sectors (notably chemicals), the expansion of the scope of tariff bindings, and the reduction of peak tariffs. To gain political acceptance for cuts in its peak tariffs, the US negotiators needed to package those commitments in sectoral deals that offered compensating benefits for domestic producers affected by the cuts. In other words, the United States was willing to reduce peak tariffs, but only if other major trading countries committed to reciprocal liberalization. Given the political sensitivity to such deals, the US approach implicitly was strongly biased toward a status quo outcome.

As a practical matter, the US approach was not terribly different from past rounds. The rationale for the tariff-cutting formula was to commit countries, through a relatively automatic mechanism, to a single package of tariff cuts, and thus discourage efforts to maintain peak tariffs. Once the formula was agreed, the bulk of the negotiations devolved into haggling about which products to exempt or give special treatment. In essence, the US approach skipped over the preliminary step of setting a formula and went directly to the detailed product-specific talks that have always been the heart of tariff negotiations.

As a result, the Uruguay Round followed an ad hoc approach to tariff liberalization; efforts focused on problems of tariff peaks and tariff escalation, as well as on expanding the scope of tariff concessions bound (i.e., locked in) in a country's GATT schedules. At the end of the midterm review of the Uruguay Round in April 1989, ministers mandated tariff cuts to average about one-third, either through a formula approach or through a request-and-offer approach.[1] However, tariff liberalization also

---

1. The ministerial agreement called for "overall reductions at least as ambitious as that achieved by the formula participants in the Tokyo Round" (*GATT Focus* no. 62, May 1989, 2).

Table 7 Average tariff cuts achieved in the Uruguay Round for industrial goods

Country or group	Imports from MFN origins (billions of dollars)	Trade-weighted average tariff (percentages)		Average tariff cut (percentages)
		Pre-Uruguay Round	Post-Uruguay Round	
Developed countries	736.9	6.3	3.9	38
Canada	28.4	9.0	4.8	47
European Union	196.8	5.7	3.6	37
Japan	132.9	3.9	1.7	56
United States[a]	420.5	4.6	3.0	34
Developing countries[b]	305.1	15.3	12.3	20
Economies in transition	34.7	8.6	6.0	30

a. Based on data provided by USTR.
b. Based on bound rates, not applied rates.

Source: Hoda (1994).

progressed through so-called "zero-for-zero" negotiations, which sought to eliminate all tariffs in specific product sectors. In the few sectors where these ambitious results emerged, the problems of tariff peaks and tariff escalation were effectively addressed.

Average Tariff Cut

Overall, the Uruguay Round will cut developed countries' tariffs by an average of 38 percent, lowering their average tariff to 3.9 percent. The average Uruguay Round tariff cut is somewhat higher than that achieved in the Kennedy and Tokyo rounds.[2] The overall depth of cut for the United States is about 34 percent; for the European Union, 37 percent; for Canada, 47 percent; and for Japan, 56 percent (table 7). All major trading countries have agreed to cut tariffs on industrial goods by more than the target amount agreed at the midterm review.

Above-average tariff cuts are taking place in seven product groups: metals; mineral products, precious stones, and metals; electric machinery; wood, pulp, paper, and furniture; nonelectric machinery; chemicals and photographic supplies; and "other" manufactured articles, which together account for 71 percent of developed countries' imports. Below-average cuts are made in four product groups: textiles and apparel; leather, rubber, footwear, and travel goods; fish and fish products; and transport equip-

---

2. However, this simple comparison overlooks the fact that a one-third cut in tariffs yields far greater economic benefits when the initial average duty is 30 percent than when it is 6 percent.

ment. In general, the cuts are phased in over five years, in equal annual increments, starting in January 1995.

Tariffs on US imports of nonagricultural commodities will decrease from a pre–Uruguay Round trade-weighted average level of 4.6 percent to 3.0 percent. The average cut in tariffs benefiting US merchandise exports is about 43 percent: from a pre–Uruguay Round level of 9.2 percent to 5.2 percent after all cuts are implemented (see tables 3 and 4).

Zero-for-Zero Commitments

In some specified product sectors, the main industrialized countries have gone beyond the average cuts in industrial tariffs and reduced their tariffs to zero. For their part, the developing countries tried to make substantial reductions in the same products.

Zero-for-zero commitments covered the following sectors: pharmaceuticals (subject to immediate elimination); construction equipment, steel, distilled spirits, certain furniture, medical equipment, and farm machinery (subject to a phase-in period of five years); beer (subject to a phase-in period of eight years); and toys and paper (subject to a phase-in period of ten years). These commitments generally apply to products at a disaggregated level (i.e., four- to six-digit Harmonized System levels) and are therefore more product- than sector-specific. For the United States, the product sectors affected by the zero-for-zero commitments accounted for about $31 billion, or 6.7 percent, of total 1989 imports.

Peak Tariffs

At the July 1993 Quad meeting, the United States, the European Union, Canada, and Japan committed themselves to reduce their peak tariffs (i.e., import duties of 15 percent or more) on average by at least 50 percent. These reductions affect mainly textiles and apparel, and ceramics and glassware. However, final commitments in this area cut the global share of imports subject to tariff peaks by only 2 percentage points, from a pre–Uruguay Round share of 7 percent to 5 percent after all cuts have been implemented.

The United States will cut its peak tariffs, which currently average 23.3 percent, by only 11.5 percent, to a post–Uruguay Round level of 20.7 percent—leaving the protection through peak tariffs of many sectors intact. For example, the trade-weighted average tariff on US apparel imports will be cut by only 9 percent, from 19.3 percent to 17.5 percent.

Tariff Bindings

One of the main objectives of the market-opening efforts in the Uruguay Round was to reduce uncertainty about future tariff levels by increasing the number of bound tariff rates—in other words, to widen the range of products for which governments were committed not to raise the levels of tariffs. This was of particular importance for the developing countries, which prior to the Uruguay Round negotiations had made very few such commitments.

The Uruguay Round ensures that virtually all imports of developed countries (99 percent) will enter under bound rates, as well as almost 60 percent of the imports of developing countries. Of all world trade in industrial products, 88 percent will be subject to bound rates, up from 70 percent (table 8).

Duty-Free Trade

Tariffs present administrative as well as economic burdens. The elimination of tariffs thus can relieve a lot of technical problems that can directly or indirectly bias trade flows. The share of imports of industrial goods being granted duty-free treatment by developed countries will more than double as a result of the Uruguay Round, from 20 percent to 44 percent (table 8). This will not only have a direct effect upon the competitiveness of US exports, but will also make US imports cheaper, benefiting US consumers as well as US manufacturers who use imported inputs.

Tariff Escalation

Another accomplishment of the tariff package is to reduce the discrimination against exports of processed products that results when countries apply increasingly higher tariffs on products as the level of processing increases. Such tariff escalation effectively works as a disincentive to exporting products with a higher value-added content as opposed to raw materials. Tariff escalation will largely be eliminated for paper products, for products made from jute, and for products made from tobacco, and has been reduced for products made from wood and metals. Overall, the difference in tariffs applied to the unprocessed and the processed versions of industrial products will be reduced by an average of 37 percent (News of the Uruguay Round, *Increases in Market Access Resulting from the Uruguay Round*, 12 April 1994 Geneva: GATT).

Tariff Harmonization

Chemicals tariffs will be harmonized downward (i.e., reduced to low common levels). Currently applied rates on some chemical products will be eliminated, while those on most other chemicals will be bound at or below 6.5 percent. As a result, the United States will lower its average

Table 8 Tariff bindings on and duty-free trade in industrial goods before and after the Uruguay Round

Country or group	Imports from MFN origins (billions of dollars)	Percentage of tariffs bound		Percentage duty-free	
		Pre-Uruguay Round	Post-Uruguay Round	Pre-Uruguay Round	Post-Uruguay Round
Developed countries	736.9	94	99	20	44
Canada	28.4	100	100	21	39
European Union	196.8	100	100	24	38
Japan	132.9	89	96	35	71
United States	297.3	99	100	10	40
Developing countries	305.1	15	58	52	49[a]
Economies in transition	34.7	74	96	13	16

a. The post–Uruguay Round decrease in the percentage of duty-free imports is due to ceiling bindings on tariff lines with zero base duties.

Source: Hoda (1994).

tariff on chemicals from 5.2 percent to 3.7 percent, a cut of about 28 percent, affecting about $15 billion, or 3.2 percent, of 1989 merchandise imports. The phase-in period for these cuts varies from 5 to 15 years, depending on the pre–Uruguay Round tariff level. However, several important developing countries (e.g., Argentina, Brazil, India, Indonesia, Thailand, and Venezuela) were reticent to substantially lower their high tariffs and did not participate in the harmonization commitment.

Assessment

The overall depth of cut accomplished in the Uruguay Round exceeds those achieved in both the Kennedy and the Tokyo Rounds, as well as the commitment made at the Montreal midterm review to cut tariffs by an average of at least one-third. The Uruguay Round succeeded in reducing tariff escalation in important product sectors, and harmonized chemical tariffs at low levels in most developed country markets (but not in some key developing countries). Tariffs on a number of industrial goods have been eliminated altogether. However, the Uruguay Round industrial tariff liberalization package fails to achieve substantial cuts in peak tariffs, particularly in the textile and apparel sector.

Government Procurement

The new Government Procurement Agreement (GPA) reinforces rules to secure open and nondiscriminatory access to public tenders for the procurement of goods and services. When it enters into force on 1 January 1996, the GPA will supersede the GATT procurement code that has been in effect since 1981. Although the GPA will not have many new signatories, it will significantly expand the list of public agencies of existing members subject to international rules, including for the first time subcentral governments (e.g., states and provinces) and public utilities, and extend the coverage of obligations to the procurement of services. Overall, the GPA obligations will apply to several hundred billion dollars annually in government purchases.[1]

The new code is one of four plurilateral agreements under the umbrella of the WTO, which do not require the participation of all WTO signatories (i.e., the GPA provisions apply only to its signatories).[2] However, the settlement of disputes on GPA matters between signatories will follow the procedures of the Dispute Settlement Understanding of the WTO, although some special rules set out in GPA Article XXII will apply (e.g., dispute panel members must be from countries that are signatories of the GPA). In addition, each signatory must introduce a challenge procedure in its national legislation through which foreign tenderers can seek redress against a domestic purchasing entity for procurement practices that are in violation of the GPA.[3]

The GPA annexes list the government entities that are subject to the agreement: central governments, subcentral governments, and other governmental entities (e.g., public utilities). The GPA applies to contracts of goods or services procured by central governments worth more than SDR 130,000 (this is comparable to the existing code, whose initial threshold value of SDR 150,000 was lowered to SDR 130,000 in 1988). For subcentral governments the threshold varies but is generally about SDR 200,000 (for the United States and Canada the threshold value is SDR 355,000); for utilities the threshold is about SDR 400,000. Construction services are

---

1. Ballpark estimates of the potential value of contracts that will be covered range up to $400 billion annually, which represents a sizable increase in the existing code coverage (see Hoda 1994, 11).

2. To date, 22 countries have indicated their intention to sign the GPA: Austria, Canada, the 12 member states of the European Union, Finland, Israel, Japan, Korea, Norway, Sweden, Switzerland, and the United States. However, Korea may delay implementation of the GPA until 1997. Hong Kong participated in the GPA negotiations but decided at the last minute not to sign the agreement.

3. Such challenges could potentially delay the award of contracts, unless "overriding adverse consequences for the interests concerned, including the public interest" present just cause for not taking rapid interim measures "to correct breaches of the Agreement and to preserve commercial opportunities" (Article XX:7).

generally subject to a threshold of SDR 5 million.[4] Contracts tendered by covered entities above these thresholds are open to international competition. The thresholds are not adjusted for inflation and consequently will be reduced in real terms over time. As a result, the new rules will apply to more and more government procurement with each passing year.

By way of comparison, the government procurement provisions of the North American Free Trade Agreement (NAFTA) set thresholds for covered procurement that are generally lower (i.e., entail more comprehensive coverage) than those established in the GPA. Contracts tendered by federal departments and agencies worth more than $50,000 for goods and services ($25,000 for Canada and the United States), and worth more than $6.5 million for construction, are subject to the NAFTA rules. Government enterprises are bound by the rules for goods and services contracts worth more than $250,000, and for construction projects worth more than $8 million. However, unlike the new GATT procurement agreement, the NAFTA does not cover procurement by subnational governments, and the thresholds are adjusted for inflation every two years, starting in January 1996. Moreover, Mexico is not a signatory to the GATT procurement code and has not agreed to adhere to GPA disciplines.

GPA and the GATS

Like GATT Article III:8(a), the General Agreement on Trade in Services (GATS) explicitly excludes procurement by government agencies. Article XIII of the GATS states that its most-favored nation (MFN), market access, and national treatment provisions do not apply to "laws, regulations or requirements governing the procurement by governmental agencies of services purchased for governmental purposes." However, the GATS does oblige countries to launch new negotiations on services procurement within two years after the WTO enters into force.

In the interim the GPA provides the only discipline on government procurement of services. Unlike the existing code, the GPA specifically covers services procured by government entities. However, the obligations apply only to those entities listed in the national schedules of the GPA signatories. The GPA rules are likely to serve as a precedent for future GATS negotiations on government procurement issues. A GATS government procurement agreement may expand the number of government entities subject to multilateral discipline, depending on the outcome of the talks. More important, its obligations will apply to all WTO members, not just those that are GPA signatories.

---

4. Converted to US dollars—at the 31 December 1993 rate of SDR 1.3736 to the dollar— these new thresholds are about $179,000 for central governments, $275,000 for subcentral governments, $549,000 for utilities, and about $6.9 million for construction contracts.

Market Access Commitments

Table 9 summarizes the market access commitments of the European Union, the United States, Japan, and Korea; the commitments of the member states of the European Free Trade Association (EFTA) closely follow those of the European Union. In general, the opportunity to bid on procurement by central governments of goods and construction services is offered on an MFN basis, while other services contracts are accorded only to those countries that put forward reciprocal offers. Obligations regarding subcentral governments and public utilities are heavily conditioned on access to other markets.

For example, Japan accords MFN treatment to all other signatories except the United States and Canada regarding contracts procured by subcentral governments and public utilities. However, it exempts the telecommunications sector, as well as electricity and transportation safety projects, from this general MFN commitment. Korea excludes the EU and EFTA countries from its offer on airport and urban transportation projects until these countries grant reciprocal access in these sectors.

To a large extent, the GPA negotiations were dominated by the European Union and the United States, which together account for a substantial share of the procurement contracts that will be covered by GPA rules. Above-threshold contracts for central government procurement are of roughly equivalent value in both markets: about $52 billion annually for the European Union and $57 billion for the United States (table 10). However, data on procurement by subcentral governments and public utilities differ widely, with the most pronounced discrepancy arising in construction by subcentral governments ($74 billion for the European Union versus $16 billion for US states and major cities). Note, however, that the final GPA commitments of the European Union and the United States do not cover all contracts included in the estimates in table 10. Moreover, the thresholds upon which these estimates are based are generally lower than the actual GPA thresholds, and thus overstate the actual sales opportunities generated by the GPA.

Procurement at the subfederal level and by public utilities provoked the most heated discussion. In January 1993 the European Community implemented a new Utilities Directive, which mandates a 3 percent price preference for European bidders on EC contracts if the home markets of non-EC bidders do not offer equitable access in that sector for EC firms (article 29 of the directive). The directive also permits EC utilities to reject any bid with less than 50 percent EC content. US negotiators demanded that US firms be exempted from the price preference (especially for telecommunications contracts), while EC negotiators sought better access to subfederal contracts in the United States as well as to telecommunications contracts awarded by private US companies.

Table 9 Market-access commitments for government procurement by the European Union, the United States, Japan, and Korea[a]

	Goods	Services	Construction
European Union[b]			
Central governments	Threshold: SDR 130,000 MFN treatment Air traffic control equipment excepted	Threshold: SDR 130,000 Reciprocal access Air traffic control equipment excepted	Threshold: SDR 5 million MFN treatment Air traffic control equipment excepted
Subcentral governments	Threshold: SDR 200,000 MFN treatment Canada excepted	Threshold: SDR 200,000 Reciprocal access US and Canada excepted	Threshold: SDR 5 million Reciprocal access US and Canada excepted
Public utilities	Threshold: SDR 400,000 MFN treatment for procurement of electricity projects and maritime, inland port, and other terminal facilities Canada excepted	Threshold: SDR 400,000 Reciprocity for procurement of electricity projects and maritime, inland port, and other terminal facilities Canada excepted	Threshold: SDR 5 million MFN treatment for procurement of electricity projects and maritime, inland port, and other terminal facilities Canada excepted
United States[c]			
Central government[d]	Threshold: SDR 130,000 MFN treatment FAA contracts excepted	Threshold: SDR 130,000 Reciprocal access FAA contracts excepted	Threshold: SDR 5 million MFN treatment FAA contracts excepted
Subcentral governments[e]	Threshold: SDR 355,000 MFN treatment for procurement by 37 states only[f]	Threshold: SDR 355,000 Reciprocity for procurement by 37 states only[f]	Threshold: SDR 5 million (for Korea: SDR 15 million) MFN treatment for procurement by 37 states only[f]

continued next page

Table 9 Market-access commitments for government procurement by the European Union, the United States, Japan, and Korea[a] (continued)

	Goods	Services	Construction
	Canada, Japan, and EFTA member countries excepted National treatment of EU bids on contracts procured by North Dakota and West Virginia and 7 of the 24 largest US cities[g]	Canada, Japan, and EFTA member countries excepted National treatment of EU bids on contracts procured by North Dakota and West Virginia and 7 of the 24 largest US cities[g]	Canada, Japan, and EFTA member countries excepted National treatment of EU bids on contracts procured by North Dakota and West Virginia and 7 of the 24 largest US cities[g]
Public utilities[h]	Threshold: SDR 400,000 MFN treatment for procurement by the New York and New Jersey Port Authority, the Port of Baltimore, and New York Power Authority, as well as power generation projects funded by the REA[i] Canada, Japan, and EFTA member countries excepted Threshold: SDR 182,000 MFN treatment for procurement by Tennessee Valley Authority, Power Marketing Administrations, and St. Lawrence Seaway Canada, Japan, and EFTA member countries excepted National treatment of EU bids on contracts tendered by Massachusetts Port Authority	Threshold: SDR 400,000 Reciprocity for procurement by the New York and New Jersey Port Authority, the Port of Baltimore, and New York Power Authority, as well as power generation projects funded by the REA[i] Canada, Japan, and EFTA member countries excepted Threshold: SDR 182,000 Reciprocity for procurement by Tennessee Valley Authority, Power Marketing Administrations, and St. Lawrence Seaway Canada, Japan and EFTA member countries excepted National treatment of EU bids on contracts tendered by Massachusetts Port Authority	Threshold: SDR 5 million (for Korea: SDR 15 million) MFN treatment for procurement by the New York and New Jersey Port Authority, the Port of Baltimore, Tennessee Valley Authority, Power Marketing Administrations, St. Lawrence Seaway, and New York Power Authority, as well as power generation projects funded by the REA[i] Canada, Japan, and EFTA member countries excepted National treatment of EU bids on contracts tendered by Massachusetts Port Authority

Japan

Central government	Threshold: SDR 130,000 MFN treatment	Threshold: SDR 130,000 Reciprocal access	Threshold: SDR 4.5 million (for architectural, engineering, and other technical services: SDR 450,000) MFN treatment
Subcentral governments[j]	Threshold: SDR 200,000 MFN treatment US and Canada excepted	Threshold: SDR 200,000 Reciprocal access US and Canada excepted	Threshold: SDR 15 million (for architectural, engineering, and other technical services: SDR 1.5 million) MFN treatment US and Canada excepted
Public utilities[k]	Threshold: SDR 130,000 MFN treatment US and Canada excepted	Threshold: SDR 130,000 Reciprocal access US and Canada excepted	Threshold: SDR 15 million (for architectural, engineering, and other technical services: SDR 450,000) MFN treatment US and Canada excepted

Korea[l]

Central government[m]	Threshold: SDR 130,000 MFN treatment	Threshold: SDR 130,000 Reciprocal access	Threshold: SDR 5 million MFN treatment
Subcentral governments[n]	Threshold: SDR 200,000 MFN treatment Canada excepted	Threshold: SDR 200,000 Reciprocal access Canada excepted	Threshold: SDR 15 million MFN treatment Canada excepted
Public utilities	Threshold: SDR 450,000 MFN treatment Canada excepted	Reciprocal access	Threshold: SDR 15 million MFN treatment Canada excepted

continued next page

Table 9 Market-access commitments for government procurement by the European Union, the United States, Japan, and Korea[a] (continued)

FAA = Federal Aviation Administration; REA = Rural Electrification Administration

a. Countries may improve their commitments until the GPA enters into force on 1 January 1996. Because Canada has not yet specified its final offer for subcentral governments and public utilities, most countries do not extend benefits to Canada in these areas. Country exceptions are generally conditioned on improved market access offers by such countries.

b. Telecommunications contracts are not included.

c. Telecommunications contracts are not included. US set-asides on behalf of small and minority-owned businesses are exempt. The US offer includes, inter alia, the following services: transportation (except when incidental to procurement of supplies), dredging, overseas military services procurement, public utilities services, R&D services, and printing services (Annex II only).

d. Except Japan for contracts procured by the National Aeronautics and Space Administration.

e. State mass transit and highway improvement projects that receive federal funding, are exempted from these commitments. States may still apply restrictions that promote the general environmental quality in that state, as long as such restrictions are not disguised barriers to international trade.

f. Including the five most populous states (California, Pennsylvania, New York, Florida, and Texas).

g. Chicago, Detroit, Boston, Dallas, Indianapolis, San Antonio, and Nashville.

h. Airport projects that receive federal funding are exempt from these commitments.

i. "Buy American" restrictions on all REA-funded projects are waived.

j. Except electricity and transportation safety projects.

k. Several utilities are exempt, notably, NTT (telecommunications) and the railways (transportation safety projects).

l. Benefits are not extended to the European Union, Austria, Norway, Sweden, Finland, and Switzerland, as regards railroad contracts.

m. Except the European Union, Austria, Norway, Finland, Sweden and Switzerland, as regards airport and urban transportation projects.

n. Except the European Union, Austria, Norway, Finland, Sweden and Switzerland, as regards urban transportation.

Sources: GATT (1994), US Department of State (1994), Deloitte & Touche (1994).

Table 10   Estimated value of EU and US procurement contracts above GPA thresholds, excluding telecommunications entities, 1993 (billions of 1993 dollars)[a]

	Goods	Services	Construction	Total
European Union[b]				
Central governments	19.2	11.4	21.0	51.6
Subcentral governments	23.5	8.9	73.7	106.1
Public utilities	18.9	9.0	16.2	44.1
Total	61.6	29.3	110.9	201.8
United States				
Central governments	26.1	27.5	3.8	57.4
Subcentral governments[c,d]	11.3	14.8	15.6	41.7
Public utilities[d,e]	2.0	1.8	4.1	7.9
Total	39.4	44.1	23.5	107.0

a. The final GPA commitments of the European Union and the United States do not cover all contracts included in these estimates. Moreover, the thresholds upon which these estimates are based are generally lower than the actual GPA thresholds, and thus overstate the actual sales opportunities generated by the GPA.
b. Values were converted at a rate of $1.21 to the ECU.
c. Includes procurement by all 50 states and the 24 largest US municipalities. In its final offer the United States granted MFN treatment to its subcentral government procurement market only in 37 states (including the five largest). The EU is granted national treatment in two additional states, as well as in 7 of the 24 largest US municipalities; however, in these states and cities not all state or local government entities are subject to the GPA rules.
d. These estimates contain no adjustment for procurements subject to small and minority-owned business preference and set-asides programs, or for construction procurements subject to Buy American provisions, thereby overstating the value of the market open to foreign bidders.
e. Includes only contracts tendered by public utilities of 20 of the 24 largest US municipalities.
Source: Deloitte & Touche (1994).

In May 1993 an interim EC-US Memorandum of Understanding committed both sides to open up central government procurement of services and construction contracts, as well as their utilities procurement markets for heavy electrical equipment. However, the failure to include the EC telecommunications market led to US imposition of sanctions on an estimated $19 million of European exports to the United States; this was followed by EC counterretaliation covering $15 million in US exports.[5] Despite the overall agreement on the Uruguay Round, efforts to break the US-Europe impasse on procurement issues failed again in December

---

5. However, in June 1993 the Office of the US Trade Representative announced its intention to withdraw sanctions against German goods after Germany unilaterally decided to drop the price preference for telecommunications procurement (*International Trade Reporter*, 16 June 1993, 974). The German action triggered a sharp internal dispute among the EC member states.

Table 11 Estimated value of final EU-US agreement of 13 April 1994 (billions of 1993 dollars)

	United States	European Union
Central governments (MFN)	56.2	51.4
Subcentral governments		
MFN	17.6	23.2
Non-MFN	3.2[a]	0
Electrical utilities		
MFN	3.9[b]	28.0
Non-MFN	21.8[c]	0
Other public utilities	0.5[d]	0.7[e]
Total	103.2	103.3

a. Procurement by North Dakota, West Virginia and seven US cities; access granted to European Union only.

b. Procurement by New York Power Administration, Power Marketing Administrations, and Rural Electrification Administration.

c. Procurement by privately owned utilities, on behalf of which no obligations are undertaken; access granted to European Union only.

d. Procurement by port authorities of New York & New Jersey and Baltimore (MFN), and Massachusetts (EU only).

e. Contracts for maritime, inland port, or other terminal facilities only.

Sources: EU press release 22/94, 15 April 1994; US Department of State (1994).

1993, as each side refused to extend to the other the benefits of offers outside of central government procurement.

In a compromise reached on 13 April 1994 in Marrakesh, the United States and the European Union finally agreed to expand the interim agreement, matching each other's offer almost dollar for dollar. The value of contracts covered by this agreement is around $103 billion for each side (table 11).

The European Union agreed to grant US firms access to its subcentral government procurement market for goods worth about $23 billion, and procurement by electric power utilities valued at about $28 billion. However, it continues to deny the United States access to its procurement market for telecommunications and other public utilities, as well as to services and construction contracts procured by subcentral governments.

The United States agreed to bind nearly all procurement by 37 states of goods and services (including construction), worth about $18 billion per year. This includes procurement by the five largest states: California, Illinois, New York, Florida, and Texas. In addition, the United States accords national treatment to the European Union for the procurement of two more states. The United States also agreed to grant EU suppliers access to the procurement of 7 of the 24 largest US municipalities (Chicago, Detroit, Boston, Dallas, Indianapolis, San Antonio, and Nashville), worth about $3 billion annually. However, certain Buy American programs and minority and small business set-asides are maintained.

Like that of the Europeans, the US offer regarding procurement by public utilities is also quite limited. Most US states maintain federally mandated rules that keep non-US firms from bidding on utilities contracts, in particular for rural electrification, mass transit, and airport and highway improvement.[6] Buy American restrictions on federally sponsored programs vary widely from program to program and therefore complicate assessments of the total procurement open to foreign bidders.

Building on the 1993 memorandum of understanding, both sides agreed to add electrical servicing contracts to their previous offers to cover heavy electrical equipment in their schedules. In addition, the United States agreed to add the New York Power Authority to its list of covered electrical entities, and to waive Buy American restrictions for contracts procured by rural electrical utilities. The overall value of procurement opportunities in this sector is estimated at $26 billion to $28 billion annually for each side (table 11).

In the public utilities area (other than telecommunications and power generation), the United States has agreed to bind goods and services (including construction) contracts procured by several major marine ports and airports (e.g., the New York & New Jersey Port Authority). The European Union opened up its procurement market for ports and terminal facilities. The overall value of this part of the offer is estimated at $0.5 billion to $0.7 billion annually for the United States and the European Union, respectively.

Because telecommunications procurement is still excluded from the GPA, US trade sanctions will remain in effect. Also, a range of federally mandated Buy American programs in such sectors as mass transit, highway and airport improvement, and wastewater treatment will be maintained. Bilateral negotiations are expected to continue in the area of telecommunications in the hope that both sides will improve their offers before the GPA enters into force on 1 January 1996.

Assessment

Overall, the GPA represents an important reinforcement of multilateral disciplines on government procurement. Coverage is extended to both services contracts and contracts procured by subnational government

---

6. For example, the Federal-Aid Highway Funds to the States program grants a 25 percent price preference to bids that propose to use domestic steel and iron; the Federal Mass Transit Grants to the Cities program adds 25 percent to the bid price of proposals that include less than 50 percent American components; the Airport Improvement Program Grants program adds 25 percent to the bid price of a contract if less than 60 percent of its components are not manufactured and assembled domestically; and the Rural Electrification Administration (REA) adds 6 percent to the price of the nondomestic component part of the bid price when awarding loans and loan guarantees to electric authorities.

entities, albeit at somewhat higher contract thresholds than apply to central governments. However, the market access commitments of the signatories fall short of expectations; access to contracts procured by subcentral government entities and public utilities is only applied to those signatories that extend reciprocal offers. Moreover, except for Korea, no countries committed themselves to the new obligations of the GPA that were not already signatories of the GATT procurement code.

Hence the major defect of the GPA is that, unlike for most other GATT codes, participation remains optional. As a result, nonsignatories are not even bound to its rules on transparency. Transparency may very well be the most important obligation in a multilateral regime on government procurement procedures; apart from encouraging continued negotiations to lower remaining national preferences, it would help eliminate conditions that invite corruption.[7]

Nonetheless, in the aggregate, several hundred billion dollars annually in government purchases will be opened to international competition, with additional gains possible if ongoing negotiations involving public utilities and telecommunications bear fruit. Furthermore, the GPA establishes a foundation for prospective GATS negotiations on government services contracts, which would commit all WTO members to open procurement guidelines and thus significantly expand the universe of contracts subject to multilateral rules.

---

7. Transparency becomes increasingly important when one considers the government procurement practices of China and other economies in transition, where purchases by state-owned enterprises are substantial.

Trade Rules

Antidumping

The GATT has long recognized the right of countries to act unilaterally to counter imports priced at "less than their normal value" (i.e., dumped) when such imports cause or threaten injury to, or retard the establishment of, a domestic industry. Dumping occurs when the export price of a good is lower than the price in the producer's home market, or, if the home market price cannot be determined, when the export price is lower than the price of the same or a comparable product in a third market, or lower than the exporter's cost of production (including "reasonable" selling costs and profit).

GATT Article VI allows countries to offset injurious dumping by imposing antidumping duties. In principle, the duty should be no higher than needed to remedy the injury to the domestic industry, but in practice the duty usually is equal to the margin of dumping.

Rules governing the determination of dumping and injury are by nature arbitrary, and the existing rules have not kept pace with the increasing complexity of international production and trade. The three most recent GATT rounds have sought to update and embellish the antidumping rules, both to address problems that have arisen in specific cases and to resolve disputes arising from differences in interpretation of GATT rules by the various national agencies that administer antidumping laws.

Nonetheless, a wide range of normal business practices—practices that are perfectly legal *within* a country—are now considered dumping when they occur *between* countries. Findings of dumping now occur in cases where a firm sells into a foreign market, even on a sporadic or regional basis, at a lower price than it sells at home; where it fails to fully recover its costs and make a healthy profit on its sales abroad; or where it does not allocate its R&D and advertising costs to an exported product in a manner satisfactory to the importing country.

Under current rules, national authorities are allowed a great deal of discretion in calculating dumping margins and assessing injury, but small changes in the rules can yield important advantages for firms contesting dumping cases. During the Uruguay Round negotiations, lobbyists for exporters and import-competing industries worked feverishly to promote changes in the definitions and methodologies that governments may use in their investigations, in the hope that such changes would improve the chances of their industry to win a prospective case, even if marginally, or to reverse the finding of a previous case that had gone against them.

The Increasing Use of Antidumping Laws

Antidumping cases have become the preferred channel of import-competing industries to petition for protection against foreign suppliers. Not only has the number of cases grown substantially, but the number of countries instituting antidumping measures also has soared. In the early 1960s GATT member countries (in total) undertook fewer than a dozen cases per year (Finger and Fung 1993, 2). But between 1985 and 1992 more than 1,000 cases were initiated, and more than 40 countries now have antidumping laws in place.

There are several reasons for the increasing resort to antidumping actions, besides the obvious one, namely, that the volume of world trade has itself grown rapidly. First, national laws have been amended, particularly in the United States and Europe, to accommodate a very broad definition of dumping. Under these standards, few cases are lost because of lack of evidence of dumping.[1] Second, the very initiation of an antidumping case casts a cloud over trade, both because the liability for penalty duties that accused exporters face is uncertain and potentially large, and because there is concern that national authorities will interpret the rules so as to favor the domestic constituents seeking import relief. Third, antidumping laws have been used in countries such as Mexico as a safety valve for domestic protectionist pressures generated by broad-based trade liberalization programs.

The United States, the European Union, Canada, and Australia have consistently been the primary users of antidumping measures (in the 1990s Brazil and Mexico have joined this elite group). Between 1 July 1985 and 30 June 1992, these four accounted for more than 80 percent of all newly initiated antidumping investigations (953 out of 1,148 new cases).

---

1. Only 2 percent of US cases were terminated during the 1985–92 period because of a finding of no dumping (Destler forthcoming).

However, since the mid-1980s antidumping actions have been frequently undertaken by "new" users—countries that took antidumping actions for the first time in the 1980s. In 1985–86, new users accounted for fewer than 3 percent of all new investigations (5 out of 178), but by 1991–92 their share had increased to more than 25 percent (60 out of 237; GATT 1993a).

The United States has been both an active user and target of antidumping actions. From July 1985 to June 1992 the United States initiated 300 antidumping cases; injurious dumping was found in about half. Interestingly, when cases were terminated, it was usually for lack of a showing of injury, not because no dumping was found.[2] During the same period, US exporters were also a leading target of antidumping actions, with 100 cases initiated against them by foreign governments.

All members of the World Trade Organization (WTO) will be required to follow the procedures set out in the antidumping agreement. However, these obligations do not guarantee that antidumping cases, particularly in some new users, will be conducted with the rigor of investigations in the United States. The administrative agencies of many new users have neither the personnel nor the expertise required to conduct detailed investigations; they will thus have to rely on the best (i.e., limited) data available to them. In such circumstances investigations are likely to resemble a black box process, lacking in transparency. And even though exporters will have the right to contest antidumping actions, the small export markets of many of the new users may make such a challenge not worth the expense.

The Uruguay Round Antidumping Agreement

The new Agreement on Implementation of Article VI of GATT 1994 (the antidumping agreement) builds on the 1979 antidumping code negotiated in the Tokyo Round. It requires greater transparency for antidumping actions and establishes new methodological and procedural rules to govern dumping investigations by national governments. These rules draw heavily on US and EU practices (e.g., the standard of review for disputes; the sales-below-cost test; and the cumulation rules).

New Methodological Rules

The antidumping agreement refines several existing rules regarding the calculation of dumping margins. Important changes involve both the method of calculating the constructed value of imports under investiga-

---

2. According to data tabulated by Destler (forthcoming) from US government reports (which differ somewhat from the GATT data base), 36 percent of the cases were dropped because of a finding of no injury.

tion, and the method of determining the value of the home market sales with which the price of the imported good is to be compared.[3]

Allocation of Profits in Constructed Value Calculations

In calculating an exporter's cost of production, the investigating agency may include reasonable administrative and selling costs, and profit. The agreement clarifies somewhat how the importing country may charge such items in its cost calculations. The charges for administrative and selling costs and profits should be based on actual data "pertaining to production and sales in the ordinary course of trade" (Article 2.2.2).[4] If such data are not available, the charges should be based on:

- actual data from other exporters or producers of similar products;
- a weighted average of the costs and profits of other exporters of the same product; or
- any other reasonable method, as long as the amount arrived at does not exceed that for other exporters or producers of the same general category of products.

The third item gives national agencies great latitude in estimating the reasonable profit and administrative costs to be allocated to the exporter's constructed price. However, it will require some change in current US practice, which assigns a minimum 8 percent profit margin and a minimum 10 percent charge for sales and administrative costs in *all* constructed value calculations.

Price Averaging

Under the agreement, the margin of dumping should "normally" be calculated either from a comparison of the weighted-average normal value in the home market with the weighted average of prices of *all* comparable exports, or on a transaction-to-transaction basis. This provision differs from current US practice, which compares individual export prices with the average price in the home market of the exporter, and should tend to reduce dumping margins. However, the investigating agency may compare individual export prices with the average normal price, if the standard methods of comparison would not adequately take account of the impact of targeted dumping practices.

---

3. The Uruguay Round antidumping agreement requires that countries compare the export price with a constructed home market value or the price of comparable exports to third countries, if the volume of home market sales is less than 5 percent of the volume of imports.

4. The phrase "in the ordinary course of trade" opens the door to varying interpretations of which sales may be excluded from the price comparisons.

Allocation of Startup Costs

In some industries, particularly high-technology industries, the initial cost of producing a new product can be quite high at the start of the production cycle. The time period and volume of production over which such startup costs may be allocated can have a significant effect on constructed value calculations in antidumping cases. Calculations of the home market price will be inflated, and the dumping margin increased, if the costs are fully allocated over only a small volume of production.

The agreement provides some guidance to investigating agencies on this matter. It requires that cost calculations be adjusted to "reflect the costs at the end of the start-up period or, if that period extends beyond the period of investigation, the most recent costs which can reasonably be taken into account." Although the provision does not specify the types of costs that may be regarded as startup expenses, it presumably covers all costs.

Sales-Below-Cost Test

The agreement codifies the current US practice of excluding sales by an exporter in its home market at prices below its fully allocated cost of production (including administrative and selling expenses). Such sales may be disregarded when determining the average home market price, provided that the average selling price in the home market is less than the weighted-average unit cost (or that the volume of sales below unit cost is more than 20 percent of the total) and costs are not recovered over "a reasonable period of time." This rule effectively raises the average home market price against which the export price is compared, and thus increases the dumping margin.

Cumulation

When imports from several countries are subject to concurrent antidumping investigations, the agreement allows the national agency to assess the combined effects of all the imports under investigation in making its injury determination. The cumulation of imports is allowed, however, only if the dumping margin of each of the individual countries exceeds de minimis levels (see below) and the volume of imports from each country is not negligible; and if such assessment "is appropriate in light of the conditions of competition between imported products and the conditions of competition between the imported products and the like domestic product."

New Procedural Rules

The agreement refines the rules governing certain procedures for the conduct of antidumping investigations, to clarify which groups have standing to file petitions and to provide some safeguards against the abuse of antidumping laws. Of particular importance for the latter are the de minimis rules and the sunset clause. The new rules also circumscribe the types of challenges that may be made against antidumping decisions under the WTO's Dispute Settlement Understanding.

Standing

The agreement clarifies which groups have the right, or standing, to file antidumping petitions before national authorities. Petitions must be filed "by or on behalf" of the domestic industry that has been injured or threatened with injury; the "industry" has normally been defined as either all producers in the industry, or those producers who collectively account for the "major proportion" of total domestic production. The new rules sharpen these definitions, requiring petitions to be supported by a group of domestic producers who collectively account for more than 50 percent of the total production of that portion of the domestic industry expressing *either support for or opposition to* the application. However, cases may not be initiated if the group of domestic producers applying for relief against dumped imports collectively accounts for less than 25 percent of total domestic output of the product. The agreement also codifies the understanding (since the 1967 antidumping code) that employees or their representatives (e.g., unions) may file or support antidumping petitions.

Only producers and their employees have standing to file antidumping cases. However, other groups that could be affected by the imposition of antidumping measures, such as industrial users and consumer organizations, are granted the opportunity to provide relevant information regarding the effects of dumping on the import-competing industry, but not on their own economic interests.

De Minimis Rules

To deter nuisance cases where the level of relief that might be afforded under the antidumping rules is very small compared with the administrative effort and expense required to process the case, the antidumping agreement includes de minimis rules that require the dismissal of cases involving small amounts of trade or small dumping margins. An antidumping investigation must immediately be terminated if the margin of dumping is less than 2 percent of the export price.[5] Normally, investigations must also be terminated if dumped imports from the exporting country represent less than 3 percent of total imports of the product in the importing country, unless dumped imports from all countries that individually account for less than 3 percent collectively account for more than 7 percent of all imports.

---

5. Current US law contains a de minimis standard of 0.5 percent or less.

Sunset Clause

The agreement requires that all antidumping measures be reviewed periodically to determine whether the actions need to be continued. Under the so-called sunset clause, both antidumping measures and price undertakings (see next section) will expire automatically after five years, unless a review of the case determines that, in the absence of such measures, dumping and injury will continue or recur. Reviews must be initiated in advance of the sunset date and should normally be concluded within one year.

Existing antidumping orders must be reviewed within five years of the entry into force of the WTO Agreement, although the language is unclear as to whether the review must be concluded or only initiated by that date (in the latter case the order could continue for up to 12 months, i.e., until January 2001, before a decision is made to continue or rescind it). Because of the large number of antidumping measures it currently has in force, the United States will be hard pressed to complete all reviews by the sunset date, especially if it defers review of a large segment of the case load until the end of the transition period.[6] In contrast, the European Union already has a sunset provision in effect, so it will not face the same constraints.

Price Undertakings

Exporters can avoid antidumping actions by agreeing to stop dumping (i.e., to raise their prices). Such agreements, often called price undertakings, are a means of suspending ongoing or threatened antidumping cases—indeed, they are called suspension agreements in the United States. In effect, a price undertaking is an out-of-court settlement of an antidumping investigation. However, price undertakings also can be used to promote anticompetitive behavior, as Messerlin (1990) documents for the case of European chemicals.

The new antidumping rules provide guidelines for the use of price undertakings but do little to address competitive concerns. Undertakings may be sought or offered only after a preliminary affirmative determination of dumping and injury. Even if the undertaking is accepted, however, either party may request that the investigation be completed. If the final determination is negative (i.e., either no dumping or no injury is found), the agreement will immediately lapse, unless the determination is due in part to the existence of the undertaking.

Standard of Review

Disputes between WTO members on dumping matters will be subject to the procedures of the Dispute Settlement Understanding of the WTO. At

---

6. As of 30 June 1993 the United States had 279 antidumping orders in effect, the European Union had 185, Canada had 81, and Australia had 64 (OECD, 1993b, 50).

US insistence, the agreement incorporates specific guidelines for the rules to be applied during WTO adjudication. According to this special standard of review, dispute panels are only allowed to determine whether the establishment of facts by the original investigation was proper and whether the evaluation of those facts was unbiased and objective. Furthermore, if the application of a particular antidumping rule accommodates several different interpretations according to customary principles of international law, the panel may not rule against the importing country unless it did not use one of those permissible interpretations. In short, importing countries have a great deal of discretion to interpret the antidumping rules; unless the findings by the national authorities are clearly GATT-inconsistent, dispute settlement panels will have a hard time overturning a decision by any government.

The standard of review is likely to limit the number of disputes brought to the WTO concerning the calculations by national authorities of dumping margins and injury.[7] It will also limit the ability of US exporters to challenge the rulings by the growing number of countries imposing antidumping duties against their shipments. This provision will be reviewed after three years to consider "whether it is capable of general application," especially in disputes involving countervailing duties.

Anticircumvention Rules

Negotiators made extensive efforts to fashion rules governing actions taken by countries to counter the circumvention of their antidumping orders; these efforts were, however, dropped during the final stages of the negotiations. As a result, the United States, the European Union, and other countries that have anticircumvention provisions in their domestic law may continue to apply those rules as they have in the past, but they remain liable to potential WTO challenges. Indeed, a GATT panel has already ruled against EU practice in a case involving Japan. The ministerial declaration accompanying the Uruguay Round agreements recognizes the need for uniform rules on anticircumvention measures and refers the matter to the Committee on Antidumping Practices for future resolution.

Assessment

Not surprisingly, the antidumping negotiations provoked a great deal of controversy, especially in the final stages of the Uruguay Round when

---

7. However, foreign exporters can still appeal US antidumping decisions to the US Court of International Trade (under a more stringent standard of review). Such stringent judicial review is not available in most other countries as an alternative or complement to the WTO dispute settlement process.

several important changes were made to the draft agreement at the insistence of the United States and the European Union. Several of the methodological and procedural reforms in the GATT rules incorporate existing practices of the United States and/or the European Union; others require adjustments in US and EU procedures and methodologies for calculating dumping margins and assessing injury.

The Uruguay Round reforms have been criticized by some for weakening countries' ability to undertake antidumping actions, and by others for allowing national agencies too much discretion to act against exports. In fact, the new rules do a little of both, but do not change to any significant extent the perceived problems with the use or misuse of antidumping measures. More important, the changes do not alter the incentives of domestic industries to resort to antidumping actions instead of other GATT remedies to obtain import relief.

The antidumping agreement clarifies the rules for constructed value calculations in a manner that limits somewhat the scope of their interpretation. Administering agencies will face more clearly defined rules for determining both the amount of profit to be allocated to dumped imports and the amortization of startup costs. In addition, the de minimis rules and the sunset clause should reduce the number of active cases that have an insignificant trade impact, and thus remove another source of bilateral trade friction.

However, the new rules also codify practices that will tend to artificially inflate dumping margins (e.g., the sales-below-cost test). The agreement also does little to discipline the imposition of price undertakings, and it defers multilateral action on anticircumvention measures. In addition, at US insistence, the new standard of review for antidumping disputes will limit the ability of countries to challenge antidumping actions through the WTO dispute settlement procedures. This change reflects US practice but is likely to disadvantage US exporters as they face an increasing number of antidumping actions by developing countries.

In sum, the antidumping agreement will add new layers to the arbitrary rules governing the use of antidumping measures, but will do little to assuage the concerns of exporters and import-competing industries alike about the abuse of the trading rules. Indeed, as these changes promote the adoption of antidumping laws in more and more countries, the number of antidumping actions is likely to expand rapidly, leading undoubtedly to more trade disputes among WTO trading partners. In short, the agreement provides a bandage to a festering sore of trade policy; more extensive treatment will be required in future negotiations.

Subsidies and Countervailing Measures

In contrast to the antidumping agreement, the negotiation of the Uruguay Round Agreement on Subsidies and Countervailing Measures achieved notable improvements in existing GATT rules. The Tokyo Round Code on Subsidies and Countervailing Measures, adopted in 1979, enacted a comprehensive ban on nonagricultural export subsidies but only began to develop rules to discipline the trade-distorting effects of domestic subsidies. The new agreement expands the list of prohibited practices, strengthens multilateral disciplines on domestic subsidies, and clarifies the rules for the application of measures to counteract the effects of another country's subsidies (countervailing measures). The agreement focuses only on measures that affect nonagricultural trade; farm subsidies, the largest component by far of the global subsidy problem, were exclusively addressed in the agreement on agriculture.

The Uruguay Round Agreement

The new agreement on subsidies and countervailing measures improves upon the Tokyo Round code in several important respects. First, the agreement contains a detailed definition of subsidy that establishes the types of practices covered by the new obligations. Second, it expands the illustrative list of prohibited practices appended to the original subsidies code, strengthens the disciplines on domestic subsidies, and creates a new category of nonactionable subsidies granted for specified purposes that are immune to countervailing measures as long as the subsidies do not cause serious adverse trade effects. Third, the agreement reforms rules for the conduct of countervailing duty investigations and institutes procedural and methodological changes akin to those incorporated in the antidumping agreement (e.g., a de minimis rule and a sunset provision). Finally, unlike the Tokyo Round code, the agreement requires most developing countries that are members of the World Trade Organization (WTO) to adhere to all its subsidy obligations after a short transition period.

Definition of a Subsidy

The Uruguay Round agreement includes for the first time a comprehensive definition of a subsidy (Article 1). A subsidy is defined as "a financial contribution by a government or any public body within the territory of a Member," or a private body acting on its behalf, that confers a benefit to the recipient. The financial contribution can take several forms:

- direct transfers of funds or liabilities (e.g., grants, loans, equity infusions, and loan guarantees);

- forgone or uncollected government revenues (e.g., tax credits) other than agreed border tax adjustments;

- provision of goods and services other than general infrastructure on concessional terms;

- income and price supports.

The agreement distinguishes between subsidies that are generally available to all enterprises or industries in the country (e.g., income tax cuts) and those that are granted only to specific recipients. Generally available subsidies are not considered trade distorting per se and thus are not actionable (that is, they are not liable to countervailing measures). A subsidy is considered specific if "the granting authority, or the legislation pursuant to which the granting authority operates, explicitly limits access . . . to certain enterprises" (Article 2.1a), or if the subsidy is in practice only available to certain enterprises, even though it is nominally open to all enterprises (Article 2.1c). Furthermore, all export subsidies are deemed to be specific subsidies (Article 2.3). The "specificity test" set out in Article 2 of the Uruguay Round accord generally follows US practice.

However, if a granting authority establishes automatic eligibility criteria or conditions for access to a subsidy program which "are neutral, which do not favor certain enterprises over others, and which are economic in nature and horizontal in application," then the subsidy will be considered generally available (Article 2.1b). In other words, subsidies only meet the specificity test if they are applied de facto to a targeted group of enterprises.

Two other aspects of the subsidy definition deserve emphasis. First, it includes financial contributions provided by *any* governmental body within the territory, including subfederal governments and parastatal agencies, or by a private firm acting on the direction of the government. Second, it excludes governmental actions that might implicitly confer an advantage but do not involve the transfer of funds or of goods or services (e.g., lax regulatory enforcement). In particular, the definition strikes down the ill-conceived notion (raised during the US debate over the North American Free Trade Agreement) that "eco-duties" could be applied against imports from countries whose environmental laws or practices are not up to US standards (Hufbauer and Schott 1993).

Prohibited Subsidies

The Uruguay Round agreement builds on the already strong disciplines on export subsidies established in the Tokyo Round code. The agreement prohibits all subsidies benefiting nonagricultural products that are granted contingent on export performance. This obligation covers both existing and new subsidies and encompasses all the practices detailed in the illustrative list of export subsidies in Annex I of the agreement. In addition, the agreement prohibits another class of subsidies, namely, those contingent on the use of domestic instead of imported goods.

The list of prohibited subsidy practices appended to the Uruguay Round agreement is identical to the list included in the Tokyo Round subsidies code, with one important exception. Item (h) of the list (relating to "the exemption, remission, or deferral of prior-stage indirect taxes") has been revised to allow taxes on fuels and other forms of energy used as inputs in the production process to be exempted, remitted, or deferred as if they were physically incorporated in the final product (as specified in Annex II). This change opens a potentially important loophole, not for the developing countries for which it was designed but for major industrial countries, whose energy-intensive export industries could benefit from the rebate of new energy taxes (for example, carbon taxes) that might be introduced in the future.

Subsidies do not always fit the mold of the proscribed practices in the illustrative list. To help WTO members determine whether specific practices conform with the new obligations, the agreement establishes a Permanent Group of Experts (PGE), comprised of five independent persons knowledgeable about the trade effects of subsidies. The PGE has two main functions: to assist dispute settlement panels and to provide advisory opinions to member countries. Upon the request of a panel, the PGE will analyze evidence regarding the existence and nature of subsidies and render a determination as to "whether the measure in question is a prohibited subsidy," which will be binding on all the disputing parties (Article 4.5). If the PGE rules that a subsidy falls into the prohibited category, the measure must be withdrawn within a time period specified by the dispute panel. The PGE may also provide member countries with confidential advisory opinions "on the nature of any subsidy" that it either proposes to introduce or already maintains (Articles 24.3 and 24.4).

Actionable Subsidies

Whereas export subsidies are prohibited per se and thus automatically subject to countermeasures, certain other subsidies are actionable only if they demonstrably distort trade. The agreement sanctions countermeasures against subsidies that cause the following "adverse effects":

- injury to the domestic industry of another signatory;
- nullification or impairment of GATT benefits;
- "serious prejudice" to the interests of another signatory.

Unlike the Tokyo Round subsidies code, the Uruguay Round agreement provides comprehensive guidelines for the determination of the trade effects of subsidies in both the home and third-country export markets. The agreement thus fills a large gap in GATT subsidy obligations. Countervailing duties provide relief against subsidized imports, but GATT rules previously had been unable to define how a country could react against subsidies used as a surrogate for tariffs to protect the home market against imports, and against domestic subsidies that allow exporters to outbid suppliers from other countries in third-country markets. The Uruguay Round accord allows countries to take action against foreign subsidies in those circumstances, by defining the types of adverse effects that seriously prejudice their trading interests (Article 6). Serious prejudice is presumed to exist if:

- the total ad valorem subsidization of a product exceeds 5 percent of the recipient's annual sales of that product, or 15 percent of the total invested funds for startup firms (Annex IV);

- subsidies cover operating losses of an industry or an enterprise, unless they are one-time and nonrecurrent measures to facilitate adjustment;

- governments provide direct debt forgiveness or grants for debt repayment;

and the effect of the subsidy is to displace or impede imports from the home market, exports to a third-country market, or undercut or suppress prices in the home market. The agreement presumes that serious prejudice does not exist if there are no demonstrable trade effects (i.e., neither the price nor the volume of exports is affected), or if there are special circumstances (e.g., natural disasters, strikes) that preclude adverse trade effects, or if there are explicit arrangements (e.g., price undertakings) that limit trade in the subsidized good.

The provisions regarding serious prejudice apply for five years and may then be extended, modified, or terminated. They do not apply to agricultural subsidies covered by Article 13 (the "peace clause") of the Agreement on Agriculture, which are not liable to countermeasures for nine years (i.e., until 2004).

Nonactionable Subsidies

The most controversial aspect of the Uruguay Round agreement is the classification of a small category of subsidy programs as generally exempt from countervailing measures. The nonactionable subsidies specified in the agreement encompass three types of activities: research and precompetitive development activities (R&D), regional aids, and adaptation of existing plants to new environmental requirements.

The agreement permits R&D subsidies provided the assistance covers no more than 75 percent of certain specified costs of industrial research or 50 percent of certain specified costs of precompetitive development activity. The assistance must be spent only on personnel, equipment, land and buildings, and overhead costs, and these costs must be directly incurred for the permissible research activity and not used for commercial activity. These provisions apply neither to the civil aircraft industry nor to "fundamental research" conducted by higher education or research establishments that is not linked to industrial or commercial objectives.

The safe harbor for R&D subsidies was substantially broadened in the final weeks of the negotiations to accommodate new technology initiatives envisaged by the Clinton administration. The exemptions for specific research costs were increased from 50 percent to 75 percent and from 25 percent to 50 percent for development activities. Moreover, the scope of the covered activities was expanded from the definitions included in the draft agreement compiled by GATT Director General Arthur Dunkel. The most notable change was from "applied research" in the Dunkel draft to "pre-competitive development activity" in the final text. The change broadened the scope of activities covered by the safe harbor provision from development prior to creation of any prototype, to development up to and including creation of the first noncommercial prototype.[1]

The second class of exempt subsidy programs involves regional aids. The agreement allows assistance to disadvantaged regions within a member country that is provided under a general framework of regional development, that is characterized as nonspecific, and that meets the following neutral and objective criteria: income per capita, household income per capita, or GDP per capita must be less than 85 percent of the territory average; or the unemployment rate of the disadvantaged region must be at least 110 percent of the territory average.

Finally, the safe harbor covers subsidies provided to support investment in pollution control and other environmental infrastructure. The agreement exempts from countervailing measures assistance to promote compliance with environmental requirements in existing facilities, provided that the subsidies are one-time and nonrecurring, are limited to 20 percent of the cost of adaptation, do not cover replacement and operating costs, are linked to a firm's planned reduction of nuisances and pollution, and are available to all firms that can adopt new equipment or production processes.

In theory, the rules are designed to establish a safe harbor for specified programs that member countries regard as desirable and therefore worthy

---

1. "Pre-competitive development" covers the "translation of industrial research findings into a plan, blueprint, or design for new, modified or improved products, processes or services whether intended for sale or use, including the creation of a first prototype which would not be capable of commercial use." The Dunkel definition of "applied research" did not differentiate between applied and development activity and did not state that industrial research could be translated into a plan or a first prototype.

of protection against countermeasures. In practice, subsidies are to a large degree, fungible and thus may be used by recipient firms for a variety of purposes. Indeed, critics such as Senator John C. Danforth (R-MO) argue that the designation will encourage countries to use subsidies for these purposes and increase trade distortions.

To prevent the abuse of the safe harbor, the agreement contains several safeguards. First, the agreement contains a sunset clause for the provisions on nonactionable subsidies. The obligations of Article 8 of the agreement apply provisionally for five years, at which time a decision must be made whether to extend or modify them (Article 31). In addition, the exemption for specified R&D subsidies will be reviewed within 18 months of the entry into force of the WTO (Article 8.2, footnote 25).

Second, otherwise nonactionable subsidies are actionable if they cause "serious adverse effects" that result in "damage which would be difficult to repair" (Article 9). In such an event the subsidizing country must modify its program to remove those effects, or be liable to countermeasures.

Third, the agreement affords close monitoring of eligible subsidies. Nonactionable programs must be notified in advance of implementation, and notifications must be updated annually. Members may request a review of a notification in order to determine whether the conditions have been met. Disputes over notifications (that is, over eligibility of the program for safe harbor treatment) are subject to binding arbitration.

Developing Countries

GATT disciplines on export subsidies have been only infrequently applied to developing countries. The reason was straightforward: most developing countries could not afford to subsidize their exports or domestic producers to the extent necessary to distort trade flows.

The Tokyo Round was the first GATT negotiation to attempt to extend discipline on subsidies to the developing countries. Article 14 of the subsidies code recognized the right of those countries to provide subsidies consistent with their trade and development needs. However, the code also established a mechanism for developing countries to schedule commitments voluntarily to phase out export subsidy programs over a specified transition period. Several countries undertook such commitments, in many cases as part of an arrangement with the United States to resolve bilateral trade disputes.[2] Most of these commitments became dead letters with the onset of the debt crisis in the early 1980s.

The Uruguay Round agreement greatly expands the multilateral obligations of developing countries with respect to subsidies. Within five years

---

2. The texts of these commitments are reproduced in Hufbauer and Erb (1984).

(eight years for the least-developed countries), developing countries must adhere to the obligation not to grant subsidies contingent on the use of domestic goods. Within eight years, developing countries will be required to adhere to all other GATT obligations regarding the use of export subsidies on nonagricultural products.[3] Moreover, during the transition period export subsidies may not be increased and must be phased out progressively. However, the least-developed countries and other developing countries with per capita GDPs less than $1,000 are exempted from the prohibition on subsidies that are contingent on export performance.

Furthermore, the agreement contains a competitive need test that requires developing countries to apply GATT obligations more quickly for those products that garner a significant share of world markets. During the transition period, developing countries must accelerate the phaseout of export subsidies if the products benefiting from those subsidies account for at least 3.25 percent of world trade for two consecutive years. In those circumstances the subsidies must be eliminated within two years (eight years for the poorest countries).

Countries that are transforming into market economies are allowed seven years to comply with the export subsidy obligations, and debt relief measures are not presumed to cause serious prejudice (Article 29). These members are subject to the same remedies as developing countries for other actionable subsidies.

Countervailing Measures

Provisions of the Uruguay Round agreement concerning the imposition of countervailing measures mirror in most respects those of the agreement on antidumping. The rules regarding standing to file countervailing duty (CVD) petitions and participation in CVD investigations are identical to those of antidumping cases. Like the antidumping agreement, the accord includes de minimis and sunset provisions and allows cases to be suspended if the exporting country accepts specific undertakings. Unlike the antidumping agreement, it does not include a standard of review for dispute panels, although a ministerial declaration recognizes "the need for the consistent resolution of disputes arising from antidumping and countervailing duty measures."

Under the de minimis rule, investigations must be terminated if the amount of the subsidy is less than 1 percent ad valorem (2 percent in cases involving developing countries), or if the volume of subsidized imports is negligible (or less than 4 percent of total imports of the like product in cases involving developing countries, unless the cumulative

---

3. During these transition periods the subsidies may not be presumed to cause serious prejudice, but they remain liable to countervailing duties if they benefit goods that injure a domestic industry in the importing country.

share of developing countries represents more than 9 percent of total imports).

The agreement also provides for CVDs to be terminated no later than five years after their imposition (or from the date of their most recent review) unless "the expiry of the duty would be likely to lead to continuation or recurrence of subsidization and injury." Outstanding CVD orders must be reviewed within five years of entry into force of the WTO.

As in antidumping, the agreement tends to encourage the use of undertakings to resolve CVD cases. Undertakings, including price undertakings, can lead to the suspension or termination of CVDs or provisional measures if the exporting country agrees to eliminate or limit the subsidy or the exporter agrees to increase prices to forestall injury. Undertakings may not be promulgated until after preliminary determinations are made of subsidy and injury.

Assessment

In contrast to the agreement on antidumping, the new accord on subsidies and countervailing measures significantly strengthens the GATT's anti-subsidy rules. The agreement expands the list of prohibited practices and clarifies rules for countervailing measures against subsidies that cause adverse trade effects in home and third-country markets. Moreover, unlike the Tokyo Round subsidies code, the new disciplines will apply to almost all WTO members because of the WTO's single undertaking and the requirement that developing countries (except the least developed) accept all subsidy disciplines after a five- to eight-year transition period.

In essence, the agreement comprises a basic trade-off: stronger disciplines on export and domestic subsidies in return for the creation of a safe haven for certain "desirable" subsidies that support R&D, pollution control investments, and regional development programs not targeted on specific industries. Although concerns have been raised about the potential for expanding subsidies in these categories, the new accord contains ample safeguards to prevent the abuse of the safe harbor provisions.

Safeguards

In the Tokyo Round the GATT negotiators failed to reach agreement on a code of conduct governing the use of measures pursuant to Article XIX to provide temporary relief against imports that were causing or threatening serious injury to a domestic industry—so-called safeguard measures. The Agreement on Safeguards achieved in the Uruguay Round resurrects many of the provisions drafted during the previous negotiations and adds a new and important proscription on the use of voluntary export restraints (VERs) and comparable interindustry arrangements.

Throughout the GATT era, Article XIX safeguards have not been the instrument of choice of GATT members to impose import protection, for various reasons. Some countries find the "serious injury" threshold too high, and the implicit requirement to pay compensation to or face retaliation from affected exporters too damaging to their trading interests. Many countries find it easier and less costly to target their trade restraints on specific exporters rather than all foreign suppliers. Most major trading countries, however, have been deterred from invoking Article XIX less by its requirements than by the availability of less onerous and more flexible channels of protection. These have included coercing trading partners to accept VERs and other so-called gray area measures, as well as frequent recourse to unilateral import relief actions under Article VI (i.e., antidumping and countervailing duties).

Similarly, most developing countries have not resorted to Article XIX because those countries have had few tariff bindings and thus could raise their tariffs without violating their GATT obligations. Developing countries have committed to a significant increase in their tariff bindings in the Uruguay Round (albeit at levels generally well above currently applied rates), but they are still unlikely to invoke Article XIX because they have both the unfettered right to raise tariffs to their bound levels, and virtual carte blanche authority to impose new tariffs or quotas under the less onerous conditions of Article XVIII, which allows developing countries to impose safeguards for balance of payments reasons.[1]

Through May 1993 countries had notified 151 safeguard actions under Article XIX.[2] Almost a third of these measures have been imposed since the conclusion of the Tokyo Round in 1979. During the last 14 years the European Community has made the most frequent use of safeguard

---

1. Article XVIII has been greatly abused over the years, giving rise to the charge that existing GATT rules allow developing countries to free-ride on the GATT system. Balance of payments safeguards should have been revised in the Uruguay Round to prevent their use as devices of sectoral protection, and to ensure that they were time-limited, but developing countries resisted significant reforms. However, some countries such as Korea and Brazil have reduced their reliance on these safeguards.

2. For a complete list of the Article XIX notifications, see the GATT's Analytical Index. The data presented in this section reflect revisions to the index through May 1993.

actions, invoking Article XIX a total of 18 times (of which 13 involved processed foodstuffs). In contrast, the United States has invoked Article XIX safeguards on only four occasions since 1979 (involving porcelain-on-steel cookware, preserved mushrooms, motorcycles, and specialty steel). In short, Article XIX has *not* been a dead letter, but its use pales in comparison with actions taken pursuant to other import relief provisions of the GATT.

Key Provisions of the Agreement

The bulk of the Agreement on Safeguards spells out the conditions under which countries may impose temporary import protection in contravention to the bound obligations in their GATT schedules. To invoke this "escape clause," as Article XIX safeguards are sometimes called, countries must demonstrate that imports are causing or threatening serious injury to a domestic industry. All measures must be notified immediately to the GATT Committee on Safeguards, and ample opportunity must be provided for consultations with countries whose trade is adversely affected.[3] Like the provisions of GATT Article XIX, the new rules indicate no preference as to whether the safeguard measures should be in the form of tariffs or quantitative restrictions. However, if quotas are imposed, they should not reduce the volume of imports below the annual average for the last three representative years.

Overall, the Agreement on Safeguards establishes clear rights and obligations regarding the imposition of Article XIX safeguard actions, including extensive notification and consultation requirements. It also contains cross-cutting constraints and incentives that will, on balance, temper the use of such measures.

First, the agreement reaffirms that safeguard actions must be applied against imports from all sources (i.e., on a most-favored nation basis). The efforts of some countries to allow the selective (i.e., non-MFN) application of any safeguard measure, which caused the collapse of the Tokyo Round negotiations, were largely rebuffed. However, the agreement does allow countries in certain circumstances to act only against selected countries whose imports "have increased in disproportionate percentage in relation to the total increase of imports of the product concerned in the representative period" (Article 5:2b). In other words, countries may effectively discriminate between strong new entrants and traditional suppliers in allocating quotas. The flexibility to impose such "selective" safeguards seems designed to protect against competitive exporters in Asia and East-

---

3. These obligations are sharply truncated in critical circumstances where the immediate imposition of protection is necessary to prevent "damage which it would be difficult to repair" (Article 6). In such cases countries should employ tariffs rather than quotas.

ern Europe. In particular, it seems to presage a strategy for dealing with import surges from China. However, such measures may be applied for a maximum of four years and may not be extended.

Nonetheless, the agreement does ban the most virulent form of selective actions, namely, VERs, which were arguably the most pernicious form of protection in the 1970s and 1980s, as well as most other discriminatory import relief actions. Countries commit not to "seek, take or maintain any voluntary export restraints, orderly marketing arrangements or any other similar measures on the export or the import side" (Article 11:1b). Existing gray area measures must be phased out within four years (or by 31 December 1999 for the EU-Japan VER on automobiles). In addition, countries agree not to "encourage or support the adoption or mainte- nance" of interindustry arrangements comparable to the governmental measures proscribed above.[4] This strong prohibition on the use of VERs and comparable arrangements is one of the major achievements of the Uruguay Round.

Second, the agreement sets out a definition of "serious injury" that clarifies the injury threshold that must be met before safeguard actions can be imposed. The agreement defines serious injury as "significant overall impairment in the position of a domestic industry," lists criteria to be evaluated in determining injury, and requires that the determination exclude "factors other than increased imports [that] are causing injury to the domestic industry at the same time." Moreover, safeguard measures must be applied only to the extent necessary "to prevent or remedy serious injury and to facilitate adjustment"—a degree of refinement that few countries are willing or able to meet. These provisions clearly indicate that the serious injury standard establishes a much higher threshold than the "material injury" standard for Article VI actions that has been applied by major trading countries.

Third, safeguard measures may be applied for a period of up to four years, with the opportunity for up to an additional four years if the action continues to be needed to "prevent or remedy serious injury," the industry is shown to be adjusting, and the action complies with obligations regard- ing compensation and special treatment for developing countries. Devel- oping countries may impose safeguard measures for a maximum of 10 years, including extensions. Previously the only constraint on the duration of a safeguard measure had been the admonishment that it should be "temporary." Under the new rules, actions in place for more than one year must be "progressively liberalized at regular intervals," and actions taken for three years or more must be reviewed to determine whether the measure can be liberalized more quickly. Existing safeguard actions

---

4. Enforcement of such obligations should be abetted by third-country notification rights and by regular monitoring by both the Committee on Safeguards and the Trade Policy Review Body.

must be terminated after they have been in force for eight years, or by January 2000, whichever comes later.[5]

In addition, the agreement prevents countries from circumventing the time limits on safeguard measures by prohibiting the reimposition of protection on the same product for a period of time equal to the original safeguard action, but in no event less than two years. However, temporary safeguards that were imposed for six months or less may be reinstated after one year, as long as actions are not taken on the same product more than twice in a five-year period. Here again, developing countries are subject to less rigorous obligations and may reimpose actions on the same product after a period equal to half the duration of the previous measure (but not less than two years).

Fourth, the agreement restricts the use of safeguard actions applied by developed countries against imports from developing countries. Safeguard measures may not be imposed on a product from a developing country if those imports do not exceed 3 percent of total imports of that product, and imports from developing countries with less than a 3 percent import share collectively account for no more than 9 percent of total imports of the product concerned.

Finally, the agreement seeks to encourage compliance with its new rules by limiting the liability of countries taking actions in conformity with the terms of the agreement to retaliation or compensation claims from affected exporting countries. As in current practice, compensation is voluntary, but if affected exporters are not compensated for trade displaced by the safeguard action, they are free to retaliate. However, this right is waived for the first three years that an action is in effect, provided that the action was taken because of increased imports and conforms to the obligations of the agreement.

Interestingly, the agreement does not oblige countries invoking Article XIX to require the domestic industry benefiting from the protection to specify an adjustment program to be implemented during the initial term of the safeguard action. This omission means that import-competing industries will be less likely to adjust. Consequently, the duration of safeguard actions generally will be longer, and more measures will need to be extended beyond the initial four-year time period (during which time the protected industry only has to provide evidence that it is, in some undefined way, "adjusting"). Although affected exporters could retaliate after three years, GATT experience indicates that such actions would be few and far between. In sum, the new rules increase the chances that safeguard actions will remain in effect for the maximum eight-year period.

---

5. According to the GATT's Analytical Index, a total of 13 safeguard actions were in effect as of 31 May 1993.

Assessment

By removing the threat of retaliation for three years, banning the use of alternative gray area measures, omitting an adjustment requirement for at least four years, holding open the prospect of a total of eight years of protection, and allowing selective application of safeguards in limited circumstances, the negotiators sought to provide incentives for countries to use Article XIX. However, for the main users of such measures—the European Union and the United States—the only real attraction of the agreement is the ability to act against import surges from new trading powers like China. And in most cases the rigorous serious injury threshold will offset the reduced risk of retaliation. On balance, the agreement offers scant incentive to resort to the new rights and obligations under GATT Article XIX instead of other import relief measures such as antidumping. Accordingly, safeguards are likely to continue to play a minor role in international trade relations.

New Issues

The General Agreement on Trade in Services

Despite its growing significance in global commerce, trade in services has not been subject to a multilateral set of rules governing its fair and nondiscriminatory conduct. Worldwide services exports grew at an annual rate of almost 15 percent from 1982 to 1992, compared with a 9.8 percent annual increase in merchandise exports over the same period. In 1992 world exports of commercial services were valued at about $1 trillion, accounting for more than one-fifth of total world exports of goods and services.

The United States is the leading exporter of commercial services: in 1992 US firms exported services worth more than $162 billion. On the import side the United States ranked second after Germany, with 1992 imports reaching almost $108 billion.[1] These data explain in large measure why the United States was the *demandeur* of the services negotiations in the GATT and why the US private sector placed a high priority on their successful conclusion.

The General Agreement on Trade in Services (GATS)—one of the agreements to be implemented under the umbrella World Trade Organization (WTO)—for the first time establishes a broad multilateral framework of rules to govern trade in services, as well as commitments to liberalize specified barriers to services trade and investment. The GATS also includes a provision mandating future negotiations aimed at the progressive elimination of barriers that discriminate against foreign service pro-

---

1. The figures cited in this section are from GATT (1993).

viders that were not fully addressed in the Uruguay Round. The GATS will be administered by the Council for Trade in Services, operating under the General Council of the WTO, and consultations and dispute settlement will be governed by the provisions of the Dispute Settlement Understanding of the WTO.

The GATS consists of three main components:

- a set of general obligations that apply to all services;

- sectoral annexes detailing how the rules apply to specific sectors;

- specific commitments regarding market access and national treatment that apply to a subset of services, on a sector-by-sector and country-by-country basis.

The general framework obligations do not confer market access commitments for any service sector. Sector-by-sector commitments to liberalize trade in services must be specified in national schedules. In general, most of the schedules commit not to impose new restrictions that discriminate against foreign service suppliers—that is, they impose a "standstill" or ceiling on existing measures. In sectors that have no existing restrictions, this obligation effectively prohibits the institution of new controls and binds significant levels of liberalization. This obligation is particularly significant for developing countries that are just beginning to develop new high-technology service industries (e.g., business and computer services).

Effective rollback of current trade barriers has been achieved only in a very limited number of service sectors and remains the main objective for future negotiations. However, the GATS does require that negotiations be launched no later than five years after the WTO enters into force, that is, by January 2000 (and be held periodically thereafter) with the goal of increasing the level of general commitments already undertaken by the GATS members in their individual schedules (GATS Article XIX).

The services negotiations grappled, and are still grappling, with the problem of how to preserve the integrity of the framework of general rules, including the general obligation to conduct trade in services on a most-favored nation (MFN) basis, while simultaneously encouraging countries to liberalize barriers to services trade. The United States has been reluctant to accord unconditional MFN treatment to all signatories in all sectors, arguing that such a commitment would guarantee access to the relatively open US market and reduce US leverage to gain reciprocal access to foreign markets. US negotiators regarded the threat of withholding MFN in the financial services, maritime, and basic telecommunications sectors as leverage to ensure that other countries engage seriously and expeditiously in the reciprocal reduction of trade barriers. In contrast, most other countries were content to accept a framework code that essentially established a standstill on existing market access, in the hope that future negotiations would focus on trade liberalization. In the end, the MFN issue has been put on hold for these sensitive sectors, while negotiations on market access continue for a period of time even after the WTO has entered into force.

General Obligations

In principle, the GATS applies to trade in all commercial services and affects measures taken by central, regional, and local governments. The GATS defines trade in services as the supply of services through any of four modes of delivery: cross-border supply of a service, movement of the consumer to the country of the supplier, movement of the supplier to the country of the consumer (i.e., establishment of legal presence), and temporary movement of natural persons employed by the supplier to the country of the consumer. However, the significance of this very broad definition of trade—broader than the definition for merchandise trade— is determined by the schedules of specific commitments offered by each country.

Because of this broad definition, the GATS goes an important step further than the GATT: it involves both cross-border trade *and* investment in services. However, the obligations on services are not as comprehensive as under the NAFTA, which contains separate chapters on investment issues as well as a chapter on cross-border trade in services.

As in the GATT, the core obligation of the GATS is MFN treatment— the requirement that each member immediately and unconditionally grant other members treatment no less favorable than that given any other country (Article II). However, countries can temporarily avoid this obligation with regard to specified measures affecting particular service sectors, if those sectors are listed in the Annex on Article II Exemptions of the GATS (see below) on the date the GATS enters into force.[2] In other words, a country has a one-time opportunity to deny MFN treatment to other GATS members for specific service sectors. In principle, these exemptions should not exceed 10 years, and they are subject to subsequent negotiations. Moreover, all exemptions granted for a period of more than five years are subject to review five years after the entry into force of the WTO. However, there is no obligation to remove the exemption after the 10-year period.

Unlike the GATT, the GATS does not contain a general national treatment obligation.[3] National treatment applies only to those service sectors

---

2. MFN exemptions for the financial services sector can be taken up to six months after the entry into force of the WTO, and until the spring of 1996 for the basic telecommunications and maritime sectors.

3. In some respects, regulations on services sector activities provide protection for domestic industries just as tariffs do on merchandise trade. In those cases, granting national treatment effectively provides free access to the market (comparable to zero tariffs).

that are listed in a country's schedule of commitments (Article XVII).[4] In contrast, the NAFTA applies its national treatment provision to all service sectors unless they are specifically excluded (i.e., included on a "negative" list), whereas the GATS accords national treatment only to service sectors that are specifically included (a "positive" list). In this respect, the GATS is not a general but a "special agreement on services."[5]

The GATS recognizes a country's right to impose domestic regulations relating to qualification requirements and procedures, technical standards, and licensing requirements. Countries agree to provide impartial and objective review of administrative decisions affecting trade in services (Article VI). Moreover, for sectors in which they have undertaken specific commitments in their national schedules, members also commit to administer their policies "in a reasonable, objective, and impartial manner," and to ensure that their standards, qualification, and licensing requirements are "based on objective and transparent criteria" and "not more burdensome than necessary to ensure the quality of the service." To that end, members should take into account relevant international standards in setting their national requirements.

The GATS encourages but does not require mutual recognition or harmonization of "standards or criteria for the authorization, licensing or certification of services suppliers," whether granted autonomously or negotiated on a bilateral basis. To ensure that such arrangements do not discriminate among service suppliers from different countries, the GATS requires that other members be offered comparable rights through accession to any negotiated agreement or its equivalent (Article VII). In setting their requirements for the provision of services, countries should follow multilaterally agreed criteria and should cooperate "with relevant intergovernmental and non-governmental organizations towards the establishment and adoption of common international standards and criteria for recognition and common international standards for the practice of relevant services trades and professions."

Articles VI and VII provide particularly important benefits for the professional services sector. If a country schedules a commitment in this sector, service providers must be ensured adequate and fair procedures to verify their competence and accredit them to perform their services in that country. Both articles also encourage the development of common international standards of practice to facilitate future trade in professional services, as well as mutual recognition of standards applied by other countries that serve comparable objectives.[6]

---

4. National treatment is defined as treatment no less favorable than that accorded to like domestic services and service providers, unless identical treatment would actually worsen the competitive position of foreign service suppliers vis-à-vis domestic firms (Article XVII).

5. I owe this observation to Richard Snape of Monash University in Australia.

6. In some sectors such as accounting services, private-sector initiatives have already generated draft proposals on certification and licensing issues for consideration by governments.

Other general obligations of the GATS set forth provisions comparable to those in the GATT regarding transparency, preferences for regional trading partners, safeguards, government procurement, general exceptions, and subsidies:

■ Transparency. The GATS requires all relevant measures affecting trade in services to be published or otherwise made publicly available, including those international agreements to which the member is a signatory (Article III). The information notified to the GATS should help firms better understand the conditions under which they may conduct business and expose trade barriers to be addressed in future negotiations.

■ Economic integration. Article V, the GATS equivalent of GATT Article XXIV, exempts members of free trade areas or customs unions from the MFN obligation for preferences granted to their regional partners. Like GATT Article XXIV, the agreement must encompass "substantial sectoral coverage,"[7] must provide for elimination of virtually all discrimination, and must not increase barriers to the trade of nonmember countries. In addition, Article V ensures that subsidiaries of third countries that are established in the preferential trading area receive the full benefits of the regional pact.

■ Emergency safeguards. By July 1998, provisions on emergency safeguards are supposed to have been negotiated and implemented (Article X).[8] In the interim, any member may modify or withdraw a specific commitment one year after it is introduced, if it demonstrates that such emergency action is required. Normally, countries must wait three years before they may modify their schedules (GATS Article XXI).

■ Transfers and balance of payments safeguards. GATS Articles XI and XII mirror the revised GATT Article XVIII(b) by allowing countries to restrict international transfers and payments only for balance of payments purposes. However, the use of such restrictions must be temporary and phased out progressively; countries retain the right to invoke dispute settlement procedures to challenge balance of payments measures.

■ Government procurement. GATS Article XIII specifically excludes government procurement of services from the MFN, market access, and national treatment obligations. However, the GATS commits countries to initiate negotiations on government procurement of services by January 1997. Until these negotiations are concluded, the only rules govern-

---

7. "Substantial" is defined in terms of the "number of sectors, volume of trade affected and modes of supply" (Article V:1a).

8. Because most countries oppose a safeguards provision in the GATS, the prospects for a successful negotiation on this issue are limited.

ing services procurement will be those of the revised Government Procurement Agreement (GPA), a plurilateral accord that is expected to enter into force on 1 January 1996 but only applies to a limited number of signatories.

- General and security exceptions. In a manner analogous to GATT Articles XX and XXI, members may take exceptions from their GATS obligations to protect public order or human, animal, or plant health or life; to ensure compliance with laws or regulations; or for national security reasons, provided that the exceptions are applied in a nondiscriminatory fashion and are not disguised restrictions on trade in services (Articles XIV and XIV bis).

- Subsidies. The GATS does not contain specific obligations on subsidies except for a general commitment to consult if subsidies distort trade. Instead, GATS Article XV suggests that negotiations be held on how to deal with subsidies and countervailing duties in the services sector, but establishes no schedule for initiating or completing such talks.

- Monopolies and exclusive suppliers. The GATS commits members to ensure that any monopoly supplier or group of exclusive suppliers does not act inconsistently with the MFN requirement and the specific commitments of the GATS (Article VIII:1). In addition, countries agree not to allow monopoly suppliers to abuse their dominant market position through actions that are "inconsistent with such commitments" (Article VIII:2).

- Business practices. GATS Article IX requires members to enter into consultations to eliminate restrictive business practices—other than monopoly and exclusive supplier systems—that restrain competition and thereby restrict trade in services.

Sectoral Annexes

The annexes to the GATS are an integral part of the agreement. They interpret and apply the rules of the general framework agreement to specific sectors:

- Annex on Article II Exemptions. This annex specifies the exemptions from the MFN provision that are taken at the time the GATS enters into force. In principle, exemptions should not exceed 10 years and are subject to negotiation in subsequent trade liberalization rounds. Moreover, the Council for Trade in Services (CTS) will review all exemptions granted for more than five years, beginning no more than five years after the WTO has entered into force. In its review the CTS will "examine whether the conditions which created the need for the exemption still prevail." However, the CTS cannot order the termination of an exemption based on this review.

- Annex on Movement of Natural Persons Supplying Services under the Agreement. This annex applies the GATS to the entry and temporary stay of persons who are employed by service suppliers of another WTO member country, and of citizens of another WTO member country who are employed by a domestic service supplier. National schedules of specific commitments have to be submitted by 31 December 1995.

- Annex on Financial Services. This annex applies to insurance, insurance-related services, banking, and other financial services. Members are not precluded from taking measures for "prudential" reasons or to ensure the integrity and stability of their financial systems. Dispute settlement panels will be required to have the necessary expertise relevant to the specific financial service under dispute. Negotiations on finalizing the parts of the national schedules relating to financial services will continue for six months after the entry into force of the WTO. During that period the MFN obligation will apply to financial services and must be maintained unless the country takes an Article II exemption. During the last 60 days of this period, any country may include MFN exemptions in its schedule and may improve, modify, or withdraw all or part of the commitments on financial services offered. Thus, commitments on financial services could be sharply curtailed if the extended negotiations fail to yield improved market access commitments.

- Annex on Air Transport Services. This annex applies the GATS to the following scheduled and nonscheduled services: aircraft repair and maintenance services, selling and marketing of air transport services, and computer reservation system services. However, specific market access and national treatment commitments must be negotiated, as in other sectors. The annex specifically excludes measures affecting traffic rights and services directly related to the exercise of traffic rights, and it acknowledges the precedence of existing bilateral aviation agreements.

- Annex on Telecommunications. In this annex each member is required to provide all service suppliers—foreign or domestic—access to any public telecommunications transport network and service offered within or across its borders for the supply of a service included in its schedule.[9] The annex requires that countries accord MFN and national treatment to all foreign service suppliers seeking access to and use of public telecommunications transport networks and services, but does not require such treatment for cable or broadcast distribution of radio and television programming. Service suppliers are permitted to use

---

9. These obligations are particularly important for the financial services industry, including nonbank companies.

their own equipment and operating protocols, provided they comply with certain technical specifications.[10] Developing countries may impose "reasonable" conditions to strengthen their domestic telecommunications infrastructures and to increase their participation in international trade in telecommunications services. However, such conditions must be specified in the country's GATS schedule, making them more transparent and subject to future negotiations.

- Annex on Negotiations on Basic Telecommunications. Basic telecommunications are not part of the telecommunications annex or of the market access and national treatment provisions. Instead, the United States, the European Union, and other countries with major telecommunications markets have agreed to continue negotiations on reciprocal liberalization of basic long-distance and international telecommunications services, with an effective deadline of 30 April 1996, either to implement the results of the negotiations or to apply the GATS (e.g., to invoke an MFN exemption).

- Annex on Negotiations on Maritime Transport Services. In the case of maritime services (international shipping, auxiliary services, and access to and use of port facilities), negotiations will continue until June 1996, at which time WTO members will implement the results of these negotiations or other actions recommended in the final report of the negotiating group. In the meantime the GATS does not apply, nor is it necessary to list MFN exemptions. Until the date upon which the results of the negotiations take effect, members may improve, modify, or withdraw commitments without offering compensation.

Specific Commitments

Each country may also append to the GATS a schedule of binding specific commitments relating to market access, national treatment, and other practices (e.g., on qualifications, standards, and licensing matters) affecting access to its market. The specific commitments apply only to the services that are mentioned in a country's schedule—a positive list—to the extent that they are not limited or otherwise qualified in the schedule.[11] The market access provision includes a list of those measures that a

---

10. These obligations are qualified by the right of national regulators to impose nondiscriminatory standards "to safeguard the public service responsibilities" of suppliers of basic telecommunications services, and to "protect the technical integrity" of telephone networks.

11. However, the national schedules might be better described as a hybrid between a positive and a negative list: countries must positively list sectors to be covered by the rules, but once selected, those sectors are accorded full market access (i.e., no regulatory barriers and national treatment) unless the country negatively lists reservations to specific practices.

member is not allowed to adopt or maintain, unless these policies are specifically mentioned in the country's schedule.

As mentioned above, the national treatment obligation applies only to those sectors included in a country's schedule of market access concessions. The market access obligation requires members to provide any foreign service supplier treatment no less favorable than that provided under the terms, limitations, and conditions specified in its schedule (Article XVI). In addition, it prohibits new or increased restrictions and establishes a baseline for future liberalization efforts.

To date, more than 80 countries have submitted national schedules of commitments to the GATT Secretariat, in the following service sectors:[12]

- Advertising. Over 40 countries have filed commitments on advertising. The European Union and other European countries (including the new democracies of Eastern Europe), Japan, and Korea have agreed not to maintain or introduce any restrictions on market access or national treatment. Several Asian and Latin American countries have made the same commitment, although in their case it is subject to some conditions and exceptions. Chile, Colombia, Costa Rica, Egypt, India, Indonesia, New Zealand, Pakistan, and the Philippines failed to make any commitments in the advertising sector.

- Audiovisual services. The framework agreement in its entirety applies to the audiovisual sector. However, no adequate commitments on audiovisual services have been made by the European Union, which represents the biggest export market for the United States.[13] In the waning weeks of the negotiations the United States and the European Union engaged in a bitter dispute over audiovisual services. At issue was not current US access to the EU market (US firms dominate most European markets and generate $3.5 billion in revenue annually, or more than half the foreign earnings of the US entertainment industry), nor was the issue of admission taxes, used to subsidize European production, a major cause of irritation. Rather, the fierce debate focused on whether the highly restrictive quota regime mandated in the European Broadcast Directive would be extended to new technologies and transmission mechanisms and to distribution channels. The European market is expected to experience explosive growth over the next decade, as new technologies expand the range of services available to a broad segment of the population and blur the distinction between entertain-

---

12. The sources for these data are Industry Sector Advisory Committee on Services for Trade Policy Matters (ISAC-13, 1994) and Office of the US Trade Representative, draft summaries of GATS schedules of commitments, June–July 1994 (processed).

13. In contrast, Korea, Japan, Singapore, Malaysia, and Thailand made important commitments, with only a few limitations on market access and national treatment affecting the four modes of supply.

ment and information flows. This latter point is particularly relevant in explaining the bitterness of the US-EU dispute, and the fear that US firms will not be able to participate in, or will face severe constraints on, growth in this sharply expanding market.

■ Construction and engineering. According to data compiled by the Office of the US Trade Representative through July 1994, 39 countries have scheduled commitments for engineering professional services, 34 for architectural services, and 38 for construction services. Most countries require that foreign service suppliers establish a domestic commercial presence in order to benefit from the liberalization commitments.

■ Financial services. Negotiations on specific commitments in the financial services sector will continue into 1995 (with a deadline of six months after the entry into force of the WTO). In the meantime the United States is free to use trade remedies provided for in its national statutes to pressure other countries into bilaterally negotiated commitments on financial services. Indeed, the Clinton administration supported the Fair Trade in Financial Services Act with just such a purpose in mind, although that bill was subsequently dropped by the Congress. Ministers also adopted at Marrakesh a separate Understanding on Financial Services that clarifies and expands upon the provisions of the financial services annex with regard to market access and national treatment obligations in this sector. The understanding provides an alternative means to the annex of scheduling national market access commitments. Commitments scheduled according to this understanding must be consistent with the provisions of the financial services annex and be applied on an MFN basis.

■ Professional services. Fifty-two countries—all of the member countries of the Organization for Economic Cooperation and Development (OECD) and 28 developing and newly industrialized countries, together representing over 90 percent of the world market—have scheduled commitments on accounting, auditing, and tax services. In addition, 49 countries have scheduled commitments on management consulting, and 57 countries on computer services. A separate ministerial decision also recommended that the Council for Trade in Services establish a working party to make sure that the principles embedded in GATS Articles VI (domestic regulation) and VII (recognition of qualifications and standards) do not constitute barriers to trade in professional services, with first priority assigned to accountancy.

■ Value-added telecommunications. These services include, inter alia, electronic mail, voice mail, on-line information and data base retrieval, and electronic data interchange. Most major US trading partners made some commitments in this sector. Generally, countries agree not to impose significant market access and national treatment restrictions, with the few exceptions relating to the presence of natural persons as the mode of supply.

- Tourism. More than 80 countries have scheduled commitments on travel and tourism, the largest service sector, including obligations not to impose new restrictions on foreign travel or on foreign ownership or operation of tourism-related businesses, and not to set limits on the amount of funds international travelers may take abroad.

- Other private services. Additional initial commitments have been made by more than 80 countries in a number of other service sectors (e.g., distribution, environmental, education, health care, land and maritime transport, and legal services). These sectors account collectively for about $20 billion of US exports each year (ISAC-13, 1994, 24).

Modification of Schedules

GATS Article XXI allows members to withdraw or modify any commitment in their schedules at any time after three years have elapsed since that commitment entered into force. Such modification or withdrawal has to be notified no later than three months before the intended date of its implementation. On request of any member affected by the modification or withdrawal, the country is required to negotiate an appropriate compensation (in a manner analogous to GATT Article XXVIII procedures), which is to be extended on an MFN basis. If the parties cannot agree on the compensation, the affected member may refer the case to arbitration. Until the arbitral finding with regard to compensation is issued, the national commitment under review may not be modified or withdrawn. If the commitment is changed in the absence of or contrary to an arbitral ruling, countries affected by the measure may modify or withdraw substantially equivalent benefits solely with respect to that member.

Dispute Settlement

The Dispute Settlement Understanding (DSU) of the WTO will apply to services, ensuring that the more expeditious procedures for resolving disputes developed in the Uruguay Round will apply to trade in services. Because the DSU is an integrated mechanism that applies to all WTO agreements, it explicitly allows cross-sector retaliation between goods and services sectors, under certain specified conditions (see the chapter on dispute settlement in this study).

The Unfinished Agenda

The GATS explicitly commits members to ongoing services negotiations to expand both the coverage of rights and obligations under the agreement and specific market access commitments. Negotiations are scheduled to continue on a wide range of issues and service sectors:

- Emergency safeguards. The GATS mandates that additional negotiations to establish emergency safeguard provisions be completed and implemented within three years after the WTO has entered into force (i.e., by 1 January 1998).

- Government procurement. Members are required to launch negotiations on government procurement two years after the entry into force of the WTO (i.e., by 1 January 1997).

- Financial services. Negotiations on specific commitments regarding financial services will have to be concluded six months after entry into force of the WTO (i.e., by 1 July 1995). During the two months prior to this negotiating deadline members may invoke MFN exemptions and "improve, modify, or withdraw" their market access commitments.

- Basic telecommunications. Negotiations on basic telecommunications services—except for any specific commitments already inscribed in a member's schedule—will continue until 30 April 1996.

- Maritime transport services. Negotiations on MFN exemptions and commitments in this sector must be completed by 1 July 1996.

- Movement of natural persons. One month after the entry into force of the WTO, countries will reopen negotiations to further liberalize the movement of natural persons, with a scheduled deadline five months later (i.e., by 1 July 1995).

- Subsidies. Recognizing that subsidies can have a trade-distortive effect, the GATS suggests that negotiations be held on how to deal with subsidies and countervailing duties in the services sector. However, the agreement does not establish a schedule for initiating or completing such talks.

Assessment

The GATS establishes multilateral rights and obligations on trade in services. As a result, substantial volumes of international trade will be subject for the first time to multilateral rules; trade policies affecting service sectors will be notified to the WTO, facilitating consultations and the resolution of disputes; and a foundation will be laid for future negotiations to improve market access. However, the agreement encompasses only barebones requirements: countries are not obligated to extend national treatment unless they specify in their national schedules that they will do so, and they may invoke "temporary" exemptions from their MFN obligations.

The GATS achieved only mixed results with regard to improved rules and market access commitments in particular service sectors. The scope of specific market access commitments varies by sector, from extensive (e.g., in professional services) to minimal (e.g., in audiovisual services). Sectoral rights and obligations provided in the telecommunications annex are especially important, since access to the telecommunications network is critical to the provision and use of information and other value-added services by a broad range of goods and services industries. However, results in other important sectors such as financial services and maritime services are incomplete and show little promise for further gains in the negotiations scheduled to end in 1995 and 1996, respectively.

Finally, the GATS links services trade disputes to the integrated dispute settlement mechanism of the WTO, thereby implicitly allowing for cross-retaliation between goods and services sectors. In other words, if there are no comparable services against which to retaliate, a country may retaliate in a services trade dispute against the merchandise trade of the offending country.

Investment

Negotiations on investment issues in the Uruguay Round ended before they really got started. Because of strong opposition from Brazil, India, and other developing countries, the Punta del Este Declaration launching the Uruguay Round restricted the scope of the GATT talks to addressing "the trade restrictive and distorting effects" of a narrow range of trade-related investment measures (TRIMs). As a result, the negotiations covered only those issues related to GATT Articles III (regarding national treatment) and XI (regarding the elimination of quantitative restrictions). Important investment issues such as the right of establishment were omitted, and investment incentives were relegated to the subsidies negotiations.

Ironically, despite their initial reluctance to include investment issues in the GATT talks, many developing countries unilaterally liberalized their investment regimes during the course of the Uruguay Round as part of broad-based market-oriented reforms. In a sense, these countries began to compete in a global "beauty contest" to see which could design the most attractive (i.e., open) policies to lure foreign investors. Encumbering restrictions on foreign direct investment gave way to investment incentives. Because of the constraints on the TRIMs negotiations, countries have not locked in these reforms in their GATT schedules. However, the sea change in national policies toward foreign direct investment bodes well for future GATT negotiations. Indeed, one may speculate that if the Uruguay Round had started in 1990, the developing country reforms of the late 1980s could have been codified and substantial new global disciplines on investment policies could have been developed.

To its credit, the Uruguay Round Agreement on Trade-Related Investment Measures (the TRIMs accord) affirms the global trend toward more-open investment policies that emerged in the 1980s. It transforms existing GATT practices—including the 1983 panel ruling on the Canadian Foreign Investment Review Agency (FIRA)[1]—into contractual obligations undertaken by all WTO members, and thus represents a modest achievement. Overall, however, the TRIMs accord should be seen only as a tentative first step toward a multilateral investment regime.

By way of comparison, the North American Free Trade Agreement (NAFTA) included comprehensive rights and obligations regarding investment issues. For example, the NAFTA commits its signatories to accord both national treatment and MFN treatment to foreign investors,

---

1. The TRIMs accord codifies the 1983 GATT panel ruling that FIRA's local-content requirements were inconsistent with GATT Article III:4. However, the same panel did not rule that export performance requirements were GATT-illegal, and noted that developing countries could in principle invoke GATT balance of payments safeguards to justify local-content requirements.

whereas the TRIMs accord deals only with the GATT's national treatment obligation. The NAFTA provisions on performance requirements are more demanding than the TRIMs accord, banning all new export performance, domestic-content, domestic-sourcing, trade-balancing, product-mandating, and technology transfer requirements, and requiring existing TRIMs to be phased out within 10 years. However, the NAFTA does allow some non-trade-related performance requirements such as employment targets. The NAFTA broke new ground for the settlement of investment disputes by providing for binding arbitration in an international forum rather than in local courts; the TRIMs accord directs disputes on investment matters to be settled under the Dispute Settlement Understanding of the WTO. In sum, the NAFTA establishes significant precedents for future GATT negotiations on investment issues and could even serve as a model for a prospective "GATT for Investment" (see Bergsten and Graham forthcoming).

The area where the TRIMs agreement achieved the most progress was in proscribing measures that are "inconsistent with the obligations of national treatment" and "the general elimination of quantitative restrictions" of GATT Articles III and XI. The agreement includes an illustrative list of GATT-prohibited measures, specifically barring local-content, trade-balancing, and foreign-exchange-balancing requirements. The brevity of the list and the omission of the important category of export performance requirements underscore the limited scope of the accord.

The TRIMs agreement requires countries to notify the Council for Trade in Goods, within 90 days after the WTO has entered into force, of all TRIMs that are not in conformity with GATT obligations, including those applied by regional and local governments. Developed countries must then eliminate notified measures within two years. Developing countries have five years to eliminate their prohibited TRIMs, and least developed countries seven years. However, the agreement acknowledges that developing countries may deviate from these obligations, if they are taking measures consistent with GATT safeguards for balance of payments purposes.

To forestall a rash of new measures before the new rules take effect, the agreement states that TRIMs that are introduced within 180 days before the WTO enters into force are not eligible for the transition period. However, countries may impose a prohibited TRIM on new investments for the duration of the relevant transition period, if such action is deemed necessary to avoid disadvantaging existing investments that are subject to a TRIM. In other words, a country can offset the implicit advantage accorded to new investors vis-à-vis established investors whose operation is constrained by TRIMs that are being phased out.

In sum, the Uruguay Round accord on TRIMs represents only a small first step toward international discipline on the nexus of trade and investment issues. However, the agreement does mark a place for future GATT talks by committing the WTO member countries to review the operation of the TRIMs accord within five years and to "consider whether it should be complemented with provisions on investment policy and competition policy." In the interim, discussion of the nexus of competition policy and trade issues should be expanded in the OECD and introduced into regional discussions such as the Asia Pacific Economic Cooperation initiative. When the TRIMs review occurs, the WTO members would do well to build on these efforts, as well as the precedents established in the investment chapter of the NAFTA, and to expand the scope of TRIMs rights and obligations to include, inter alia, establishment and competition policy issues.

Intellectual Property

The negotiators of the Uruguay Round Agreement on Trade-Related Aspects of Intellectual Property Rights (the TRIPs agreement) wrestled over the interrelated and sometimes cross-cutting objectives of promoting innovation and facilitating the diffusion of technology. Most industrial countries (especially the United States) argued that strengthening intellectual property rights was needed to achieve both goals. In contrast, other countries expressed concern that such strengthening would inhibit the diffusion of technology from developed to developing economies.

Like the agreement on investment measures, the TRIPs accord was initially negotiated along a North-South divide but soon refocused on North-North issues. Developed countries cited the need for GATT disciplines to combat the piracy and misappropriation of new technologies that reportedly cost their industries billions of dollars of revenues that could otherwise be rededicated to research and development. Developing countries argued that strong rules would impose heavy and disproportionate costs on their economies; they also maintained that strong rules would hamper their ability to acquire new technology by inhibiting national policies that force compulsory licensing of patents or other working requirements to promote local production through joint ventures with foreign firms.

However, since the launch of the Uruguay Round, many newly industrializing countries have begun adopting new laws and regulations to strengthen the protection of intellectual property. These reforms have had two key objectives: to encourage inflows of foreign direct investment embodying foreign technologies and to promote economic development by expanding domestic innovation.

As with any negotiated text, the TRIPs agreement melded the interests of both developed and developing countries and therefore fully satisfied neither. In the end, developing countries were willing to trade their support for the TRIPs accord for improved access to industrial markets in agriculture and light manufacturing products. Compromises that watered down the market access commitments in those areas consequently strengthened developing country demands to maintain the provisions of the TRIPs accord that allow them more time to meet its obligations.

General Rules

The TRIPs agreement incorporates (by reference) most of the provisions of four existing international agreements on the protection of intellectual property rights: the Paris Convention for the Protection of Industrial Property, and its Stockholm Act of 1967; the Berne Convention for the Protection of Literary and Artistic Works, and its Paris Act of 1971; the

International Convention for the Protection of Performers, Producers of Phonograms and Broadcasting Organizations, also known as the Rome Convention (1961); and the Treaty on Intellectual Property in Respect of Integrated Circuits, or IPIC (1989). However, countries are not required under the TRIPs agreement to join these intellectual property conventions. Countries are allowed to implement legislation that guarantees more protection than is required by the TRIPs agreement as long as it does not contravene any TRIPs provisions.

The TRIPs accord breaks new ground by establishing for the first time a comprehensive set of global trade rules for the protection of copyrights, patents, trademarks, industrial designs, trade secrets, semiconductor layout designs, and geographical indications. Its comprehensive standards are substantially higher than those embodied in current international intellectual property conventions (administered primarily by the World Intellectual Property Organization), and its provisions on enforcement are more rigorous. However, the accord also includes contentious provisions that afford long transition periods for developing countries and inadequate protection for patents in the development pipeline.

The agreement embraces the principles of national and most-favored nation (MFN) treatment. National treatment is defined as "treatment no less favorable than [accorded] to [a country's] own nationals with regard to the protection of intellectual property rights," unless exceptions were already taken under other intellectual property conventions noted above.[1] The MFN provision is a novelty in intellectual property rights agreements: any advantage a country gives to another country automatically applies to all other countries, even if such treatment is more favorable than that which it gives to its own nationals.[2]

Copyright

The copyright provisions of the TRIPs agreement incorporate by specific reference the economic provisions of the Berne Convention (1971). The TRIPs accord explicitly extends protection to computer software and databases, as well as sound recordings, performances, and broadcasts. Broadcasts are protected for 20 years. Computer programs, movies, performances, and sound recordings receive 50 years of protection.

The agreement also extends copyright protection in the area of rental rights. Authors of computer programs and producers of sound recordings

---

1. This qualification of the general national treatment obligation is especially important in the area of copyrights (see below).

2. The MFN obligation does not apply in cases where conflicts arise with provisions of existing intellectual property conventions, or "in respect of the rights of performers, producers of phonograms and broadcasting organizations not provided under this Agreement" (Article 4:c).

are provided an exclusive right to authorize or prohibit the commercial renting of their works to the public.[3] However, these rental rights do not apply to movies, unless there is evidence of "widespread copying of such works which is materially impairing the exclusive right of reproduction" (Article 11). Performers are also protected against bootlegging of their performances.

The copyright protection afforded to performers, producers, and broadcasting companies in Article 14 of the TRIPs agreement recognizes that many countries have adopted "neighboring" or "related" rights protection in this area under the Rome Convention. In brief, copyright protection is afforded to works such as books or songs, and neighboring rights protect, inter alia, the performers and performances of copyrighted material (Acheson and Maule 1994). These neighboring rights are now specifically covered by the TRIPs accord.

The TRIPs accord incorporates the relevant provisions of, inter alia, both the Rome and Berne conventions, including their respective exclusions. In contrast to the Berne Convention (for literary and artistic works), the Rome Convention (for performers, producers of phonograms, and broadcasting companies)—to which the United States is not a signatory—is based on reciprocity instead of national treatment. By allowing a choice between the two conventions with respect to the protection of performers, producers, and broadcasting companies, the TRIPs accord does not guarantee across-the-board national treatment. For that reason, for example, the revenues that France collects on the sales of blank tapes to compensate producers and performers for copying can continue to be denied to US performers and producers, because the United States does not have a similar compensation program and therefore does not qualify for reciprocal treatment under the neighboring rights obligations of the Rome Convention.

Such ambiguity may trigger future disputes with respect to the provision of national treatment for "new" subject matter or neighboring rights, or "new" beneficiaries of new or old rights. Some countries might argue that these are outside the coverage of the existing copyright and neighboring rights conventions, and that therefore they are not bound by the obligation to provide national treatment to foreign owners of such rights.

Patents

In addition to the general obligation to comply with Articles 1 through 12 of the Paris Convention (1971), all product or process inventions—

---

3. In addition, if a country has in place a system of equitable remuneration of rightholders for rentals of records—i.e., rental revenues are to be shared among creators, performers, and producers—that system may be maintained as long as copying from such rentals does not cause material damage to the copyright owners (Article 14.4).

regardless of whether they are imported or produced locally—receive 20 years of patent protection measured from the date the application was filed. This obligation applies only to filings after the entry into force of the World Trade Organization (WTO), and thus excludes patent applications for products in the development pipeline.

However, countries may deny patent protection for certain inventions (Articles 27.2 and 27.3). The most important of these involve "diagnostic, therapeutic and surgical methods for the treatment of humans or animals"; and plants and animals (other than microorganisms) and biological processes (other than microbiological processes) for their production. In addition, countries must provide patent or *sui generis* protection for plant varieties. These provisions, which will be reviewed four years after the WTO enters into force, provide a very narrow scope for patentability of biotechnological inventions and are very likely to be the subject of future disputes—especially considering the high level of protection that both the United States and the European Union provide for biotechnology inventions.

Countries that are allowed to delay the provision of patent protection for pharmaceutical and agricultural chemical products under transition rules must still set out application procedures as if such protection were already available. After the transition period has expired, those countries must grant applicants that filed during the transition period patent protection for the remainder of the patent term, counted from the filing date (Article 70.8). In addition, such countries must grant exclusive marketing rights (generally for five years) until a decision is made on the patent application, if a patent application was made and granted in another country (Article 70.9).

Compulsory licensing is not prohibited, but detailed conditions are established regarding, inter alia, notification, remuneration, and judicial review. Compulsory licensing of semiconductor technology is only allowed "for public non-commercial use" or to remedy anticompetitive practices (Article 31:c) and must afford adequate compensation to the rightholder.

Trademarks

Trademarks and service marks are protected for seven years and are renewable indefinitely for additional seven-year periods. Although actual use is not required to *file* for registration of a trademark, registration of the mark and extension of the period of protection may be dependent on use (Article 15.3). If actual use is required to *maintain* a registration, the registration may be cancelled only if the trademark has not been used for three years (Article 19.1). The agreement prohibits compulsory licensing of trademarks and other requirements, such as those requiring that foreign trademarks be linked with a local trademark, which would diminish the value of the mark as an indication of source (Article 20). However, the same provision does allow for requirements that prescribe the use of a company trademark along with the trademark of the specific product in question—for example, in Brazil, pharmaceutical firms are required to place the company logo alongside the product trademark on the packaging label, subject to a specified font size.

Geographical Indications

The TRIPs accord requires members to prohibit the use of an indication that could mislead the consumer as to the true origin of the good. However, with regard to wines and spirits, countries are allowed to continue to use geographical indications that may contravene obligations in this area if the usage is of long standing—for example, common existing names such as champagne and burgundy may continue to be used even if the product does not originate from those geographical regions (Article 24:4). The agreement mandates further negotiations to establish a "multilateral system of notification and registration of geographical indications for wines" to reclaim these widely used geographical indications as protectable matter. The TRIPs Council (established as part of the WTO) will hold its first review of the application of this section two years after the WTO enters into force.

Other Intellectual Property Rights

Industrial Designs

New or original industrial designs (including textile designs) are protected for 10 years against the unauthorized making, selling, or importing of copies for commercial purposes.

Designs of Integrated Circuits

The TRIPs provisions extend to 10 years the protection of layout designs of integrated circuits provided by the IPIC agreement of 1989 to products that incorporate protected integrated circuit designs. Unintentional violators are required to pay royalties as soon as they receive notice of the infringement. Unlike under the IPIC agreement, compulsory licensing is not allowed.

Trade Secrets

Industries that protect valuable commercial information through trade secrets receive protection against misappropriation and unauthorized use of these secrets, provided they take reasonable steps to guard them. The TRIPs provisions include protection of trade secrets against third-party acquisition and protection against abuse of proprietary test data submitted by firms to government agencies.[4]

Anticompetitive Practices in Contractual Licenses

The TRIPs agreement acknowledges that certain licensing practices or conditions (e.g., "tie-in" clauses in franchising contracts), which may restrict competition and trade, can violate intellectual property rights. Countries may adopt remedies against such practices, provided that they do not violate the other provisions of the TRIPs agreement. If a foreign firm engages in anticompetitive behavior in violation of the host country's national regulations, the host country may consult with the home country government to seek compliance of the offending firm with its national regulations.

Implementation

Developed countries are given one year to implement the agreement. Developing countries and economies in transition must provide national treatment and MFN treatment within one year, but will have an additional four years to implement most of the remaining obligations of the agreement. For provisions concerning patent protection for pharmaceutical and agricultural products, developing countries that currently do not provide patent protection are given an additional nine years instead of four. Least developed countries have a total of 11 years to implement intellectual property rights protection. However, at the end of the one-year transition period, all countries—including developing countries—must accept the national treatment and MFN obligations.

From the standpoint of chemical, pharmaceutical, computer, and other firms in developed countries, these long transition periods amount to the surrender of huge amounts of royalties and fees over an extended period of time. These firms foresee a "legitimate" trade emerging in pirated software and videos, knock-off pharmaceuticals, and imitation fashion goods. Such activities are likely to provoke sharp trade friction among

---

4. This provision applies to pharmaceutical or agricultural chemical products which utilize "new chemical entities" (Article 39.3).

WTO members, particularly regarding the appropriate usage of Section 301 or other national statutes to counter unfair trade practices.

In contrast to the World Intellectual Property Organization (WIPO), which was never empowered to enforce intellectual property conventions, the TRIPs Council will monitor the operation of the agreement and facilitate consultations and dispute resolution on matters relating to intellectual property rights. Because of its enforcement provisions, the TRIPs accord may well become a focal point for efforts to revise and augment intellectual property rights and obligations. The future agenda for intellectual property negotiations is likely to be force-fed with the unresolved issues arising from the dispute settlement process.

Nonetheless, the WIPO will continue to have a role to play with regard to the evolution of the intellectual property rights regime. Its expertise should be useful to the TRIPs Council in interpreting existing intellectual property conventions and in administering the TRIPs provisions, as well as in developing new TRIPs rights and obligations. In that regard, the TRIPs Council will engage in consultations with the WIPO within one year after its first meeting to make appropriate arrangements for mutual cooperation (Article 68).

Enforcement and Dispute Settlement

The TRIPs agreement requires each country to maintain adequate procedures and remedies under its domestic law to counter misappropriation and piracy of intellectual property; these procedures and remedies must be available to foreign rightholders. Remedies must include cease-and-desist orders (to stop infringement), payment of damages (against counterfeiting and piracy), and impoundment and/or destruction of goods that are found to be in violation or of the machines with which they were made.

Disputes involving the TRIPs agreement will be settled under the Dispute Settlement Understanding (DSU) of the WTO. However, the accord places a five-year moratorium on disputes involving measures that do not conflict with the "letter" of the provisions of the TRIPs agreement, but which nevertheless are alleged to nullify or impair the "spirit" of the concessions under the agreement (so-called nonviolation, nullification and impairment disputes).

This moratorium on nonviolation disputes could hamper the United States' ability to reap immediate benefits from the agreement, especially in the case of developed countries, which are required to implement the TRIPs provisions after one year. For example, for five years after the entry into force of the WTO, cases could not be brought against countries that fail to permit the transfer of royalties from the commercial exploitation of an intellectual property right. During this five-year period the TRIPs

Council will examine these nonviolation cases and make recommendations as to how related disputes should be settled.

Comparison with the NAFTA

The intellectual property provisions of the NAFTA were designed with the pending TRIPs agreement in mind. In most respects the TRIPs accord affords roughly the same protection for intellectual property as does the NAFTA. However, the NAFTA does provide more protection in several areas: for copyrights by granting full national treatment; for patents by extending the coverage of patentable material to products that are in the approval pipeline; and for trademark and industrial design registrations and/or renewals by providing protection for 10-year periods instead of the 7 years offered by the TRIPs accord. Trademarks, however, have to be used to maintain registration under the NAFTA. After two years of nonuse, the registration may be cancelled; in the TRIPs accord this period is three years in those countries where actual use is required to maintain registration of a trademark.

The transition periods in the TRIPs accord are significantly longer than those granted in the NAFTA. The intellectual property provisions of the NAFTA had to be fully implemented when the agreement entered into force, whereas the TRIPs accord affords the least developed countries up to a maximum of 11 years' delay in implementing its provisions). However, it should be noted that the range of differences between the obligations negotiated in NAFTA and the protection already available in Canada, Mexico, and the United States was not as great as the differences between the final TRIPs obligations and the protection available in many of the more than 120 countries that will undertake obligations under the TRIPs accord.

Assessment

In the 1980s the enormous expansion in world trade elevated intellectual property rights to new prominence in trade policy. Many firms turned increasingly to foreign markets to earn economic returns on their intellectual property assets, either exporting those products to or investing directly in foreign markets where they often encountered different levels of intellectual property protection. In contrast, newly industrializing countries—relying heavily on imported technology for their economic growth—remained wary of intellectual property rights and feared that protection of intellectual property would raise domestic prices for key inputs and consumption goods while simply transferring profits outside the country.

The TRIPs accord sets standard terms for protection of patents, copyrights, and trademarks, and protects new forms of intellectual property such as semiconductor layout designs and biotechnology patents. Most important, the TRIPs accord fills a wide gap in existing intellectual property conventions by setting out extensive obligations for the enforcement of intellectual property rights both at the border and within the domestic market. The agreement contains some shortcomings (notably the excessively long transition periods for developing countries, and inadequate protection for patents in the pipeline), but on balance it achieves important new obligations with regard to patents, trademarks, copyrights, and trade secrets that supplement existing intellectual property conventions.

Institutional Issues

Dispute Settlement

The willingness of countries to undertake new rights and obligations under international trade agreements depends importantly on whether those rights can be enforced. Developing a strong multilateral dispute settlement mechanism was thus a critical objective of the Uruguay Round talks.

The Uruguay Round negotiations sought to remedy three basic flaws in the GATT dispute settlement mechanism: the overly long delays from the establishment to the conclusion of panel proceedings; the ability of disputants to block the consensus needed to approve panel findings and authorize retaliation; and the difficulty in securing compliance with panel rulings. Interim reforms adopted at the midterm review of the Uruguay Round in 1989 set some new time limits for GATT panels but did not relieve many other problems. The provisions of the Understanding on Rules and Procedures Governing the Settlement of Disputes (the Dispute Settlement Understanding, or DSU) codify (i.e., make permanent) those reforms and remedy many of the other shortcomings of the existing GATT system.

The New Dispute Settlement Procedures

The DSU establishes a unified system to settle disputes arising under all multilateral and plurilateral trade agreements covered by the World Trade Organization (article 1 and Appendix 1 of the DSU). It applies to all new disputes taken to the WTO after its entry into force (article 3.11).

In brief, the Uruguay Round reforms expedite the decision-making process, institute a new appeal procedure for panel rulings, and implement new procedures to promote compliance with WTO decisions. Time limits for forming a panel, conducting a panel review, and issuing findings are reduced to ensure that disputes do not languish and that WTO violations are remedied more quickly. A new standing appellate body is established to review appeals of panel rulings, and procedures are created to set time periods for compliance, to monitor compliance actions, and to allow automatic retaliation in the event of noncompliance (subject to disapproval by consensus of the members of the Dispute Settlement Body, the new body created under the WTO Agreement charged with administering dispute settlement rules and procedures). From start to finish, the dispute process should not take more than 20 months—and less if the panel decision is not appealed (see figure 1).

As under existing provisions in GATT Article XXIII, the DSU also can adjudicate disputes involving measures that nullify or impair benefits accruing to a WTO member but do not violate any provision of the WTO agreements. However, in such "nonviolation" cases a panel ruling cannot require the withdrawal of the disputed measure, but it can make a nonbinding recommendation as to a mutually satisfactory adjustment as a final settlement of the dispute (article 26.1).

Because WTO obligations encompass a broader range of trade and investment in goods and services than the GATT, and because of the ambiguity of numerous national liberalization commitments, one should expect a sharp increase in the incidence of trade disputes over time. The WTO legal office will have to be expanded accordingly to support the increased work load. Similarly, legal resources to administer and utilize the dispute settlement system will have to be upgraded within national governments (see Hudec 1994).

Panel Procedures

The DSU affirms the right to establish a panel expeditiously to consider complaints. Disputants can no longer delay the process interminably by haggling over the terms of reference of a panel or the selection of panel members.

Panels are established automatically if initial consultations do not quickly resolve the dispute. Within 30 days, members must be selected and agreement reached on the terms of reference of the panel review. Panels will normally be composed of three persons, from within or outside government, recommended to the disputing parties by the WTO Secretariat. From establishment of a panel to issuance of the panel report should normally take six to nine months (articles 12.8–9).

Figure 1   Dispute settlement procedures and deadlines under the WTO

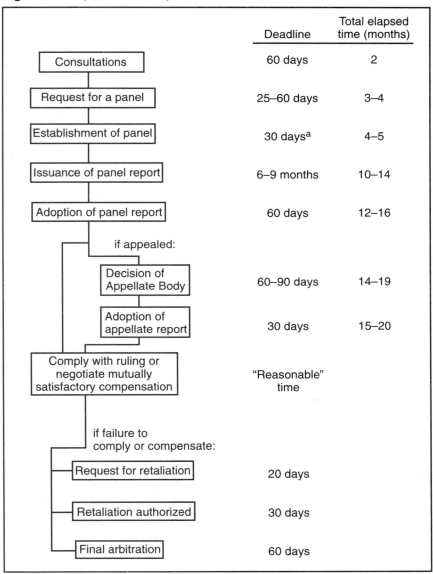

	Deadline	Total elapsed time (months)
Consultations	60 days	2
Request for a panel	25–60 days	3–4
Establishment of panel	30 days[a]	4–5
Issuance of panel report	6–9 months	10–14
Adoption of panel report	60 days	12–16
if appealed:		
Decision of Appellate Body	60–90 days	14–19
Adoption of appellate report	30 days	15–20
Comply with ruling or negotiate mutually satisfactory compensation	"Reasonable" time	
if failure to comply or compensate:		
Request for retaliation	20 days	
Retaliation authorized	30 days	
Final arbitration	60 days	

a. Maximum time allowed to agree upon the terms of reference and the composition of the panel.

Unlike under past procedures, panel reports will be automatically approved unless the decision is appealed (articles 16.4).[1] The new rules reverse the approval procedure: whereas in the past approval could be delayed indefinitely by the opposition of only one government (even by the "guilty" party) because reports had to be accepted by consensus, now a consensus will be required to block approval.

In short, the new procedures give panels more authority to decide cases and to recommend remedial action. However, because panel rulings are binding and countries can no longer block the proceedings, the new rules do provide some important safeguards against legal errors in panel decisions, notably through the institution of a new appellate process.

New Appellate Procedures

Panel rulings are subject to review by a new, standing Appellate Body, which will issue decisions normally within 60 days regarding "issues of law covered in the panel report and legal interpretations developed by the panel" (article 17.6). The Appellate Body will be composed of seven persons, each appointed for a four-year term; three of the members will serve on any particular case. The findings of the appellate body are adopted automatically unless the DSB decides by consensus against such action (article 17.14).

New Compliance Procedures

If the panel recommendations have not been fully implemented within a reasonable period of time (agreed to by the disputants or imposed by an arbitrator), and subsequently no satisfactory compensation has been agreed, the complaining country has the right to retaliate by suspending the application of WTO obligations to the offending country (article 22.2).[2] Here again, the new rules reverse the presumption that countries must receive a positive vote before they can act unilaterally. Retaliation is automatically authorized unless the DSB decides by consensus against such action (article 22.6).

---

1. Panel determinations are not like US court rulings. They are binding only on case participants and do not necessarily have strict precedental effect on future cases (Jackson 1994).

2. In principle, parties should comply immediately with a panel's rulings and recommendations. If that is deemed impracticable, compliance must occur within a "reasonable" time, which is determined in one of three ways: as proposed by the member concerned and approved by the DSB; as agreed between the parties concerned within 45 days after adoption of the panel or appellate report; or as determined through binding arbitration within 90 days after adoption of the panel or appellate report. In the case of arbitration, a guideline is provided which recommends that the reasonable period of time to implement panel or appellate report not exceed 15 months from its adoption.

Because the DSU integrates the mechanisms of the constituent agreements under the umbrella of the WTO, it implicitly allows cross-sector retaliation. However, the rules prescribe that retaliation should normally entail suspension of concessions or obligations that affect the sector subject to the dispute (article 22.3). If that is not practicable or effective, concessions or obligations may be suspended in other sectors under the same agreement. Ultimately, if that is still not satisfactory, concessions or obligations under another covered agreement may be suspended (that is, cross-retaliation is permitted).

Implications for the United States

Strengthening the GATT's dispute settlement procedures was one of the key US objectives at the start of the Uruguay Round. In fact, "more effective and expeditious dispute settlement mechanisms and procedures" topped the list of "principal trade negotiating objectives" codified in section 1101 of the US Omnibus Trade and Competitiveness Act of 1988. However, as the United States has increasingly become a defendant as well as a plaintiff in GATT disputes, congressional support for stronger multilateral procedures has become more ambivalent.[3]

Do the new rules significantly increase the constraints on the United States' ability to impose trade measures to defend its trading interests? In the past, US retaliation in cases that involved trade covered by GATT obligations would have been in violation of the GATT, if the action was taken without prior multilateral authorization. Under the new rules, the authorization to retaliate will be forthcoming, but limited to a specific response determined by the panel.

Furthermore, under existing rules, if a dispute panel found the United States in violation of its GATT obligations, the United States could simply block adoption of the panel report and avoid formal censure. Under the DSU the United States can no longer block adoption of the panel report. However, it can still choose to ignore its findings, because panel rulings are not self-executing in US law. In other words, if WTO decisions require changes in US law, new legislation would need to be enacted to bring US practice into compliance. The WTO cannot compel the United States to pass such legislation. However, inaction could result in the United States being in violation of its international obligations.

The costs of noncompliance with WTO rulings fall into three categories. First, countries whose trade is adversely affected by the US violation

3. From the start of the Uruguay Round through May 1993, the United States was taken to the GATT 31 times and filed 52 complaints against foreign trade practices (data from the GATT's Analytical Index). Along with the European Union, the United States has been the main laggard in delaying panel procedures and implementing panel decisions.

would have the right to retaliate. However, most countries simply do not present the United States with a credible threat of retaliation; the US market is too important for them to risk escalating the trade dispute. With the notable exceptions of the European Union, Canada, and perhaps Japan, no country is likely to subject the United States to such drastic action. A second cost of noncompliance is that the United States would have a harder time pressing cases against other WTO members. Its ability to act under the DSU would not be compromised in a legal sense, but its ability to apply moral suasion would be diminished. Third, noncompliance by a major trading country would undercut confidence in the rules-based system as a whole and raise anew concerns about system erosion.

In sum, the WTO can reprimand but not severely punish violations by major trading powers. When they regard it as necessary, big countries can still abuse the system. However, such actions are not without cost and will tend to erode confidence in and support for the global trading system.

One possible safeguard against big power abuse, which was not raised during the Uruguay Round, would be to impose penalties against frequent violators of the DSU rules. Following the model of automobile driving infractions, "points" could be assessed against a country each time it fails to comply with a panel decision. If a country incurred three points over a five-year period, its "license" to retaliate pursuant to a panel ruling in its favor would be temporarily revoked.[4] In this manner, pragmatic and effective costs could be imposed against delinquent countries.

Implications for Section 301

Section 301 of the US Trade Act of 1974, as amended, is designed to promote the enforcement of US rights under international trade agreements and to coerce foreign countries into eliminating unfair trade practices that adversely affect US trading interests. In most instances the use of section 301 has been consistent with US obligations under the GATT;[5] indeed, the law itself allows cases to be dropped if a GATT ruling finds the US complaint to be unwarranted (section 301:2A).

Increasingly, however, section 301 cases have been brought against practices that are not covered by GATT disciplines, or that fall into a gray area which GATT jurisprudence was unable to clarify, or that lingered because GATT dispute procedures were blocked by the country accused of the unfair trade practice. In brief, defects in the GATT dispute settlement

---

4. This scheme could be characterized as the trade policy equivalent of "three strikes and you're out!"

5. However, the United States has sometimes threatened actions that would have violated its GATT obligations if implemented. For a detailed analysis of these cases see Bayard and Elliott (1994).

process and broad loopholes in the coverage of GATT obligations encouraged the United States to respond unilaterally under section 301.

Constraints on US unilateralism were a major objective of many participants in the Uruguay Round, and the DSU does contain provisions that require the United States to win a WTO case before it may act unilaterally to impose trade sanctions—unless the case does not involve issues covered by the WTO.[6] However, the claims of European and other negotiators that the Uruguay Round accord defanged section 301 are grossly exaggerated.

In practice, the DSU does not require the renunciation of, or even major modifications in, section 301. To the contrary, the new rules align DSU time limits more closely with US law. The United States can continue to use section 301 to bring WTO cases, to implement retaliation (which will now be automatically approved by the WTO) if countries fail to comply with panel rulings, and to institute unilateral challenges against foreign practices in cases not subject to WTO obligations.

However, US action under section 301 will be constrained in two respects. First, the circumstances in which the United States can act unilaterally without first going through WTO procedures have been sharply reduced because of the expanded coverage of WTO obligations. Second, the US response will be conditioned in part by the specific recommendations contained in the panel report.

On balance, the authority to act to defend US trading rights will be enhanced. The improved multilateral process should make resort to unilateral actions far less necessary, and should turn section 301 into a procedure for initiating US complaints to the WTO and implementing multilaterally authorized retaliation.

Assessment

In sum, the DSU establishes an integrated dispute settlement mechanism that fulfills the need for effective and expeditious procedures to resolve disputes arising in the broad range of agreements subsumed under the WTO umbrella. The DSU requires the prompt establishment of panels and sets strict deadlines for their resolution of disputes. It facilitates the approval of panel rulings by requiring a consensus to block reports, and thus prevents disputing parties from blocking the implementation of WTO rulings. It establishes a new Appellate Body empowered to review panel decisions and overturn ill-considered findings. Finally, it strengthens retaliation rights as part of improved compliance procedures, including

---

6. In essence, DSU paragraph 23 involves a basic bargain: in return for the more expeditious processing of disputes and the more automatic right to retaliate after a panel ruling, WTO members are required to use and abide by the DSU provisions when seeking redress for any violation of WTO obligations.

near-automatic authority to retaliate (including cross-retaliation among sectors) if countries do not comply with panel rulings.

Reform of the dispute settlement process should promote more expeditious compliance with panel rulings and thus encourage the use of multilateral procedures. Given the ambiguity of many of the new trading rules and market access commitments negotiated in the Uruguay Round, the new dispute settlement system is likely to be put to the test early and often.

The World Trade Organization

The GATT was originally crafted as a reciprocal trade agreement that would eventually be subsumed under the charter of the International Trade Organization (ITO), a comprehensive set of multilateral rights and obligations negotiated immediately after World War II.[1] The ITO was designed to be the trade component of the postwar Bretton Woods institutions, with a well-defined organizational structure like those of the World Bank and the International Monetary Fund (Kenen 1994). However, the ITO charter was never ratified, and the GATT has effectively served in its place ever since.

Succeeding GATT rounds have significantly expanded the scope of world trading rules, but the Uruguay Round was the first negotiation that has strengthened the institutional foundation of the world trading system.[2] After decades of provisional application, the Uruguay Round Final Act transforms the GATT into a permanent international institution, the World Trade Organization (WTO), responsible for governing the conduct of trade relations among its members.

The Agreement Establishing the World Trade Organization can be best described as a "mini-charter."[3] It turns the GATT from a trade accord serviced by a professional secretariat into a membership organization. In most respects the WTO Agreement simply establishes a legal framework that ties together the various trade pacts that have been negotiated under GATT auspices. Most of the provisions of the WTO Agreement involve procedural rules that govern the activities of the organization. Simply put, the WTO does not recreate the ITO.

GATT obligations remain at the core of the WTO. However, the WTO Agreement requires that its members adhere not only to GATT rules, but also to the broad range of trade pacts (with a few exceptions noted below) that have been negotiated under GATT auspices during the past two decades (e.g., the Tokyo Round codes and arrangements and the new accords on services, investment, and intellectual property negotiated in the Uruguay Round).

This "single undertaking" does not require much of countries like the United States that already adhere to almost all the existing pacts, but it ends the free ride of many GATT members that benefited from, but refused to join, new agreements negotiated in the GATT since the 1970s. Many

---

1. Robert E. Hudec and John H. Jackson provided very useful comments on this section.

2. Efforts in the 1950s to negotiate a charter for an Organization for Trade Cooperation met the same fate as the ITO (GATT, Basic Instruments and Selected Documents, 3/S [1955], 231–52).

3. The term is that used by John H. Jackson, whose recommendations in 1990 provided the intellectual underpinning for the Canadian and European proposals for a WTO (then called the Multilateral Trade Organization). See Jackson (1990).

countries, especially developing countries, will now have to undertake substantial new trade obligations that they had not adopted in previous GATT rounds. In this sense, the WTO Agreement entails a higher level of commitment than the existing GATT, which allowed countries to decline membership in new accords and maintained wide-ranging exemptions from other obligations.

Apart from the establishment of an integrated dispute settlement mechanism, and the requirement that members adhere to almost all its constituent accords, the WTO Agreement entails few new substantive trade obligations. Indeed, the Uruguay Round accords could have been implemented without the creation of the WTO, but the management of the diverse agreements would have been much more difficult, particularly regarding the resolution of disputes.

The WTO arrived late on the Uruguay Round agenda; draft proposals to establish the new organization did not surface until the runup to the Brussels ministerial in December 1990 and were not fully elaborated until the latter half of 1991. The issues that the WTO was designed to address, however, were in mind from the start of the round, namely, how all the various agreements would fit together; what countries would assume which obligations; and whether there would be a common dispute settlement mechanism among the different accords.

The WTO in Brief

The WTO is often described as an umbrella organization. Its charter covers the agreements that resulted from the Uruguay Round talks: the GATT 1994, including the agreement on trade-related investment measures and the Tokyo Round codes (Annex 1A to the WTO Agreement); the General Agreement on Trade in Services, or GATS (Annex 1B); and the agreement on Trade-Related Aspects of Intellectual Property Rights, or TRIPs (Annex 1C). These agreements are binding on all members. The WTO Agreement also consolidates the dispute settlement provisions of those different accords into one common dispute settlement mechanism (Annex 2) and administers the trade policy review mechanism (TPRM) provided for in Annex 3. In addition, the WTO incorporates four plurilateral agreements (the civil aircraft agreement, the government procurement agreement, and the meat and dairy arrangements), the obligations of which apply only to their signatories, not to all WTO members (Annex 4).

In one important respect, the exception of the plurilateral agreements from the single undertaking of the WTO is a notable flaw, since it allows most countries to avoid obligations regarding key economic activities such as government procurement.[4] However, the existence of Annex 4 in

---

4. Besides the United States and the European Union, only 9 other countries are likely to sign the new agreement on government procurement.

Figure 2 Structure of the World Trade Organization

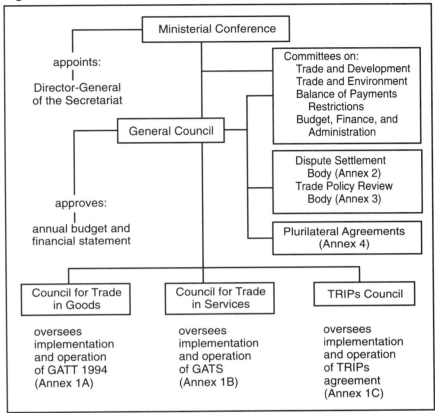

the WTO Agreement does add flexibility to the WTO system by allowing trade pacts to be developed among a subset of countries as a way station toward their future extension to the entire WTO membership. Indeed, the plurilateral accords in Annex 4 could provide a precedent for dealing with the new issues emerging on the WTO agenda (Jackson 1994).

In that regard, the new institutional structure of the WTO facilitates the conduct of continuing trade negotiations mandated in the Uruguay Round Final Act, as well as future talks in areas covered by the GATT 1994, the GATS and TRIPs agreements, and new issues affecting the trade relations of WTO members (see figure 2). For that reason, claims by environmental and consumer groups that the WTO poses a new obstacle to consideration of their concerns in world trade talks seem totally without merit. Quite the contrary, as the creation of the new Committee on Trade and Environment demonstrates, the WTO establishes an umbrella under which environmental issues can be added much more readily to the agenda of the world trading system.

The WTO also removes certain procedural relics of the GATT system, including the protocol of provisional application of the GATT and the so-called grandfather rights that exempted from GATT disciplines domestic legislation enacted prior to 1947 (or the date of accession for new GATT members) that violated multilateral trade obligations. Existing GATT Article XXV waivers that are not covered by the Uruguay Round accords, which are listed in Annex 1A of the WTO Agreement (e.g., the US-Canada Auto Pact, the Caribbean Basin Economic Recovery Act, and the Andean Trade Preference Act), must be terminated within two years of the entry into force of the WTO, unless extended pursuant to the provisions of Article IX of the WTO Agreement. In addition, a special provision in the general interpretative note to the WTO Agreement (Annex 1A, paragraph 1:e) continues to exempt the US Jones Act (which restricts cabotage to US carriers) from WTO obligations.

GATT signatories that deposit schedules of commitments for the revised agreement that emerged from the Uruguay Round (the GATT 1994) and the GATS are eligible to become original members of the WTO.[5] These countries have up to two years to deposit their schedules of commitments; however, if a country deposits its schedule after the entry into force of the WTO, the commitments still must be implemented counting from the date on which the WTO entered into force (WTO Article XIV:2).

As under the GATT and most other international agreements, members may withdraw from the WTO six months after notifying the director general of their intention to do so. In addition, members may invoke the so-called nonapplication clause of the WTO Agreement (analogous to GATT Article XXXV) to deny the benefits of the WTO agreements to a particular country. However, this provision may only be invoked at the time the targeted country becomes a member of the WTO or if such nonapplication already has been invoked—and is still effective—under Article XXXV of the GATT.

In other words, if a non-GATT member accedes to the WTO, existing members have a one-time opportunity to invoke nonapplication against the new member at the time of its accession. This provision was used extensively against Japan when it entered the GATT several decades ago, and could be invoked by the United States against China if US law prevents the extension of most-favored nation (MFN) treatment on a permanent basis.

The WTO is headed by a Ministerial Conference, which will meet at least once every other year to direct the work of the WTO. A General Council will be established to oversee the operation of the agreements.

---

5. As of 30 June 1994 the GATT had 123 members. In addition, GATT accession working parties have been established for another 20 or so countries and territories. If these countries accede to the GATT before the WTO enters into force, they will also qualify as charter members of the WTO.

The General Council will itself act as a Dispute Settlement Body and a Trade Policy Review Body. The General Council will also establish subsidiary bodies such as a Goods Council, a Services Council, and a TRIPs Council to administer agreements in those areas. Both the Ministerial Conference and the General Council will be composed of representatives of all members.

The Ministerial Conference will establish a Committee on Trade and Development, a Committee on Balance-of-Payments Restrictions, and a Committee on Budget, Finance, and Administration. In addition, the ministerial meeting in Marrakesh in April 1994 decided to establish a new Committee on Trade and Environment at the first meeting of the General Council of the WTO. The ministers commissioned a preparatory subcommittee to begin work immediately on a broad range of trade and environmental issues.

The WTO Secretariat will comprise most of the existing GATT staff, and the new WTO director general will be appointed by the Ministerial Conference. The GATT traditionally has placed tight restraints on secretariat functions and initiatives, forcefully implemented through tight budgets. Although the trade policy review mechanism has clearly enhanced secretariat responsibility for assessing member country trade policies, the WTO staff is likely to remain small compared with those of the World Bank, the International Monetary Fund (IMF), and the OECD Secretariat.

Small can be beautiful (and efficient), but the size of the WTO staff will undoubtedly constrain activities in two areas. First, the added responsibilities imposed on the WTO Secretariat by the Uruguay Round accords, especially regarding dispute settlement and trade policy reviews, will strain the already lean resources for legal and economic analysis. Second, staffing constraints could limit the scope of joint activities that might be undertaken with other international economic institutions.[6] In particular, it could effectively undercut the intent of the hortatory, but nonetheless important, declaration in the Final Act encouraging the director general of the WTO to review with the heads of the IMF and the World Bank possible cooperative efforts to help promote "greater coherence in global economic policymaking."[7]

Organizational Problems

There are two major problems in the provisions for the WTO: its voting procedure and the absence of a management council.

---

6. Various provisions mandate joint efforts with the IMF, the World Bank, and the World Intellectual Property Organization. In contrast, the Uruguay Round accords do not explicitly mention institutional linkages with international environmental and labor organizations.

7. In that regard, the WTO will have to outgrow some old bad habits from the GATT. For example, data on the tariff results of the Uruguay Round were initially denied to the World Bank after the Marrakesh meeting because a major participant blocked the transfer.

Voting Rights

As under the GATT, WTO decisions will normally be made by consensus (i.e., decisions become effective if no member officially objects). If a consensus cannot be reached, matters will be decided by majority vote.

Although the one-country, one-vote rule has been standard GATT practice since 1948, concerns have been raised regarding the WTO's unweighted voting procedures. The one-country, one-vote procedure has provoked fears that "majority" decisions would discriminate against the major trading nations and undercut their sovereignty. Unflattering comparisons have been made between WTO procedures and the unweighted majority voting system of the UN General Assembly, and charges have been leveled that the unweighted voting system poses the risk of a "tyranny of the majority."[8]

In almost every respect, these concerns are more theoretical than real. The GATT has almost always acted by consensus (thus affording a big-power veto). When votes have been taken, they have not exhibited UN-style block voting. In addition, however, important checks and balances were added to the voting rules that effectively institute a "big power" block on all but the most mundane WTO decisions. Although the Uruguay Round negotiators refused to allow major trading countries a veto in WTO votes, similar to that of the five permanent members of the UN Security Council, procedural safeguards were added to the WTO Agreement that should mitigate most potential problems.

To minimize the "tyranny of the majority," the United States insisted on modifications in the amendment procedures to ensure that major trading countries can prevent the WTO from instituting new obligations or amending existing rules that would undercut the negotiated results of prior trade rounds. The size of the blocking minority depends on the type of issue subject to the vote (i.e., interpretations of existing obligations; waivers; and amendments). For interpretations of any of the agreements, and for waivers of an obligation (which are subject to annual review), the rules require a three-fourths majority of the WTO members. Amendments generally require a two-thirds majority. However, if an amendment would "alter the rights and obligations of the members," it generally would apply only to those countries that accept it.[9] Amendments to WTO Articles IX (on decision making) and X (on amendments) and to the MFN provisions of the GATT 1994, the GATS, and the TRIPs agreement can only take effect upon acceptance by all members.

---

8. Critics have cited the imbalance between participation in world trade and WTO voting rights. The United States, the European Union, Canada, and Japan together accounted for 64 percent of world merchandise exports in 1992 (*International Trade Statistics*, GATT 1993).

9. In rare instances the Ministerial Conference can require (by a three-fourths majority vote) WTO members to accept the amendment or withdraw from the WTO.

A related (albeit minor) concern relates to the voting rights of regional blocs. Although it had only one vote in the GATT, the European Union will have 12 votes, one for each of its member countries (soon to be increased to 16 votes with the entrance of Norway, Sweden, Finland, and Austria) in the WTO. In comparison, the United States and Japan have only one vote each. The former Soviet Union will have more than a dozen votes when its constituent states accede to the WTO in coming years.[10]

Management

Mirroring current GATT practice, WTO operations will be directed by a Council comprised of all current members. Like the GATT, the WTO is likely to suffer from slow and cumbersome policymaking and management.

Simply put, an organization with more than 120 member countries cannot be run by a "Committee of the Whole." Mass management does not lend itself to operational efficiency or serious policy discussion. Past attempts to operate a GATT steering group—the CG-18—failed badly. The group was essentially a microcosm of the Committee of the Whole, with all its warts and blemishes.

Member countries must be prepared to delegate responsibility for the management of WTO operations to a small steering committee of WTO members. Otherwise those countries that resist broadening WTO trade discussions or object to particular initiatives (such as new negotiations) will continue to be able to delay WTO decisions.

Both the International Monetary Fund and the World Bank have executive boards to direct the executive officers of the organization, with permanent participation by the major industrial countries and weighted voting. The WTO will require a comparable structure to operate efficiently. Attempts to form a small executive body, including proposals put forward in the "Functioning of the GATT System" group during the Uruguay Round, were unsuccessful, and the political orientation of smaller GATT members remains strongly opposed to the concept. These organizational challenges remain to be tested.

In the absence of WTO reforms, the United States and other major trading countries may well continue to resort to ad hoc, extralegal processes like the Quad (an informal group consisting of the United States, the European Union, Canada, and Japan). Alternatively, the United States and the European Union could simply cut their own deal (as they did in the Uruguay Round on agriculture) and insist that others accept it.

---

10. The anticipated entry of China and Russia into the WTO in the near future will also complicate political considerations inherent in the decision-making process.

Assessment

The WTO significantly strengthens the institutional foundation of the world trading system. By restructuring the GATT into a membership organization and requiring all members to adhere to all its constituent accords, the WTO substantially reduces the free-rider problem that has plagued many of these pacts since their inception. After a relatively short transition period, all developing countries will have to assume all WTO obligations.

Concerns about flaws in WTO voting procedures have been grossly exaggerated. In most cases, WTO decisions will be made by consensus. Where votes are taken, numerous procedural safeguards have been included to preclude the "tyranny of the majority." In particular, WTO decisions cannot alter the substantive obligations undertaken by a member country unless that country agrees to the changes.

The major problem with the WTO provisions is the failure to establish a management council to direct the work of the director general and the WTO Secretariat, thus leaving the weak management structure of the GATT intact. To operate efficiently, the WTO needs an organizational structure comparable to that of the IMF or the World Bank, with an executive board on which the major industrial countries have permanent participation.

Because of its weak management structure, the WTO will start off at a sharp disadvantage in dealing with the IMF and the World Bank. Efforts to expand consultations and joint initiatives between the three organizations, as explicitly encouraged in the WTO Agreement, are likely to be significantly constrained as a result.

Trade Policy Review Mechanism

The 1988 Montreal midterm review of the Uruguay Round established, on an interim basis, a trade policy review mechanism (TPRM) to review periodically the trade policies and practices of GATT member countries. Up to that point national trade policies had seldom been subject to international review in a manner comparable to that exercised by the Organization for Economic Cooperation and Development and the International Monetary Fund over macroeconomic policies. Such review can contribute to the better formulation and execution of trade policies by analyzing the costs and benefits of national practices and by exposing potential problems before they fester into trade disputes.

The objectives of the TPRM are codified in Annex 3 of the Agreement Establishing the World Trade Organization: to provide greater transparency of national laws and practices, "to contribute to improved adherence by all Members to [WTO] rules, disciplines and commitments" (paragraph A.i), and "to examine the impact of a Member's trade policies and practices on the multilateral trading system" (paragraph A.ii). Although the TPRM encourages greater transparency of national trade policies, it is by no means intended "to serve as a basis for the enforcement of specific obligations under the Agreements or for dispute settlement procedures, or to impose new policy commitments on Members" (paragraph A.i). The TPRM reviews take the form of simple consultations and do not attempt to judge the consistency or conformity of national practices with the world trading rules.

The Uruguay Round Final Act establishes a Trade Policy Review Body (TPRB) to administer the TPRM, which is accorded permanent status. The TPRB reports to the WTO General Council and is responsible both for the implementation of the TPRM and for reporting annually on developments in the international trading system. In that context the TPRB is also the repository of all notifications that countries are obliged to make under the various WTO pacts. The TPRB is also required to appraise the operation of the TPRM within five years after the WTO has entered into force, that is, in 2000.

The TPRB examines on a regular basis the national trade policies and other economic policies of member countries that affect the world trading system. Reviews will continue to be carried out every other year for the four largest trading areas in terms of world market share (currently, the European Union, the United States, Japan, and Canada); every four years for the next 16 largest trading nations; and every six years for other developing countries (with exceptions for the least developed countries).

In essence, the TPRM reviews are seminars on national trade policies, with discussions based on two papers: a full report presented by the country under review, and an independent analysis by the WTO Secretariat based on information provided by the country concerned and on other data available to the TPRM staff. Together, the two reports provide a useful trade policy retrospective but offer few comments or criticisms regarding the prospective evolution of those policies.

The TPRM reports, together with the minutes of the review meeting of the TPRB, are published promptly after the review. However, these reports are not widely circulated and seldom provoke more than a passing mention in the business pages. In other words, the TPRB debate remains an academic exercise, with little impact on the domestic trade policy debate of member countries.

Multilateral surveillance of national trade policies under the TPRM serves two useful purposes: it examines how a country is meeting its international obligations and what barriers obstruct the free flow of goods and services. But TPRM reviews do little to expose the cost of protection, propose adjustment measures to unravel existing protection, or recommend alternative domestic policies that could be adopted in lieu of trade restraints. Without these additional ingredients, TPRM reviews will do little to encourage adjustment by protected industries or to promote political support within countries to dismantle trade barriers.

What additional steps should be taken? First, international surveillance of trade policies should have a domestic counterpart (perhaps akin to the Australian Industries Commission) that could educate the public on the costs and benefits of national trade policies and offer independent policy prescriptions. Domestic analysis and debate on trade policies are needed to complement the TPRM reviews. The GATT "Wisemen's" Report of 1985 (Leutwiler et al. 1985) suggested that countries conduct the domestic equivalent of a TPRM that could inter alia tabulate a "protection balance sheet" for national trade policies. Such reports would be valuable both to demonstrate the cost of such measures to domestic constituents, and to compare the level of trade controls maintained by GATT member countries.

To date, no country has taken up the challenge. The TPRM accord includes only a hortatory statement that WTO members should "recognize the inherent value of domestic transparency of government decision-making on trade policy matters," and agree on a voluntary basis to "promote greater transparency within their own systems."

Second, the expanding scope of policies subject to trade policy reviews complicates the task of compiling national reports and will require additional resources for the TPRM. The TPRM staff is likely to remain too small to be able to handle this growing task; indeed, it is already stretched thin by the large number of reviews it must produce each year.

To overcome this resource constraint, the WTO should rely more heavily on private and semipublic research institutions to do this analysis on a regular basis. Gary Hufbauer and Kimberly Elliott (1994) have done so for the United States and will extend their analysis to Japan and other countries in the near future, but such studies of the cost of protection need to be updated regularly and coordinated by the WTO.

In sum, the TPRM has made a positive, but limited, contribution to the international surveillance of trade policies. The Uruguay Round agreement extends the TPRM indefinitely and reconfirms its existing terms of reference and reporting requirements. However, the TPRM accord provides only hortatory encouragement for the formation of domestic surveillance bodies to parallel and complement the work of the TPRM. It thus makes few improvements on the interim TPRM established at the Montreal midterm review.

III

Summaries of Key Provisions
of the Uruguay Round Agreements

TRADE LIBERALIZATION: Agriculture

RECOMMENDATIONS

Internal support
1. Reduce current levels of domestic support by 50 percent from a base year of 1988.
2. Base reductions in internal support on an Aggregate Measure of Support (AMS), provided that (i) reductions in AMS are accompanied by cuts in export subsidies and (ii) support is not increased for any product (i.e., no "rebalancing").

Export subsidies
3. Reduce export subsidies by 50 percent from 1988 levels.

Market access
4. Convert import quotas into tariffs or tariff rate quotas.
5. Liberalize sectors that are currently shielded from import competition significantly from their existing levels of protection.

Food security
6. Encourage stockpiling, instead of trade protection, to achieve food security objectives.

RESULTS

Internal support
1. The Aggregate Measure of Support (AMS) is adopted as the benchmark for liberalization commitments. Countries agree to reduce their AMS by 20 percent over six years, in equal annual installments, from 1986–88 levels. The reduction commitment is not product-specific but covers both national and subnational subsidies.
2. The calculation of the AMS excludes specified domestic subsidies, including research and extension services, pest and disease control, inspection services, environmental and conservation programs, resource and producer retirement programs, stockholding for food security, domestic food aid, crop insurance, disaster relief, regional aids, and structural investment aid. These nonactionable subsidies are also exempted (under the so-called peace clause of Article 13) from countervailing duties, nullification and impairment actions, and serious prejudice actions under the GATT for nine years.
3. Direct payments to farmers (e.g., deficiency payments) are not considered part of the AMS, and thus not subject to reductions, if they are made under production-limiting programs and based on a fixed area and yield or number of livestock, or cover less than 85 percent of base level production.
4. A *de minimis* provision allows countries to exclude from the calculation of the AMS (i) product-specific support if it does not exceed 5 percent of the value of production of that commodity, and (ii) non-product-specific support where it does not exceed 5 percent of the value of the country's total agricultural production.
5. For developing countries, the *de minimis* level is 10 percent, and specified agricultural input subsidies are excluded from the AMS (Articles 6.2 and 6.4).

Export subsidies
6. Export subsidy expenditures are reduced by 36 percent over six years, in equal annual installments, from 1986–90 base year levels.
7. The volume of subsidized exports is cut by 21 percent over six years, in equal annual installments, from 1986–90 base year levels.
8. If exports of subsidized commodities in 1991–92 are higher than in the base period, the cuts in the volume of subsidized exports can be made from the 1991–92 level in equal annual installments (e.g., US and EU wheat). If the average level in 1991–92 exceeds the base-period average by more than 25 percent and more than 40 percent of the 1992

volume of subsidized exports is sold from intervention stocks, the volume cuts can be made from a 1986–92 base in equal annual installments (e.g., EU beef). In either case, the volume of subsidized exports after six years must be no more than 79 percent of the average 1986–90 level.

9. Minor adjustments in annual reductions are permitted in years 2 through 5, so long as the cumulative cuts to date are within 3 percent of the value and 1.75 percent of the volume commitments specified in the country's liberalization schedule (Article 9.2b).

10. For developing countries, the percentage cuts are 24 and 14 percent, respectively, in equal annual installments, over 10 years.

11. All reductions apply to specific products or product groups, generally on a four-digit HTS level. However, in some important sectors (e.g., coarse grains; fruits and vegetables), the commitments involve more aggregated groups.

12. Countries commit not to grant export subsidies on products that currently do not benefit from such assistance (Article 3:3).

13. Privately financed export aid is not covered as long as it is not mandated or arranged by the government, or not applied to products receiving other government support (e.g., domestic price supports).

14. Precise disciplines on export credits, credit guarantees, and insurance programs are not covered, but governments commit to develop internationally agreed disciplines with respect to this area.

15. International food aid should not be tied to commercial transactions and has to conform to UN Food and Agriculture Organization principles.

Market access

16. All existing nontariff barriers are converted into tariffs, which are then added to existing tariffs.

17. The total import tariffs are cut by an *unweighted* average of 36 percent in equal installments over six years (or 24 percent over ten years for developing countries), from a base of 1986–88.

18. Each individual tariff must be reduced by a minimum of 15 percent (or 10 percent over 10 years for developing countries).

19. Under certain, narrowly defined circumstances, a country may impose temporary duties (special safeguards) for up to one year on products subject to tariffication commitments.

20. Countries agree to establish "minimum access" import quotas for products or product groups where imports have faced prohibitive trade barriers, equal to 3 percent of domestic consumption and rising to 5 percent at the end of the sixth year.

21. For rice, Japan establishes a minimum access quota equal to 4 percent of domestic consumption, rising to 8 percent by the year 2000. Korea establishes a 1 percent quota, which increases by 0.25 percent annually for four years, then by 0.4 percent annually for five years, to a level of 4 percent in the year 2004. At the end of these transition periods, the countries must comply with the tariffication requirement, unless the tariffication obligation is otherwise waived in the context of negotiations regarding "continuation of the reform process" (Article 20).

22. Least-developed countries must bind their tariffs but are exempt from liberalization commitments in this area.

Sanitary and Phytosanitary (SPS) measures

23. The SPS agreement allows countries to impose trade controls "to protect human, animal or plant life or health," if the measure is based on scientific principles and is applied on a nondiscriminatory basis. The agreement encourages the use of international SPS standards but does not require that a country maintain international SPS standards; the use of stricter national standards is allowed.

Future negotiations

24. Countries agree to initiate new negotiations by the year 2000 to further "the long-term objective of substantial progressive reductions in support and protection" (Article 20).

ASSESSMENT

1. Contains historic, albeit modest, commitments to cap and reduce export and domestic subsidies. For the United States and the European Union, the accord requires significant reductions in current levels of export subsidies and "locks in" reductions in domestic supports implemented since 1986. However, the exemption of major US and EU farm income support programs from the AMS calculation will likely dilute somewhat the impact of the domestic subsidy disciplines, although budgetary constraints should prevent this loophole from being overly exploited.

2. Fixes the liberalization commitments in nominal terms without inflation adjustments so that subsidy reductions in real terms will continue even after the 6- or 10-year transition periods.

3. Requires comprehensive tariffication of nontariff barriers and 36 percent cuts in average import protection. However, the most import-sensitive products face only a 15 percent tariff cut over six years. In short, the cost of protection becomes much more transparent, but the level of protection remains high for products currently subject to nontariff measures.

4. Creates minimum access quotas for products currently blocked by comprehensive import barriers, including Japanese and Korean rice. Starts a process of reform of long-standing, intractable trade barriers but only opens a small segment of domestic markets to import competition.

5. Requires that renewed negotiations begin by the year 2000 to supplement the farm reform process.

GRADE: B +

TRADE LIBERALIZATION: Textiles and Apparel

RECOMMENDATIONS

1. Convert existing quotas to tariff rate quotas and phase out within a decade.
2. Expand quotas during the transition period by an average of 7 percent annually so that the severity of protection does not increase.
3. For developed countries, accord higher priority to the elimination of quotas than to deep tariff cuts in this sector. Newly industrialized countries should also liberalize barriers to their markets.
4. Exempt least-developed countries from quotas.

RESULTS

1. For products listed in the annex, the agreement calls for the immediate removal of quotas negotiated under the Multi-Fiber Arrangement (MFA) on products that accounted for at least 16 percent of the total volume of covered imports in 1990. The initial liberalization and subsequent reforms must include some products from each of the following categories: tops and yarns, fabrics, made-up textile products, and clothing, but the pact does not set specific shares for each category.
2. Remaining MFA quotas will be phased out over 10 years according to the following three-stage schedule:
    a) after three years, quotas will be removed on products that accounted for 17 percent of the total volume of 1990 imports;
    b) after seven years, quotas will be removed on products that accounted for 18 percent of the total volume of 1990 imports;
    c) after ten years, all remaining quota restrictions will be eliminated.
3. During the transition period, remaining quotas will be expanded according to a three-stage formula:
    a) stage 1 (first three years): quotas will be increased by at least 16 percent more than the growth rate prescribed in the bilateral agreement in the year preceding the entry into force of the WTO. So if the base growth rate was 6 percent, the quotas will expand by 6.96 percent annually;
    b) stage 2 (years 4 through 7): quota growth rates will be 25 percent higher than in stage 1;
    c) stage 3 (years 8 through 10): quota growth rates will be 27 percent higher than the stage 2 rates.
4. Swing, carryover, and carry-forward provisions in force during the base period will be maintained during the transition period.
5. MFA countries whose exports account for not more than 1.2 percent of the volume of a country's imports covered by the MFA as of 31 December 1991 will be granted higher quota growth rates during the transition period (i.e., 25 percent in stage 1 and 27 percent in stage 2).
6. Non-MFA restrictions not justified under the GATT will be brought into conformity within one year after the entry into force of the agreement or phased out progressively over 10 years according to a schedule notified to the Textiles Monitoring Body.
7. Safeguard measures can be applied against imports of a particular country that are still subject to MFA quotas and that cause or threaten serious damage to the domestic industry, subject to certain conditions:
    a) The safeguard action shall not reduce the volume of trade below the actual level of exports or imports from the country concerned during the 12-month period ending two months before the month in which a request for consultation was made.
    b) The safeguard measure can remain in place for up to three years without extension or until the product is integrated into GATT 1994, whichever comes first. Multiyear safeguards must provide for quota growth of at least 6 percent annually.

c) Safeguard measures shall not apply to developing-country exports of handloom fabrics or products of the cottage industry, or traditional folklore handicraft; textiles that are historically traded in significant quantities; and products made of pure silk.

8. Developed countries only agreed to small tariff cuts (e.g., US average cut of 9.2 percent for apparel) to complement the phase-out of quotas.

ASSESSMENT

1. Meets 10-year quota liberalization goal. However, more than half of existing quotas are not required to be removed for 10 years (since reforms are based on 1990 imports).
2. Expands quotas substantially during the transition period. Most quotas that remain in effect for 10 years will more than double from base-year levels. However, products subject to restrictive quota growth rates under existing bilateral MFA agreements may expand by only 16 percent over the decade. In addition, recourse to transitional safeguards could constrain annual import growth for the most import-sensitive products.
3. Does not exempt least-developed countries and small exporters from quotas but provides them higher quota growth rates during the transition period.
4. Maintains relatively high textile tariffs in developing countries and high tariffs on clothing in developed countries.

GRADE: B +

TRADE LIBERALIZATION: Tariffs

RECOMMENDATIONS

1. Cut tariffs by an average of one-third, as mandated by the ministers at the midterm review of the Uruguay Round, either through a formula or request-offer approach.
2. Reduce tariff escalation by requiring industrialized nations to cut tariffs on higher value-added goods.
3. Lower tariff peaks.

RESULTS

1. **Average tariff cut.** Developed countries' tariffs on industrial goods are reduced by a trade-weighted average of 38 percent—lowering the pre–Uruguay Round average tariff of 6.3 percent to 3.9 percent. The overall depth of the cut for the United States is about 34 percent; for the European Union, 37 percent; for Canada, 47 percent; and for Japan, 56 percent. The average cut in tariffs benefiting US industrial exports is about 43 percent.
2. **Phase-in.** Most reductions are phased in over five years, starting 1 January 1995.
3. **"Zero-for-zero" commitments.** Tariffs on a number of goods are eliminated: pharmaceuticals (subject to immediate elimination); construction equipment, distilled spirits, certain furniture, medical equipment, steel, and agricultural equipment (subject to a phase-in period of five years); beer (subject to a phase-in period of eight years); and toys and paper (subject to a phase-in period of ten years). Most commitments are at a disaggregated level (i.e., four- to six-digit HS level) and therefore more product- than sector-specific. For the United States, the zero-for-zero commitments affect about 6.7 percent of US imports, or almost $31.3 billion in 1989. The pre–Uruguay Round trade-weighted average US tariff on these goods was already low, at 4.6 percent.
4. **Tariff escalation.** Tariff escalation has largely been eliminated for paper products and for products made from jute and tobacco. It has also been substantially reduced for products made from wood and metals.
5. **Duty-free trade.** The share of developed countries' imports of industrial products that enter duty-free will more than double (from 20 to 44 percent). Developing countries have bound their share of imports that enter duty-free at 39 percent, and economies in transition have committed to increase the share of duty-free imports from 13 to 16 percent.
6. **Tariff harmonization.** The main industrial-country producers agreed to harmonize their chemical tariffs at low levels. Tariffs on some chemical products will be eliminated, while those on most other chemicals will be bound at, or below, 6.5 percent. The phase-in period for these cuts varies from 5 to 15 years, depending on the pre–Uruguay Round tariff level. However, several important developing-country markets are not included. The chemical tariff harmonization affects 3.2 percent of US imports, or almost $15 billion in 1989, lowering the average tariff on US chemical imports from 5.2 to 3.7 percent.
7. **Peak tariffs.** The proportion of developed countries' imports subject to peak tariffs (defined as 15 percent or more) declines from 7 to 5 percent. However numerous peak tariffs will remain, especially in the textiles and apparel sectors.
8. **Tariff bindings.** The proportion of world trade in industrial goods that is subject to bound tariff rates has increased from 44 to 83 percent. As a result, virtually all imports of the developed and transition economies will enter now under bound tariffs, as well as more than half the imports of developing countries (respectively, 99 percent and 58 percent). However, many developing countries have bound their rates at levels that exceed currently applied rates (ceiling bindings).
9. **Implications for US trade.** Overall, the 34 percent average cut in US import tariffs on industrial goods reduces the average tariff from 4.6 to 3.0 percent. On the export side, US exporters benefit from a 43 percent average cut in tariffs collected abroad on their products—reducing the average tariff from 9.2 to 5.2 percent. Based on 1989 data (1988

for exports), these cuts could result in an increase in US merchandise imports of 2.7 percent, while US exporters could expect to sell about 6.5 percent more in US industrial products abroad.

ASSESSMENT

1. Exceeds both the overall depth of the cuts achieved in the Kennedy and Tokyo Rounds (35 percent and 34 percent, respectively) and commitments made at the Montreal mid-term review.

2. Reduces tariff escalation in important product sectors through zero-for-zero results and harmonizes chemical tariffs at low levels in most developed-country markets (but *not* in some key developing countries). Tariffs on a number of industrial goods have been eliminated.

3. Fails to achieve substantial cuts in peak tariffs, much less the Quad's "best efforts" commitment of July 1993 to reduce peak tariffs by 50 percent.

GRADE: A −

TRADE LIBERALIZATION: Government Procurement

RECOMMENDATIONS

1. Expand the number of entities subject to the Government Procurement Code by extending coverage to telecommunications, transport, and electric power authorities.
2. Extend code obligations to the procurement of services.
3. Lower the contract threshold above which code rules apply.

RESULTS

1. The Agreement on Government Procurement (GPA) applies to subcentral governments (e.g., states and provinces) and other governmental entities, such as public utilities, as well as procurement by central governments already covered by the existing Government Procurement Code.
2. Unlike the existing code, the GPA specifically includes services contracts procured by government entities of the *signatories* to the GPA. However, two years after the WTO enters into force, services procurement will be the subject of negotiations under auspices of the General Agreement on Trade in Services (GATS); the results of these talks will apply to *all* WTO members.
3. The existing code applies to contracts of goods procured by central governments worth more than SDR 130,000. In general, the GPA establishes the following threshold values for goods and services:
   —central governments: SDR 130,000;
   —subcentral governments: SDR 200,000 (SDR 355,000 for Canada and the United States);
   —utilities: about SDR 400,000 (SDR 130,000 for Japan);
   —construction services: SDR 5 million (SDR 15 million for noncentral government contracts in Korea and Japan, and SDR 4.5 million for central government procurement in Japan).
4. The GPA thresholds will *not* be adjusted for inflation and thus will be reduced in real terms over time.
5. In notes to their annexes, most countries have reserved MFN derogations for contracts procured by subcentral governments and public utilities against other signatories to compel them to improve their offers before the GPA enters into force on 1 January 1996.
6. The value of the US and EU commitments is estimated at over $100 billion annually on each side. In addition, other signatories have committed to apply the new GPA rules to a broad range of their procurement markets. Estimates of the total value of contracts subject to GPA disciplines range up to $400 billion annually.

ASSESSMENT

1. Extends rules to procurement by subcentral governments, subject to a somewhat higher threshold than central governments.
2. Extends rules to government procurement of services, especially the important construction services sector.
3. Maintains contract thresholds at the lower levels incorporated in the existing code in 1988, but these thresholds will be reduced in real terms over time due to the absence of an inflation adjustment.
4. Although GPA coverage of contracts tendered by urban transport and electric power authorities is fairly substantial, these public utilities and telecommunications are subject to ongoing negotiations—with uncertain prospects.

GRADE: A −

TRADE RULES: Antidumping

RECOMMENDATIONS

1. Establish more clear and stringent criteria for the calculation of dumping (covering the range of adjustments permitted to be made to price data in comparing export and home-market prices).
2. Bar the use of price undertakings to resolve antidumping cases, to avoid promoting soft cartels that could arise in the absence of strict antitrust rules.
3. Establish new GATT rules to protect against circumvention of antidumping duties by means of slight product alterations or minor assembly ("screwdriver") operations in the importing country or a third country.

RESULTS

Methodological changes

1. **Constructed value.** If there are no significant home-market sales of the product under investigation, the export price can be compared to third-country sales or to a constructed value, which is calculated as production costs plus administrative and selling expenses plus profit, using detailed rules with regard to the determination of profits (Article 2.2).
2. **Determination of profit for constructed value.** If the constructed amount for profit cannot be based on actual data of production and sales by the exporter or producer under investigation, it should be based on: (i) the actual profit realized by other exporters or producers in the same general category of products; (ii) the weighted average of the actual profit realized by other exporters of the same product; or (iii) "any reasonable method" provided it does not exceed the profit normally realized by other exporters or producers on sales of the same general category of products in the home market (Article 2.2.2).
3. **Sales below cost.** Home-market sales that are below the fully allocated cost of production (including administrative and selling expenses) can be disregarded when determining the average home-market price, provided that the average selling price in the home market is less than the weighted average unit cost, or the portion of the volume of sales below per-unit costs is more than 20 percent (Article 2.2.1).
4. **Start-up costs.** Adjustments to cost calculations made for start-up operations "shall reflect the costs at the end of the start-up period or, if that period extends beyond the period of investigation, the most recent costs which can reasonably be taken into account by the authorities during the investigation" (Article 2.2.1.1).
5. **Price averaging.** The determination of the dumping margin shall "normally" be based on a comparison of the weighted average normal value to the weighted average of prices of *all* comparable exports, or on a transaction-to-transaction basis (Article 2.4). However, in cases of targeted dumping, individual export prices may be compared to the average normal price only if the weighted average-to-weighted average, or transaction-to-transaction, comparison would not appropriately take the impact of targeted dumping into account (Article 2.4.2).
6. **Cumulation.** The agreement allows cumulation of dumped imports subject to investigation from more than one country, provided that the dumping margin in each case is more than *de minimis* and the volume of dumped imports from each country is not negligible (Article 3.3).

Procedural changes

7. **Standing.** An antidumping petition must be submitted "by or on behalf of" the domestic industry of the like product (Article 5.4). National authorities are required to ascertain the degree of industry support for a petition before initiating an investigation. A petition is considered to have been made by or on behalf of the domestic industry if it is supported by those domestic producers that collectively account for more than 50 percent of the total

production by that portion of the domestic industry expressing *either support for or opposition to* the application. However, investigations may not be initiated if those *supporting* the complaint represent less than 25 percent of the entire domestic industry. Trade unions representing workers in an industry can file or support antidumping petitions.

8. ***De minimis* rules** (Article 5.8). An antidumping investigation must be terminated if it is determined that the margin of dumping is less than 2 percent of the export price. Investigations will also be terminated when dumped imports from an exporting country constitute less than 3 percent of imports of the same product in the importing country, unless dumped imports from all countries that individually account for less than 3 percent collectively account for more than 7 percent of the imports of the same product in the importing country.

9. **Price undertakings** (Article 8). A price undertaking may be sought or offered only after a preliminary affirmative determination of dumping and injury. If an undertaking is accepted, the investigation will nevertheless be completed on request of the exporter or the importing country. If the final determination is affirmative, the undertaking will continue. If the final determination is negative, the undertaking will lapse immediately, unless the determination was in part due to the existence of the undertaking; in that case, the price undertaking will continue.

10. **"All other" rate**. If authorities do not examine all exporters, the "all other" rate (an estimated dumping margin for the noninvestigated firms) is the weighted-average dumping margin for the exporters examined, excluding zero or *de minimis* margins and margins based on the best information available (Article 9.4).

11. **Sunset clause**. Antidumping orders and price undertakings must be reviewed every five years to determine whether injurious dumping is likely to continue or recur if the order is terminated. The review shall normally be concluded within 12 months of the date of initiation of the review (Article 11). Existing antidumping orders must be reviewed within five years of the entry into force of the WTO (Article 18.3.2).

12. **Dispute settlement: standard of review**. Under the Dispute Settlement Understanding (DSU), GATT challenges of antidumping actions are permitted only against specific abuses by the national administering agency. Panel reviews can only address whether the agency in question established the facts properly and evaluated them in an unbiased and objective fashion, even if the panel itself might have reached a different conclusion. Moreover, if the application of a particular rule "admits of more than one permissible interpretation," the action will be sanctioned "if it rests upon one of those permissible interpretations" (Article 17.6).

Anticircumvention

13. Anticircumvention provisions were deleted during the final stages of the negotiations. However, the Ministerial Declaration accompanying the agreement recognizes the need for uniform rules on anticircumvention measures and recommends that the Committee on Antidumping Practices address this issue in future negotiations.

ASSESSMENT

1. Requires adjustments in the procedures and methods used to calculate dumping margins and assess injury that, on balance, will have a relatively minor impact on the administration of antidumping statutes in the United States and the European Union.

2. Clarifies rules for constructed-value calculations by administering agencies for the determination of the amount of profit to be allocated to dumped imports and the amortization of startup costs.

3. Incorporates a sunset clause that requires outstanding antidumping orders to be revoked after a maximum of five years unless it is determined that those measures are needed to preclude injurious dumping.

4. Constrains the ability of countries to challenge antidumping actions through GATT dispute settlement procedures by limiting the terms of reference of panel reviews.

5. Does little to discipline the imposition of price undertakings and defers negotiations to develop specific rules on anticircumvention measures.

GRADE: C+

TRADE RULES: Subsidies and Countervailing Measures

RECOMMENDATIONS

1. **Prohibited subsidies**. Expand the scope of prohibited subsidies to include *inter alia* mixed credits (official credits extended on commercial terms but linked to soft loans or outright grants) and subsidies contingent on export performance or domestic sourcing. Include subsidies that give rise to a presumption of serious prejudice in the prohibited category.

2. **Actionable subsidies**. Include investment incentives as actionable subsidies and extend disciplines to parastatal and subfederal subsidies.

3. **Nonactionable subsidies**. Establish a category of nonactionable subsidies for a limited number of purposes (i.e., regional development, precompetitive R&D, environmental protection, worker adjustment assistance) that are deemed *a priori* to be noninjurious. These subsidies should be granted for a strictly defined period and be digressive within this period.

4. **Countervailing duties (CVDs)**

    a) Clarify definition of material injury with a few dispositive indicators (for example, if subsidized imports lead to lower prices or lost sales.)

    b) Allow participation of consumer and public interest groups in CVD proceedings.

    c) Establish a *de minimis* test.

    d) Proscribe or impose greater restraint on the use of price undertakings in lieu of CVDs.

    e) Require a sunset provision for CVDs after five years unless "good cause" is shown for their continuation.

    f) Establish narrowly defined anticircumvention provisions.

RESULTS

1. **Subsidies definition**. Defines a subsidy as "a financial contribution by a government or any public body," or a private body acting on its behalf, that entails direct transfers of funds (e.g., grants, loans, equity infusions, and loan guarantees); forgone or uncollected government revenues (e.g., tax credits); provision of goods and services other than general infrastructure; or income or price supports; and that confers a benefit on the recipient firm (e.g., is not offset by an onerous employment requirement).

2. **Prohibited subsidies**

    a) Prohibits nonagricultural subsidies contingent upon export performance, including those in the Illustrative List of practices specified in annex I. The list is identical to the 1979 code except that item (h) allows taxes on energy, fuels, and oil used as inputs in the production process to be exempted, remitted, or deferred as if they were physically incorporated in the final product (as specified in annex II).

    b) Prohibits subsidies contingent upon the use of domestic goods over imported goods.

    c) Establishes a Permanent Group of Experts (PGE) to assist panels by analyzing evidence regarding the existence and nature of subsidies and rendering binding determinations "whether or not the measure in question is a prohibited subsidy" (Article 4.5). The PGE may also provide member countries and the Committee on Subsidies with confidential advisory opinions "on the nature of any subsidy" (Articles 24.3 and 24.4).

3. **Actionable subsidies**

    a) Sanctions countermeasures against subsidies that cause the following "adverse effects": (i) injury to the domestic industry of another signatory; (ii) nullification or impairment of GATT benefits; or (iii) "serious prejudice" to the interests of another signatory.

    b) Serious prejudice is presumed to exist if:

    —the total ad valorem subsidization of a product exceeds 5 percent of the recipient's annual sales of that product or 15 percent of the total invested funds for startup firms (annex IV);

TRADE RULES: Subsidies and Countervailing Measures
(continued)

—subsidies cover operating losses of an industry or those of an enterprise other than one-time and nonrecurrent measures to facilitate adjustment;

—governments provide direct debt forgiveness or grants for debt repayment;

and the effect of the subsidy is to displace or impede imports from the home market, exports to a third-country market, or undercut or suppress prices in the home market. This obligation applies for five years and may then be extended, modified, or terminated.

c) Presumes that serious prejudice does not exist if there are no demonstrable trade effects (i.e., neither price nor volume of exports is affected); or if there are special circumstances (e.g., natural disasters, strikes) that preclude adverse trade effects; or explicit arrangements (e.g., price undertakings) that limit trade in the subsidized good.

d) Agricultural subsidies covered by the peace clause of the Agreement on Agriculture (Article 13) are not liable to countermeasures for nine years (i.e., until 2004).

4. **Nonactionable subsidies**

a) Obligations apply provisionally for five years, at which time a decision must be taken whether to extend or modify them (Article 31). In addition, the exemption for specified R&D subsidies (see below) will be reviewed within 18 months of the entry into force of the WTO (Article 8.2, footnote 25).

b) Encompasses generally available subsidies and specific subsidies that meet the following criteria:

—R&D: assistance that covers not more than 75 percent of certain specified costs of industrial research or 50 percent of certain specified costs of precompetitive development activity (neither provision is applicable to civil aircraft).

—Regional aid: assistance to disadvantaged regions within a member country that is provided under a general framework of regional development, that is characterized as nonspecific and that meets the following neutral and objective criteria: (i) income per capita, household income per capita, or GDP per capita must be less than 85 percent of the territory average; or (ii) the unemployment rate must be at least 110 percent of the average for the territory.

—Environmental infrastructure: assistance to promote compliance with environmental requirements in existing facilities, provided that the subsidies are one-time and nonrecurring, are limited to 20 percent of the cost of adaptation, do not cover replacement and operating costs, are linked to a firm's planned reduction of nuisances and pollution, and are available to all firms that can adopt new equipment or production processes.

c) Nonactionable programs must be notified in advance of implementation, and notifications must be updated annually.

d) Members can request a review of a notification in order to determine whether the conditions have been met. Disputes over notifications are subject to binding arbitration.

e) Nonactionable subsidies become actionable if they result in "serious adverse effects" that cause "damage which would be difficult to repair." In such an event, the subsidizing country must modify its program to remove those effects or be liable to countermeasures.

5. **Special and differential treatment**

a) Least-developed countries and other developing countries with GDP per capita less than $1,000 are exempted from the prohibition on subsidies that are contingent on export performance. Other developing countries are granted an eight-year transition period during which these subsidies cannot be increased and must be phased out progressively.

b) Developing countries are exempted for five years from the obligation not to grant subsidies contingent on the use of domestic goods (eight years for least-developed countries).

c) Developing countries must phase out export subsidies on products that have become "competitive" (i.e., that account for at least 3.25 percent of world trade for two consecutive years) within two years (or within eight years for the poorest countries).

d) Developing Country export subsidies are not actionable during the transition period unless they cause injury and may not be presumed to cause serious prejudice.

e) Remedies with regard to actionable subsidies can only be authorized if the subsidy impedes or displaces imports in the subsidizing country or if subsidized exports cause injury to domestic firms in the importing market.

f) Centrally planned members that are transforming into market economies are allowed seven years to comply with the export subsidy obligations, and debt relief measures are not presumed to cause serious prejudice. These members are subject to the same remedies as developing countries for other actionable subsidies.

6. **Countervailing duties**

a) Investigations must be initiated "by or on behalf of the domestic industry," by firms whose collective output constitutes more than 50 percent of the total production of the like product of those domestic firms expressing support or opposition to the petition. Investigations shall not be initiated if domestic producers supporting the application account for less than 25 percent of total production, whether or not producers express support or opposition to the petition.

b) Industrial users and consumer groups are afforded opportunities to provide information to the administrative agencies regarding injury, subsidy, and the causal link between them.

c) GATT proceedings for export and actionable subsidies can be invoked in parallel with national CVD proceedings; however, only one form of remedy can be imposed to offset the effect of the subsidy in the domestic market.

d) Investigations must be terminated if:
—there is insufficient evidence of either subsidization or injury; or
—the amount of the subsidy is *de minimis* (i.e., less than 1 percent ad valorem or 2 percent in cases involving developing countries); or
—the volume of subsidized imports is negligible (or less than 4 percent of total imports of the like product in cases involving developing countries, unless cumulative LDC shares represent more than 9 percent of total imports).

e) Undertakings, including price undertakings, can lead to the suspension or termination of CVDs or provisional measures if the exporting country agrees to eliminate or limit the subsidy or the exporter agrees to increase prices to forestall injury. Undertakings cannot be promulgated until after preliminary determinations are made of subsidy and injury.

f) Subsidized products that are exported to the importing country through an intermediate country will be regarded as having been shipped from the country of origin to the importing country.

g) Sunset provision: CVDs will be terminated no later than five years after their imposition (or from the date of their most recent review) unless "the expiry of the duty would be likely to lead to continuation or recurrence of subsidization and injury." Outstanding CVD orders must be reviewed within five years of entry into force of the WTO.

h) Importing countries may cumulate shipments from all countries under investigation in determining whether subsidized imports cause or threaten material injury to domestic industry.

ASSESSMENT

1. Strengthens disciplines on export subsidies by prohibiting subsidies contingent upon the use of domestic goods but opens a significant loophole by defining energy inputs as meeting the physical incorporation test, thus allowing rebates of energy taxes.

TRADE RULES: Subsidies and Countervailing Measures
(continued)

2. Defines subsidies to encompass a broad range of "financial contributions" that benefit the recipient firm, but not other governmental actions that might implicitly confer an advantage (e.g., lax regulatory enforcement).

3. Clarifies definition of serious prejudice and conditions under which it is presumed to occur.

4. Creates an extensive category of nonactionable subsidies, exempting certain R&D, regional development, and environmental subsidies (but not labor adjustment subsidies) from countermeasures for at least five years. However, these "green light" subsidies are actionable if they cause serious adverse trade effects.

5. Requires developing countries (except the least developed) to accept all subsidy disciplines after a five- to eight-year transition period.

6. Establishes a *de minimis* test and sunset provision for countervailing duty actions but fails to significantly constrain the use of price undertakings in lieu of CVDs.

GRADE: **A−**

TRADE RULES: Safeguards

RECOMMENDATIONS

Article XIX Safeguards

1. Require that safeguard actions be accompanied by structural adjustment measures for the industry seeking relief from imports. Allow safeguard actions to take the form of quotas only if complemented by adjustment requirements.

2. Lower the injury threshold from serious to material injury to encourage countries to invoke Article XIX (with adjustment requirements) rather than other safeguard-type restrictions.

3. Prohibit or severely constrain the use of selective actions, especially voluntary export restraints.

4. Bar compensation claims and retaliation against measures that conform to GATT rules.

Balance of Payments Safeguards

5. Developed countries should waive the right to invoke Article XII.

6. Use of Article XVIII by developing countries should be subject to more stringent conditions.

7. If balance of payments safeguards remain in place for more than two years, they should be linked to structural adjustment policies.

RESULTS

Article XIX Safeguards

1. Reaffirms that safeguard measures are to be applied on a most-favored nation basis, not selectively by country. These obligations do not apply, however, to import relief imposed pursuant to other GATT provisions (e.g., antidumping undertakings).

2. Notwithstanding the MFN provision cited above, the agreement allows countries to discriminate (i.e., impose selective safeguards) where increased imports from certain competitive suppliers account for a disproportionate share of the total increase of imports subject to the safeguard measure.

3. Safeguard measures must be applied only to the extent necessary "to prevent or remedy serious injury and to facilitate adjustment." If quotas are imposed instead of tariffs, they should not reduce the quantity of imports below the annual average for the last three representative years.

4. Defines serious injury as "significant overall impairment in the position of a domestic industry."

5. Safeguard measures may be applied for up to four years and may be extended for an additional four years if (a) the action is needed to "prevent or remedy serious injury," (b) the industry is shown to be adjusting, and (c) the action complies with obligations regarding compensation and special treatment for developing countries.

6. Safeguard measures imposed for more than one year must be "progressively liberalized at regular intervals," and actions taken for three years or more must be reviewed to determine whether the measure can be liberalized more quickly.

7. Safeguard measures cannot be reimposed on the same product for a period equal to the original safeguard action but in no case less than two years. However, temporary safeguards that were imposed for six months or less may be reinstated after a year, as long as actions are not taken on the same product more than twice in a five-year period.

8. Countries "shall not seek, take or maintain any voluntary export restraints, orderly marketing arrangements or any other similar measures on the export or the import side." Existing measures must be phased out within four years (or by 31 December 1999 for the EU-Japan voluntary export restraint (VER) on automobiles). In addition, countries agree not to "encourage or support the adoption or maintenance" of interindustry arrangements comparable to the governmental measures proscribed above.

9. Safeguard measures shall not be imposed on a product from a developing country, if:
—those imports do not exceed 3 percent of total imports of that product;
—imports from developing countries with less than 3 percent import share collectively account for no more than 9 percent of total imports of the product concerned.

10. Developing countries may impose safeguard measures for an extra two years and may reimpose actions on the same product after a period equal to half the duration of the previous measure but not less than two years.

11. Countries imposing safeguard measures may offer compensation to countries whose trade is adversely affected. Exporting countries waive the right to retaliate against such measures for the first three years that a safeguard action is in effect, if the measure (a) was taken because of increased imports and (b) conforms to GATT obligations.

12. Existing safeguard actions must be terminated after they have been in force for eight years, or by 1 January 2000, whichever comes later.

Balance of Payments Safeguards

13. Countries commit to prefer "price-based" measures (e.g., import surcharges, import deposit requirements) rather than quantitative restrictions, when imposing safeguard measures for balance of payments purposes.

14. Countries agree to provide time schedules for the removal of import measures taken for balance of payments purposes, but no limits are established, and the schedules can be modified at will.

15. Countries are not required to adopt structural adjustment policies.

16. Countries are not required or encouraged to waive their rights to invoke Article XII or XVIII, although Brazil and Korea, among others, have reduced their reliance on balance of payments safeguards in recent years.

ASSESSMENT

1. Contains strong prohibition on the use of VERs, a major achievement of the Uruguay Round.

2. Includes weak incentives to promote adjustment, which are offset by the long maximum duration of safeguard actions.

3. Maintains the MFN requirement in most cases, clarifies the serious injury standard, and constrains actions against developing-country imports, thus strengthening incentives for importing countries to seek other avenues of relief.

4. Waives retaliation rights for the first three years of a safeguard measure and allows selective safeguards in limited circumstances, thus removing disincentives to invoke Article XIX actions.

5. Fails to remove balance of payments justification for safeguard measures imposed by developed countries.

6. Fails to discipline balance of payments safeguards imposed by developing countries except for the hortatory commitment to "prefer" price-based measures and to set national time limits on the duration of such measures.

GRADE: B

RECOMMENDATIONS

1. Countries should establish a General Agreement on Trade in Services (GATS) to provide a framework of rights and obligations to guide the formulation of national laws, policies, and regulations affecting services and to ensure that foreign suppliers have access to markets and receive national treatment.

2. The framework should include dispute settlement provisions, preferably as part of the GATT mechanism, to permit cross-sector linkage between goods and services.

3. The GATS should liberalize trade through an evolutionary process, sector by sector, starting from the baseline of existing policies.

4. The GATS framework agreement should be supplemented by sectoral annotations elaborating how the principles enunciated in the framework should be interpreted for particular industries.

5. For financial services, the supplemental annotation should include a prudential safeguard clause to ensure that national regulators are not inhibited from imposing controls to protect the integrity of the financial system and a provision requiring that dispute settlement panels have sufficient financial expertise.

6. The coverage of the GATS should be as comprehensive as possible. GATS rules should apply to all services. Exceptions from GATS rules should be temporary, not permanent, and listed in an annex to the GATS.

RESULTS

The General Agreement on Trade in Services (GATS) comprises three main components: a framework agreement spelling out the rules on trade in services, sectoral annexes describing how the rules apply to specific sectors, and national schedules of market-access commitments and exemptions.

Framework

1. The framework establishes rights and obligations that apply to all services. The core obligation of the GATS is MFN treatment (Article II). Temporary derogations from the MFN obligation are permitted but must be listed in the Annex on Article II Exemptions and are subject to review every five years. In principle, these exemptions should not last for more than 10 years and should be subject to future negotiations.

2. Other general obligations require transparency of national measures affecting services trade, application of recognition practices in a way that does not discriminate or restrict trade, disciplines to ensure that monopolies do not violate the MFN requirement or other specific commitments, and prohibition of restrictions on international payments and transfers. In addition, the GATS allows preferences for partners in regional economic integration pacts (analogous to GATT Article XXIV).

3. Obligations regarding national treatment and market access apply only to services that are listed in a country's schedule (Articles XVI and XVII). Government procurement of services is not included but is subject to future negotiations (Article XIII).

4. GATS Article XV suggests that negotiations be held on how to deal with subsidies and countervailing duties in the services sector but establishes no time frame for initiating or completing such talks.

5. Disputes involving GATS obligations are governed by the provisions of the Dispute Settlement Understanding of the WTO (Article XXIII).

6. In addition, the accord recommends that the Council for Trade in Services establish at its first meeting:

a) A working party to examine the nexus of services trade and environmental issues and to report on the results of its work within three years after the WTO enters into force;

b) A working party to examine, report, and give recommendations on the disciplines necessary to ensure that measures relating to qualification, technical standards, and licensing in the field of professional services do not constitute unnecessary barriers to trade.

Sectoral Annexes

7. **Movement of persons**. This annex applies the agreement to the temporary entry of those who are service suppliers of a member country and to people of a member country who are employed by a service supplier of a member.

8. **Financial services**. The annex on financial services describes how the general rules of the GATS apply to insurance, insurance-related services, banking, and other financial services. In addition, it spells out a few special rules:

—Members are not precluded from taking measures for "prudential" reasons or to ensure the integrity and stability of their financial systems.

—Dispute settlement panels are required to have expertise relevant to the specific financial service under dispute.

—Countries are allowed to specify their national commitments relating to financial services either according to the provision of the annex or on the basis of an "alternative approach," as long as the latter (i) does not conflict with the provisions of the Annex on Financial Services, (ii) is applied on a MFN basis, (iii) does not prejudice the right of any other country to specify its commitments according to the provisions of the Annex, and (iv) creates no presumption as to the degree of liberalization to which a country is committing itself under the GATS. Through July 1994, most countries that have scheduled financial services commitments have used the alternative approach.

—Negotiations on finalizing the financial-services offer in the national schedules of liberalization commitments will continue up to July 1995. During the months of May and June 1995, countries may include MFN exemptions for financial services in their schedules or improve, modify, or withdraw all or part of the commitments on financial services offered.

9. **Telecommunications**.

—Countries agree that access to and use of public telecommunications transport networks and services will be available on reasonable, nondiscriminatory terms and conditions (i.e., national and MFN treatment) to all service suppliers (excluding distribution of radio and television programs).

—The agreement also allows users of these networks and services to provide enhanced or value-added services, including transborder data flows and intracorporate communications, as well as to use their own equipment and operating protocols provided they comply with certain technical specifications.

—Conditions on access and use may be imposed to (i) "ensure the security and confidentiality of messages," (ii) fulfill public service obligations, or (iii) protect the technical integrity of public networks or services.

—Developing countries may impose "reasonable" conditions, specified in their national schedules, to strengthen their domestic telecommunications infrastructure and to boost their participation in international trade in telecommunications services.

10. **Basic telecommunications services**. These services are not part of the Telecommunications Annex nor of the market access and national treatment provisions. Instead, the United States, the European Union, and other countries have agreed to continue negotiations on reciprocal liberalization of basic long-distance and international telecommunications services. The annex on negotiations on basic telecommunications services sets a deadline of 30 April 1996 to either implement the results of the negotiations or to apply the GATS (e.g., invoke an MFN exemption).

11. **Air transport services**. The annex on air transport services acknowledges the precedence of existing bilateral aviation agreements.

12. **Maritime services**. Negotiations will continue on international shipping, auxiliary services, and access to and use of port facilities, the results of which will be implemented in June 1996. In the meantime, the GATS does not apply in this sector, nor is it necessary to list MFN exemptions. Until the results of these negotiations are implemented, members may change or withdraw commitments without having to offer compensation.

National schedules

13. Complementing the framework agreement and annexes are binding commitments to market access and national treatment in services sectors that countries schedule as a result of bilateral negotiations. These schedules are an integral part of the GATS and will become effective upon entry into force of the agreement.

14. As of July 1994, more than 80 countries have scheduled market access commitments in a range of service sectors. In terms of trade coverage, the most comprehensive commitments have been made in the tourism and professional services sectors.

15. The GATS requires that new negotiations, aimed at "achieving a progressively higher level of liberalization," be launched within five years after the WTO enters into force (i.e., by the year 2000).

16. Analogous to GATT Article XXVIII, the GATS provides for the negotiated modification of national commitments, if the commitment has been in effect for at least three years. Compensation for changes must be implemented on an MFN basis (Article XXI).

ASSESSMENT

1. Most important, the GATS establishes multilateral rights and obligations for the first time on trade in services and links services trade disputes to the integrated dispute settlement mechanism of the WTO. However, the agreement encompasses only barebones requirements: countries are not obligated to extend national treatment unless specified in their national schedules and may invoke "temporary" exemptions from the MFN obligation.

2. Sectoral annexes on maritime, civil aviation, telecommunications, and financial services are subject to ongoing negotiations and possible modification. However, the telecommunications annex establishes important rights regarding the provision and use of information and other value-added services.

3. The scope of specific market-access commitments varies by sector and ranges from extensive (e.g., professional services) to minimal (e.g., audiovisual).

GRADE: B+

NEW ISSUES: Trade-Related Investment Measures

RECOMMENDATIONS

1. Develop a framework of rights and obligations that includes a prohibition on the use of six types of trade-related investment measures (TRIMs):
   — local-content requirements;
   — export performance requirements;
   — local-manufacturing requirements;
   — trade balancing requirements;
   — production mandates;
   — foreign exchange restrictions.
2. Eliminate prohibited TRIMs by a fixed date. However, where investors already subject to TRIMs would be disadvantaged vis-à-vis new entrants, new TRIMs should be allowed for a limited period before being phased out.
3. Commit to negotiate comprehensive investment rules in future GATT negotiations.

RESULTS

1. The accord prohibits TRIMs that are "inconsistent with the obligations of national treatment" and "the general elimination of quantitative restrictions" of GATT Articles III and XI. It includes an illustrative list of prohibited measures, barring local-content, trade balancing, and foreign exchange balancing requirements.
2. Notification of TRIMs that are not in conformity with GATT obligations are required within 90 days of the entry into force of the agreement. The obligation applies to TRIMs related to goods and mandated by national, regional, and local governments.
3. Developed countries must eliminate their prohibited TRIMs within two years (five years for developing countries; seven years for least-developed countries).
4. TRIMs introduced within 180 days of the entry into force of the WTO cannot benefit from the transition period.
5. Countries may impose a prohibited TRIM on a new firm for the duration of the relevant transition period if it is necessary to avoid disadvantaging existing investments that are subject to a TRIM.
6. The Council for Trade in Goods will review the operation of the TRIMs agreement by the year 2000 and "consider whether it should be complemented with provisions on investment policy and competition policy" (Article 9).

ASSESSMENT

1. Clarifies existing GATT obligations regarding local-content requirements (which were interpreted by the 1983 panel report on Canada's Foreign Investment Review Agency) and codifies the prohibition of trade balancing and foreign exchange balancing requirements.
2. Provides greater transparency of TRIMs mandated by national and subnational governments.
3. Fails to sanction export performance requirements and other trade-distorting TRIMs.
4. Lacks commitment to new negotiations but does open the door to future consideration of other investment policy issues.

GRADE: B −

NEW ISSUES: Trade-Related Intellectual Property Rights

RECOMMENDATIONS

1. Develop a TRIPs accord that contains nondiscrimination and national treatment obligations. Include minimum standards and enforcement procedures and extend protection to new areas such as biotechnology, to areas now inadequately protected, and to *sui generis* areas such as semiconductor design.
2. Extend copyright protection to computer software, data bases, and new forms of expression that may result from technological developments.
3. Derive trademark protection from use or registration, making it renewable indefinitely.
4. Provide patent protection for a standard period of 20 years from the time the patent was first granted.
5. Discourage compulsory licensing or, if allowed, let license holders receive full value for the license.
6. Include enforcement procedures that cover domestic commerce as well as international trade to fight infringement of intellectual property rights in the home market.
7. Encourage participation of developing countries by recognizing their technical problems regarding enforcement and by allowing them to continue to require compulsory licensing under limited conditions.

RESULTS

General Rules
1. The TRIPs agreement generally obliges countries to afford national treatment and MFN treatment to other WTO members, except as provided in other intellectual property conventions (Articles 3 and 4).

Intellectual Property Rights
2. **Copyrights**
   a) Explicitly extends protection of copyrights provided under the Berne and Rome Conventions to computer software and data bases, as well as sound recordings, performances, and broadcasts. Computer programs and movies are protected for 50 years, performances and sound recordings for 50 years, and broadcasts for 20 years.
   b) New protection also covers rental rights: authors of computer programs and producers of sound recordings have the right to authorize or prohibit the commercial rental of their works to the public. The same exclusive rental right applies to movies, but only if there is evidence of damaging and widespread copying. Performers are also protected against bootlegging of their performances.
   c) Existing "neighboring" rights—which protect *inter alia* the performers and performances of copyrighted material—are explicitly covered by the TRIPs copyright provisions regarding performers, producers, and broadcasting companies. However, national treatment is not guaranteed if countries respect the reciprocity standard of the Rome Convention.
3. **Patents**
   a) In addition to the general obligation to comply with the Paris Convention (1967), all product or process inventions—regardless of whether they are imported or locally produced—receive 20 years of patent protection measured from the date the application was filed (Article 33).
   b) Countries may deny patent protection for treatment methods for humans or animals; for plants, animals, and biological processes (other than microorganisms or microbiological processes); or to protect the *ordre public* (Article 27). Article 27 requires patent or *sui generis* protection for plant varieties and provides a very narrow scope for patentability of biotechnological inventions.

c) Pharmaceutical and agricultural chemical products in the "pipeline" are not protected.

d) Countries that are allowed to delay implementing patent protection for pharmaceutical and agricultural chemical products under transition rules must still set out application procedures as if such protection was already available. After the transition period has expired, those countries must grant applicants that filed during the transition period patent protection for the remainder of the patent term, counted from the filing date (Article 70.8). In addition, such countries must grant exclusive marketing rights (generally, for five years) until a decision is made on the patent application, if that product has successfully been patented in third countries during the transition period (Article 70.9).

e) Compulsory licensing is not prohibited, but detailed conditions are established regarding, *inter alia*, notification, remuneration, and judicial review (Article 31). Compulsory licensing of semiconductor technology is only allowed to remedy anticompetitive practices (Article 31.c).

4. **Trademarks**

a) Trademarks and service marks are protected for seven years, with an option to renew protection indefinitely for additional seven-year periods.

b) Actual use is not required to file for registration of a trademark, but registration may be dependent on use, as well as extension of the period of protection. If actual use is required to maintain a registration, the registration may be canceled only if the trademark has not been used for three years.

c) The agreement prohibits compulsory licensing of trademarks and requirements that foreign trademarks be linked with a local trademark.

5. **Geographical indications**

a) The TRIPs accord prohibits the use of an indication that could mislead the consumer as to the true origin of goods. Wines and spirits are subject to tighter standards: use of geographical indications for goods not originating in that area is prohibited even if confusion as to the true origin of the product could not reasonably be expected. However, with regard to wines and spirits, countries are allowed to use geographical indications that may contravene obligations in this area if the usage is of long standing (Article 24.4).

b) Further negotiations are mandated to establish a multilateral system of notification and registration of geographical indications for wines (Article 23).

6. **Industrial designs**. Protection against unauthorized making, selling, or importing copies of new or original industrial designs is provided for 10 years.

7. **Designs of integrated circuits**. The TRIPs agreement extends the 10-year protection of layout designs of integrated circuits provided by the Treaty on Intellectual Property in Respect of Integrated Circuits, or IPIC (1989), to products that incorporate protected integrated circuit designs. Unintentional violators are required to pay royalties as soon as they receive notice of the infringement.

8. **Trade secrets**. Industries that protect valuable commercial information through trade secrets are guaranteed protection against misappropriation and unauthorized use of these secrets, provided they take reasonable steps to guard them.

9. **Anticompetitive practices in contractual licenses**. The agreement acknowledges the existence of certain licensing practices (e.g., "tie-in" clauses in franchising contracts) regarding intellectual property rights, which restrict competition and trade (Article 40). Countries may adopt remedies against such practices, provided they are consistent with the other provisions of the TRIPs accord. Article 40 further requires consultations between governments to secure compliance with the national laws of the country that requested the consultations.

Enforcement and Dispute Settlement

10. The agreement requires each country to maintain adequate procedures and remedies under their domestic law to ensure effective enforcement of intellectual property rights.

These procedures must be available to foreign rightholders. Remedies range from cease-and-desist orders (to stop infringement), to monetary damages (specifically against counterfeiting and piracy), to destruction of the goods.

11. Disputes involving the TRIPs agreement will be settled under the dispute settlement procedures of the WTO. However, the agreement sets a five-year moratorium (i.e., until the year 2000) on disputes involving measures that do not conflict with the provisions of the TRIPs agreement but which nevertheless are alleged to nullify or impair concessions under the agreement ("nonviolation cases").

Implementation

12. By January 1996, all countries must accept the national treatment and MFN obligations of the agreement. Developed countries are given one year to implement the agreement (Article 65.1). Developing countries and economies in transition have an additional four years to implement their obligations (Article 65.2), except for provisions concerning patent protection for pharmaceutical and agricultural products where they are given an additional nine years (Article 65.4). Least-developed countries have an additional ten years to implement the TRIPs agreement (Article 66).

13. Developed countries agree to promote and encourage technology transfer to developing and least-developed countries through technical cooperation.

14. The TRIPs agreement falls under the "umbrella" of the WTO; all WTO members thus undertake the TRIPs obligations.

ASSESSMENT

1. Establishes a framework of rights and obligations and enforcement provisions to protect intellectual property. Extends protection to computer software, data bases, and integrated circuits, but not to some biotechnology inventions and products in the patent pipeline.

2. Provides adequate terms of protection for patents, copyrights, trademarks, and industrial designs, and useful constraints on compulsory licensing practices.

3. Requires countries to strengthen both domestic enforcement and border measures to counter misappropriation and piracy of intellectual property.

4. Affords long transition periods before developing countries are required to assume obligations (except for MFN and national treatment).

5. Sets a five-year moratorium on disputes involving nullification and impairment of a country's rights under the TRIPs accord.

GRADE: B +

RECOMMENDATIONS

1. Provide for the expeditious formation of panels on any GATT-related issue and for the binding acceptance of panel rulings, subject to review by an appellate tribunal.

2. Provide an automatic right to retaliate (i.e., without further multilateral authorization) if the offending country does not comply with panel rulings within the period prescribed by that ruling.

3. Accept cross-retaliation, allowing countries to impose sanctions against the goods or services of a country in violation of its obligations.

4. Establish guidelines for review of Article XXIII nonviolation complaints and provide authority to panels to issue nonbinding recommendations as to possible remedies.

RESULTS

1. The Dispute Settlement Understanding (DSU) establishes an integrated dispute settlement system for all multilateral and plurilateral trade agreements covered under the umbrella of the WTO (Article 1 and appendix 1). It applies to all new disputes taken to the Dispute Settlement Body (DSB) after the WTO has entered into force (Article 3.11).

2. Unless the DSB decides by consensus against establishment of a panel, panels are established automatically if consultations have not resulted in settlement of the dispute within 60 days (Article 6).

   a) Panels will normally comprise three governmental and/or nongovernmental persons, recommended to the disputing parties by the WTO Secretariat.

   b) From establishment of a panel to the issuance of the panel report should normally take six months, but in no event longer than nine months. The DSB will then adopt the report within 60 days, unless the ruling is appealed (Articles 12.8-9 and 16.4).

3. Panel rulings are subject to review by a new standing Appellate Body, which will issue decisions normally within 60 days regarding "issues of law covered in the panel report and legal interpretation developed by the panel" (Article 17.6). The Appellate Body will comprise seven persons appointed for a four-year term, of which three will serve in a particular case.

4. The findings of the panels and the Appellate Body are adopted automatically unless the DSB decides by consensus against such action (Articles 16 and 17.4).

5. If the panel recommendations have not been fully implemented within a reasonable period (agreed by the disputants or imposed by an arbitrator), and subsequently no satisfactory compensation has been agreed, the complaining country may ask permission of the DSB to suspend the application of WTO obligations (i.e., retaliate) to the offending country (Article 22.2). Such authorization will be granted unless the DSB decides by consensus against such action (Article 22.6).

6. Generally, retaliation should entail suspension of concessions or obligations that affect the same sector (Article 22.3). If that is not practicable or effective, concessions or obligations may be suspended in other sectors under the same agreement. Ultimately, if that is still not satisfactory, concessions or obligations under another covered agreement may be suspended ("cross-retaliation").

7. Disputed measures that nullify or impair benefits accruing to a WTO member but do not violate any provision of the WTO agreements ("nonviolation" cases) are subject to regular DSU discipline. However, a panel cannot require the withdrawal of the disputed measure in its ruling but can recommend a mutually satisfactory adjustment as a final settlement of the dispute (Article 26.1).

ASSESSMENT

1. Requires the prompt establishment of panels and expeditious reporting of panel findings.

2. Prevents countries from blocking the implementation of WTO rulings and provides near-automatic authority to retaliate (including cross-retaliation among sectors) if countries do not comply with panel rulings by requiring a consensus decision to block retaliation.

3. Establishes a new Appellate Body empowered to review panel decisions and overturn ill-considered findings.

4. Overall, reform of the dispute settlement process should encourage the use of multilateral procedures and promote more expeditious compliance with panel rulings.

GRADE: A

INSTITUTIONAL ISSUES: World Trade Organization

RECOMMENDATIONS

1. Provide an institutional reinforcement of the GATT through the establishment of a World Trade Organization (WTO). The WTO should deal with the legal issues involved in a restructuring of the GATT into a membership organization, strengthening the secretariat, removing the provisional character of some GATT obligations, and introducing administrative reforms.

2. Coordinate efforts of the Bretton Woods institutions to ensure the consistency and compatibility of their initiatives on trade, monetary, and development issues.

RESULTS

1. The Final Act establishes a World Trade Organization (WTO) that supersedes the GATT. The WTO is an umbrella organization that encompasses the GATT 1994 (including the TRIMs agreement and the Tokyo Round codes), the GATS, and the TRIPs agreement. The WTO includes a Dispute Settlement Understanding that consolidates the dispute settlement provisions of the different agreements into one common mechanism. It also incorporates four plurilateral agreements, the obligations of which apply to signatories only, not to all WTO members.

2. All WTO members automatically accept the obligations of all the constituent agreements (except the four plurilateral accords).

3. Current members of the GATT that deposit schedules of commitments for the GATT 1994 and the GATS are eligible to become original members of the WTO. (As of 30 June 1994, the GATT had 123 members. In addition there are 20 or so countries and territories, including China, Chinese Taipei, and the former Soviet republics, for which accession working parties have been established. If these countries accede to the GATT before the WTO enters into force, they will qualify as charter members of the WTO). These countries have up to two years to deposit their schedules of commitments.

4. The structure of the WTO will be headed by a Ministerial Conference meeting at least once every two years. A General Council, consisting of all WTO members, will be established to oversee the operation of the agreement. This General Council will also act as a dispute settlement body and a trade policy review body. The General Council will also establish subsidiary bodies such as a Goods Council, a Services Council, and a TRIPs Council to administer agreements in those respective areas.

5. The Secretariat of the WTO is headed by a director general, who is appointed by the Ministerial Conference. The Secretariat presents the annual budget and financial statement of the WTO to the Committee on Budget, Finance, and Administration. The committee reviews the budget and financial statement and makes recommendations to the General Council, which approves the budget.

6. WTO decisions will normally be made by consensus (i.e., requires that no member formally object). If a consensus cannot be reached, matters will be decided by majority vote, except in the following cases:

—Interpretations of any of the agreements require a three-fourths majority.

—Waivers of an obligation (which are reviewed annually) require a three-fourths majority.

—Amendments generally require a two-thirds majority. However, amendments to the WTO provisions on amendments and decision making, as well as to the MFN provisions of the GATT 1994, GATS, and TRIPs agreements, will only take effect upon acceptance by all members.

7. Amendments to GATT 1994, GATS, and the TRIPs agreement that "would alter the rights and obligations of the Members, shall take effect for the Members that have accepted them upon acceptance by two-thirds of the members and thereafter for each other Member

INSTITUTIONAL ISSUES: World Trade Organization
(continued)

upon acceptance by it." However, the Ministerial Conference may decide by three-fourths majority that members that have not accepted such amendments are free to leave the WTO or remain a member with the explicit consent of the Ministerial Conference. Amendments to GATT 1994, GATS, and the TRIPs agreement that "would not alter the rights and obligations of the Members, shall take effect for all Members upon acceptance by two-thirds of the Members."

8. Existing GATT Article XXV waivers (e.g., US-Canada Auto Pact; Caribbean Basin Economic Recovery Act; and Andean Trade Preference Act) must be terminated within two years unless extended under the terms of WTO Article IX. In addition, the WTO continues to exempt the US Jones Act from WTO obligations.

9. The Final Act includes a hortatory declaration encouraging the director general of the WTO to review with the heads of the IMF and the World Bank possible cooperative efforts to help promote "greater coherence in global economic policymaking." In contrast, it does not explicitly deal with institutional linkages with international environmental and labor organizations.

ASSESSMENT

1. Strengthens the institutional foundation of the world trading system by restructuring the GATT into a membership organization, requiring universal acceptance of the obligations of almost all multilateral trade agreements and establishing an integrated dispute settlement mechanism to address problems regarding all trade issues.

2. Fails to establish an executive board or other management committee to direct the work of the director general and the WTO Secretariat, thus leaving the weak management structure of the GATT intact. Institutes unweighted voting procedures but incorporates checks and balances to protect against the "tyranny of the majority."

3. Encourages consultations among the WTO, IMF, and World Bank but makes no recommendations regarding collaborative efforts or joint reports.

GRADE: B +

INSTITUTIONAL ISSUES: Trade Policy Review Mechanism

RECOMMENDATIONS

1. Establish a permanent and stronger trade policy review mechanism (TPRM), which issues analytical reports dealing with policy development as well as reviews of existing trade measures.
2. Encourage the establishment of domestic surveillance bodies to work in tandem with the TPRM and provide independent and objective analysis of trade policies, educate the public about the cost of protection, and monitor domestic adjustment programs established pursuant to safeguard actions.

RESULTS

1. The TPRM agreement codifies the system of periodic reviews of trade policies and practices that have been carried out on an interim basis since the Uruguay Round mid-term review in 1989. The reports will be reviewed by the Trade Policy Review Body (TPRB).
2. The objective of the reviews is to examine the trade policies and practices of member countries and their impact on the multilateral trading system but not "to serve as a basis for the enforcement of specific obligations."
3. WTO members "recognize the inherent value of domestic transparency of government decision making on trade policy matters" and agree on a voluntary basis to "promote greater transparency within their own systems."
4. Within five years after the WTO has entered into force, the TPRB will appraise the operation of the TPRM. It will also report annually on developments in the international trading system.

ASSESSMENT

1. Extends the TPRM indefinitely and reconfirms its existing terms of reference and reporting requirements.
2. Requires submission of a national statement of trade policy but does not mandate WTO analysis of the consistency of trade policies and measures with multilateral rules.
3. Provides only hortatory encouragement for the formation of domestic surveillance bodies to parallel and complement the work of the TPRM.

GRADE: B+

APPENDICES

Appendix A:
US Implementing Legislation

The Uruguay Round agreements are not self-executing in US law. To implement the commitments made by the United States in the negotiations, Congress needs to amend US laws or adopt new laws. Much of what was negotiated in the Uruguay Round will not require significant changes in existing US law or practice—for example, the provisions on customs valuation, trade-related investment measures (TRIMs), and preshipment inspection call for little change. However, US law will have to be adjusted to implement the Uruguay Round accords on agriculture, sanitary and phytosanitary measures, antidumping, subsidies and countervailing duties, safeguards, intellectual property rights, government procurement, and dispute settlement, among others.

This appendix discusses the main features of the Uruguay Round Agreements Act of 1994 (US House of Representatives 1994), the bill that approves and implements the trade agreements concluded in the Uruguay Round.[1] Brief references are also made to the Clinton administration's Statement of Administrative Action (SAA), which complements the legislation and describes the general administrative actions required or appropriate to implement the Uruguay Round agreements.

---

1. The bill consists of eight parts: Title I (Approval of, and General Provisions Relating to, the Uruguay Round Agreements); Title II (Antidumping and Countervailing Duty Provisions); Title III (Additional Implementation of Agreements, which covers. e.g., safeguards, government procurement, and textiles); Title IV (Agriculture-related Provisions); Title V (Intellectual Property); Title VI (Related Provisions, which include, e.g., extension of the Generalized System of Preferences); Title VII (Revenue Provisions); and Title VIII (Pioneer Preferences; for FCC licenses for new telecommunications services).

Trade Liberalization

Agriculture

Title IV of the Uruguay Round Agreements Act implements the provisions relating to agriculture and sanitary and phytosanitary measures. No changes in US law are required to implement the US obligations regarding domestic support levels, because the significant cuts of the past few years have already lowered the level of domestic support below that which the United States is committed to achieve by the end of the transition period.

The implementing legislation provides for the elimination of all quantitative restrictions on agricultural goods under section 22 of the Agricultural Adjustment Act (affecting dairy, sugar, sugar-containing products, cotton, beef, and peanuts). This commitment relates to trade with World Trade Organization (WTO) members only and will take effect on the date on which the WTO enters into force.[2] In addition, the Meat Import Act of 1979, which provides for import quotas, is repealed. The bill requires the president to take action to ensure that imports of agricultural products do not "disrupt the orderly marketing of commodities in the United States." For example, the president may impose special safeguards for commodities, such as dairy products and cotton, whose nontariff barriers were removed under the Uruguay Round agreement on agriculture. On the other hand, if the president determines that the supply of an agricultural product that is subject to a tariff-rate quota is inadequate to meet domestic demand, he may temporarily *increase* the quantity of imports subject to the in-quota duty rate.

The implementing bill includes a provision that extends the Export Enhancement Program (EEP) through 2001, and expands it by no longer targeting it exclusively against unfair trade practices.[3] Instead, the EEP should "encourage the commercial sale of US agricultural commodities in the world market at competitive prices." It is important to note that the bill does not include a commitment to fund the EEP to the maximum amount allowed under the Uruguay Round agreement. The implementing bill also extends the Dairy Export Incentive Program (DEIP) until 2002 but does not explicitly change the program requirements in the law.[4]

The implementing bill also gives the president the authority to increase tariffs on tobacco imports by up to 350 percent ad valorem above the

---

2. For wheat, this commitment takes effect either on that date or on 12 September 1995, whichever is later.

3. This provision is known as the Export Enhancement Program Amendments of 1994.

4. In contrast to current EEP language, the DEIP does not include a provision requiring it to target foreign unfair trade practices.

rates in effect on 1 January 1975, as an alternative to the domestic-content requirements imposed in the 1993 Budget Reconciliation Act. A GATT dispute settlement panel had found these 1993 provisions to violate US international trade obligations. If US tobacco tariffs are increased, however, the United States would have to negotiate appropriate compensation for affected foreign suppliers under GATT Article XXVIII.

Sanitary and Phytosanitary Measures

The implementing bill provides for increased public access to information relating to sanitary and phytosanitary measures and clarifies several US statutes in this area. It also establishes procedures for US participation in international standard-setting activities and equivalence determinations.

The president is required to designate an agency to distribute information to the public on international standard-setting activities and to publish an annual notice in the Federal Register.[5] The agency must provide an opportunity for the public to comment on such international standards, and must take these comments into consideration when proposing matters to be considered by the international standard-setting organization.

Most notable are the provisions clarifying the Poultry Products Inspection Act and the Federal Meat Inspection Act, which include a stipulation that the secretary of agriculture "may treat as equivalent to a US requirement a requirement [of an exporting country] if the exporting country provides the Secretary with scientific evidence or other information [. . .] to demonstrate that the requirement achieves the level of sanitary protection achieved under the US requirement."[6] The bill sets up an extensive procedure for determining the equivalence of foreign and domestic sanitary and phytosanitary measures. A foreign measure may not be ruled equivalent unless the agency involved determines that it provides at least the same level of sanitary or phytosanitary protection as the comparable US measure. The Food and Drug Administration may not make a determination of equivalence without taking comments from interested persons into account.

Textiles and Apparel

US participation in the Multi-Fiber Arrangement (MFA), which currently governs trade in textiles and apparel, was negotiated under the authority

---

5. In 1979 a standards information center was established in the Commerce Department to collect and make available to the public information regarding product standards. This center currently serves as the inquiry point under the North American Free Trade Agreement for sanitary and phytosanitary measures in the United States, but refers inquiries regarding agricultural products to the Department of Agriculture. The responsibilities of the existing center would be expanded under the implementing legislation to ensure that they meet the requirements under the Uruguay Round agreement on sanitary and phytosanitary measures.

6. Implementation of a similar program in the US-Canada Free Trade Agreement was blocked by special interest groups in the United States.

of section 204 of the Agricultural Act of 1956, as amended. The Uruguay Round textiles agreement replaces the MFA and provides for the gradual and complete integration of textile and apparel products into the GATT regime over a period of 10 years. It accomplishes this in two ways. First, for each of three successive phases within the 10-year period, countries are required to declare those products for which they will achieve integration (i.e., eliminate all MFA quotas) during that phase. Each country may select which products it will integrate in each phase, but products from each of four categories—tops and yarns, fabrics, made-up textile products, and clothing—must be included. Second, the existing annual growth rates for those quotas that remain in effect for part or all of the 10-year transition period must be increased, also in three successive stages.

The US implementing bill requires the secretary of commerce to publish in the Federal Register, within 120 days after the WTO has entered into force, the final lists of textile and apparel products to be integrated in each stage set out in the textiles agreement—in other words, which products the United States will integrate at the beginning of the fourth year, at the beginning of the eighth year, and at the end of the transition period. A proposed liberalization schedule must be published within 30 days after the WTO enters into force, and is subject to public hearings. Once published in the Federal Register, the final lists may not be changed except in certain specified situations (e.g., to correct technical errors). Within 30 days after their publication the Office of the US Trade Representative must notify the lists to the Textiles Monitoring Body established under the textiles agreement.

In the SAA that accompanies the implementing bill, the Committee for the Implementation of Textile Agreements (CITA), which currently supervises the implementation of US bilateral textiles agreements and the textiles provisions of the North American Free Trade Agreement (NAFTA), is directed to establish and publish the product lists.[7] In establishing these lists, the CITA has to include a "reasonable representation" of products from each of the four product groups. However, the CITA is directed to ensure that "integration of the most sensitive products will be deferred until the end of the ten-year period."

The implementing bill further amends section 204 of the Agricultural Act of 1956, which provides that the president may regulate imports from countries that are not signatories to an international trade agreement on textile or agricultural products. The amendment clarifies that the Uruguay Round textiles agreement constitutes a multilateral agreement as defined under section 204—that is, that it is an agreement between countries that collectively account for a significant part of world trade. In addition, it

---

7. The CITA has already published a list of products, accounting for 16 percent of US imports of textiles and apparel in 1990, that will be integrated into the GATT system on the date the WTO enters into force.

authorizes the president to extend the application of section 204 to countries that are parties to a multilateral agreement, but to which the United States nonetheless does not apply the agreement. Accordingly, the United States can continue to impose quotas on textile imports from non-WTO members or from WTO members for which the United States has invoked the nonapplication provision. This provision allows US negotiators extensive flexibility to deal with major suppliers that are not yet in the WTO, such as China and Taiwan.

The implementing bill further requires a change in the rules of origin for textile and apparel products for purposes of customs law and the administration of import quotas. As of 1 January 1996 the origin of these goods will be established by where the goods are assembled, not by where they are cut, subject to certain specified exceptions—for example, articles that enter under the US-Israel Free Trade Area Agreement. However, the new rules will not apply to goods sold after the implementation date if they were contracted for prior to July 1994.

In addition, the bill establishes procedures regarding the importation of textile and apparel products that are illegally transshipped. It authorizes the secretary of the Treasury to publish in the Federal Register a list of persons outside the United States against whom the Customs Service has issued a penalty claim and final decision finding them in violation of US customs law by, inter alia, "engaging in practices which aid or abet the transshipment, through a country other than the country of origin, of textiles or apparel in manner which conceals the true origin or permits quota evasion." Persons are to be removed from the list if they have not committed such violations for at least three years. The president is authorized to publish annually a list of countries in which illegal activities have occurred involving transshipped textiles or apparel. The secretary of the Treasury must require any importer from a country included in the list to show that "reasonable" care has been taken to ascertain the true country of origin. Countries are removed from the list upon demonstrating a good faith effort.

Government Procurement

Title III of the Trade Agreements Act of 1979 authorizes the president to waive restrictions, under the Buy American Act and other legislation, on federal government procurement of certain products from signatories to the 1979 Government Procurement Code (GPC). Procurement restrictions still apply to contracts valued below the thresholds set in the GPC, purchases by uncovered entities, and procurement from countries that are not signatories to the code. Small business and minority set-asides are currently unaffected by US obligations under the GPC. Pursuant to the US-Canada Free Trade Agreement and the NAFTA, Title III also includes special rules pertaining to Canadian and Mexican goods as well as services incidental to such goods. In addition, it provides for the imposition of sanctions against foreign countries that maintain significant and persistent discrimination against US goods or services in their procurement.

The new Government Procurement Agreement (GPA) negotiated in the Uruguay Round extends the coverage of GPC obligations to specified services and to subnational government entities. US government procurement of the implementing bill contains various technical amendments to conform Title III provisions to the new agreement. For example, it authorizes the president to waive Buy American requirements under the Rural Electrification Act for eligible countries (mainly the European Union).

In addition, the implementing bill amends Title III of the 1979 Trade Agreements Act to conform its sanctions authority to the time limits and criteria set out in the Uruguay Round Dispute Settlement Understanding (DSU). It requires that the president impose sanctions within 18 months after initiation of dispute settlement proceedings against signatories that are not in compliance with their obligations under the GPA. However, sanctions against signatories may only be imposed when the WTO dispute settlement procedures have been completed and the suspension of concessions has been authorized, or when the dispute settlement procedures have not been concluded within 18 months after their initiation. In addition, the president is required to report on discriminatory government procurement practices in countries that are not signatories to the GPA, for possible action under section 301 of the 1974 trade act.

Tariff Liberalization

Section 1102(a) of the Omnibus Trade and Competitiveness Act of 1988 authorizes the president to enter into trade agreements and to proclaim reductions in duties required to carry out such agreements, subject to certain narrow limitations. The implementing bill extends the president's authority to proclaim tariff reductions that exceed the limits set in section 1102(a), if the president determines them to be necessary to carry out the US schedule of tariff commitments under the Uruguay Round. However, the president is not authorized to cut tariffs beyond the scope of US commitments in the round. The bill also authorizes the president to raise tariffs on, for example, agricultural goods whose import quotas or other nontariff restrictions are replaced by new, higher tariffs.

More important, the implementing bill allows the president to negotiate and proclaim—subject to consultation with the private sector and with Congress—further tariff reductions in sectors specified in the SAA. The SAA also states US negotiating objectives with respect to these sectors, which include wood products, electronics, nonferrous metals, oilseeds, and distilled spirits. For example, in those sectors where the United States sought complete duty elimination (as part of its zero-for-zero tariff reduction initiative), the president may negotiate and proclaim future duty elimination. The president is also authorized to negotiate and then proclaim faster phaseout schedules for tariff cuts than previously agreed in the round, as well as a faster tariff harmonization schedule for chemical products.

Trade Rules

Title II of the implementing bill contains the provisions that pertain to antidumping and countervailing measures. Subtitle A includes amendments to the antidumping statute that implement the methodological changes mandated by the Uruguay Round antidumping agreement, as well as amendments to current US antidumping and countervailing duty laws that implement procedural changes agreed to in the antidumping and subsidies agreements. Subtitle B comprises amendments to US countervailing duty statutes to implement the methodological provisions of the Uruguay Round subsidies agreement.

Antidumping

Title VII of the 1930 Tariff Act, as amended, provides that antidumping duties must be imposed on imports if the Commerce Department determines that these imports are sold at "less than fair value" (i.e., dumped), and the International Trade Commission (ITC) finds that a US industry is materially injured (or threatened with material injury, or that the establishment of a US industry is materially retarded) by reason of these dumped imports.

In many respects, the Uruguay Round antidumping agreement codifies existing US practice with regard to antidumping procedures. However, some important statutory changes need to be made. Title II of the Uruguay Round Agreements Act amends US antidumping law to establish a new methodology for comparing prices, provide for sunset reviews, require average-to-average price comparisons (in investigations but not in subsequent administrative reviews), establish a special adjustment for startup production costs, establish a special provision for captive production, and amend existing anticircumvention provisions, and makes other changes to US law.[8] In general, the implementing bill brings the time limits in the US antidumping statute into conformity with the Uruguay Round antidumping agreement.

Methodological Changes

Fair Comparison. To determine whether an imported good is being dumped or is likely to be dumped into the domestic market, the agreement

---

8. For instance, the implementing bill conforms Title VII to the terminology used in the new antidumping agreement: for example, "United States price" becomes "export price," and "foreign market value" becomes "normal value."

requires that a "fair comparison" be made between the export price (or the constructed export price)[9] and the normal value. Several adjustments are made to the export price: for example, for costs involved in making goods ready for shipment, import duties that were rebated or not collected by reason of exportation to the United States, countervailing duties imposed to offset export subsidies, shipping and transportation costs, export taxes and duties, and costs of further manufacture or assembly.

Constructed Export Price. The bill includes a provision concerning the determination of dumping margins in cases where a sale is made between related companies, such as an overseas parent and its US subsidiary. In such cases the Commerce Department is authorized to deduct selling profits from the US price charged between related parties when using the price of the first purchase to an unrelated party to establish the so-called exporter's sales price (ESP).

The formula used to calculate the profit reduction could substantially inflate dumping margins in cases involving sales between related companies, by effectively lowering the price calculated for sales in the United States without making a similar adjustment to the home market price.[10] The bill requires that the profit reduction be calculated by multiplying the total worldwide profits of the firm involved by the percentage of its total expenses that are incurred in the United States.[11] This formula could result in a situation in which affiliated companies are forced to increase their intercompany transfer prices, perhaps thereby jeopardizing compliance with section 482 of the Internal Revenue Code, which requires that intercompany prices be set on an arm's-length basis. It would discriminate against foreign investment by penalizing firms that sell through related parties in the United States. If emulated by foreign governments, this formula would also adversely affect many US exporters who frequently sell to their overseas subsidiaries.

Level-of-Trade Adjustment. The bill provides for an adjustment for the level of trade in the normal value with which the constructed export price is compared. The Commerce Department has to make "due allowance for any difference between the export price . . . and the [normal value] . . . that is shown to be wholly or partly due to a difference in the level

---

9. The export price is the price at which the product is first sold before importation to an unaffiliated purchaser in the United States. The constructed export price is the price at which the product is first sold in the United States before or after importation to a purchaser not affiliated with the exporter or producer (see below). Current law distinguishes between "purchase price" (now "export price"), and "exporter's sale price" (now "constructed export price").

10. The Pro-Trade Group charges that this requirement could lead to an increase in dumping margins by 7 percent or more (*Inside US Trade*, Special Report, 23 September 1994, S-1).

11. Whether this formula yields an estimate comparable to the GATT requirement that adjustments be made for "profit accrued" is unclear and may well provoke a WTO dispute.

of trade between the export price . . . and normal value." This adjustment is based on the assumption that export sales are usually further down the distribution chain, and thus higher in price, than home market sales. The home market price should therefore be calculated at about the same level of trade (e.g., off-factory price).

However, the implementing bill contains significant barriers to applying such a level of trade adjustment. The burden of proof is placed on the exporter to show that differences in selling activities between two levels of trade warrant an appropriate adjustment to the normal value. Exporters must also demonstrate a consistent "pattern of price differences between sales at the different levels of trade." There may be some overlap in prices at the different levels, but it is unclear how much overlap is allowed. If it is established that there are different levels of trade, but no pattern of price differences can be shown, the level of trade adjustment is zero. Based on virtually identical criteria, the Commerce Department has seldom applied level-of-trade adjustments in the past.

Constructed Value. In the "fair comparison" between the (constructed) export price and the normal value, adjustments are made for, among other factors, sales below cost. The provisions in the implementing bill relating to the constructed normal value calculations mainly codify what is already US administrative practice, except for the new profit calculation (which mirrors EU practice). The constructed value is the sum of the following: costs of materials; manufacturing, selling, and general and administrative expenses; profits "in the ordinary course of trade"; and costs incurred in making the goods ready for shipment. Special adjustments are allowed, for example, for startup costs (see below).

The implementing bill eliminates the statutory minimum percentage for profit to be used in constructing a normal value. Instead, imputed profits must be based on the actual amounts incurred and realized with the sale of the product in question in the exporting country. In these calculations the Commerce Department may disregard foreign sales made at a price below the cost of production (see below). If actual data are not available, profits are determined from the actual profit realized on the foreign sale of products in the same general category of the product under investigation; or from the weighted average of the actual profit realized by other exporters under investigation on their foreign sales of the product; or may be based on any other reasonable method, "except that the amount allowed for profit may not exceed the amount *normally* realized by [other exporters] in connection with the [foreign] sale . . . of merchandise that is in the same general category of products as the subject merchandise" (emphasis added). The implementing bill does not express a preference for any of the methods permitted.

Startup Costs. The Commerce Department is required to adjust costs for a firm's startup period—when it uses "new production facilities or [produces] a new product that requires substantial additional investment—based on both fixed and variable production costs, but not marketing costs. The startup period is considered to end when the firm has achieved the level of commercial production characteristic of the merchandise, producer, or industry concerned.

Sales Below Cost of Production.   The implementing bill contains a provision that allows the Commerce Department, in determining normal value, to disregard sales that were made at prices below the cost of production, if they were made within an extended period of time—defined as normally one year, but not less than six months—in substantial quantities,[12] and if they were not at prices that would permit recovery of all costs within a "reasonable" period of time (effectively limited to one year by the SAA). The Commerce Department has "reasonable grounds to believe or suspect" that sales were made below the cost of production if an interested party provides information, based upon observed or constructed prices or costs, showing that such sales have been made. Whenever such sales are disregarded, normal value is based on the remaining sales of the exported good "in the ordinary course of trade." If few or no sales remain, the normal value is based on a constructed value.

Price Averaging.   The implementing bill provides that the Commerce Department will "normally" establish and measure antidumping margins by comparing a weighted average of normal values with a weighted average of export prices. To conform US law with the Uruguay Round antidumping agreement, the bill allows the Commerce Department to compare a weighted average of normal values with individual export prices in cases of targeted dumping. However, the bill also leaves open the possibility of comparing a weighted average with individual transactions when reviewing antidumping orders.[13]

Procedural Changes

Standing.   Following the language of the Uruguay Round agreement, the bill requires that an antidumping petition be expressly supported by a group of producers who collectively account for at least 25 percent of domestic production and represent at least 50 percent of domestic producers who either support or oppose the petition. It also stipulates that the

---

12. "Sales made at prices below the cost of production have been made in substantial quantities if (i) the volume of such sales represents 20 percent or more of the volume of sales under consideration for the determination of normal value, or (ii) the weighted average per unit price of the sales under consideration for the determination of normal value is less than the weighted average per unit cost of production for such sales."

13. In fact, the SAA expressly states that "the preferred methodology in reviews will be to compare average [normal values] to individual export prices."

position of domestic producers who are related to foreign producers or who are also importers of the product under investigation will be disregarded.

De Minimis Rules and Negligibility. The implementing bill changes the de minimis dumping margins (both for preliminary and final determinations, but not for reviews) from the current 0.5 percent to 2 percent as required by the agreement. Similarly, "negligible imports" are defined (as the new pact requires) as imports from countries that individually account for less than 3 percent of total imports of the like product under investigation, unless they collectively account for more than 7 percent of total imports of the like product.

Captive Production. In determining whether a domestic industry is materially injured by imports, the ITC must evaluate the import penetration of the US market and the financial performance of the affected domestic producers. US law is amended to address situations in which goods are produced and subsequently not sold in the market for that good (the merchant market), but instead processed into higher valued downstream products by the same producer ("captive production"). The bill provides that, where domestic producers devote significant production both to captive consumption for the production of downstream products and to merchant market sales, the ITC has to focus primarily on the merchant market for the upstream product.

Review of Determinations. The implementing bill amends the US antidumping statute to provide for three kinds of reviews of determinations of injury and dumping. The first relates to an annual administrative review, if requested, of the amount of the antidumping duty; the second to reviews, undertaken on request, based on changed circumstances; and the third to so-called sunset reviews.

Sunset Reviews. Under the agreement, all antidumping duty orders, suspension agreements, and determinations to continue an order or suspension agreement are to expire five years after they are issued or concluded, unless it is determined that "revocation of the [. . .] antidumping duty order or [suspension agreement] would be likely to lead to continuation or recurrence of dumping [. . .] and of material injury."

No later than thirty days before the five years are up, the Commerce Department must publish in the Federal Register a notification of initiation of a review. If the interested parties do not respond to the department's request to submit information for the purposes of the review, it may automatically revoke the duty order or terminate the suspension agreement.[14] The Commerce Department must issue its final determination regarding dumping within nine months after the initiation of the review; the ITC must make its final injury determination within 12 months. In "extraordinarily complicated" cases the Commerce Department and the ITC may take an extra three months to make their determinations.[15]

Antidumping duty orders that were in effect on the date on which the WTO enters into force—so-called transition orders—are subject to the sunset review. The implementing bill stipulates that the Commerce Department must begin to review transition orders three-and-a-half years after the entry into force of the WTO. Reviews have to be completed within 18 months after their initiation,[16] and all reviews have to be completed not later than six-and-a-half years after entry into force of the WTO. Hence, the implementing bill interprets the ambiguous language in the Uruguay Round antidumping agreement as meaning that reviews do not have to be concluded, but only initiated, by the end of the five-year period. Moreover, although the agreement stipulates that reviews should "normally" be concluded within one year after their initiation, the Commerce Department may take up to 18 months to conclude its review of a transition order (the initial review as well as all subsequent reviews). In the SAA, the administration claims that the longer review period for transition orders is essential to alleviate the bottleneck of reviews of transition periods every five years. Finally, the Commerce Department, in consultation with the ITC, determines the sequence of review of transition orders— to the extent practicable, older orders are reviewed first.

Anticircumvention. The Uruguay Round antidumping agreement does not include rules regarding the actions taken by countries to counter the circumvention of their antidumping orders. Countries may continue to apply anticircumvention provisions, although such actions may face potential WTO challenge.

The implementing bill strengthens the current anticircumvention provisions in US law. It provides that, in the case of circumvention of an antidumping order,[17] the imported parts or components, or the good

---

14. In case of "inadequate response" to its request, the Commerce Department may base its final determination on "the facts available."

15. If the Commerce Department extends the time for making a final determination but the ITC does not, the ITC must issue its final determination within four months after Commerce has done so.

16. However, no transition order may be revoked sooner than five years after the WTO enters into force.

17. Circumvention occurs when merchandise is sold in the United States that is subject to an antidumping order or completed or assembled in the United States from parts or components produced in the foreign country to which an antidumping order applies, if the process of assembly or completion in the United States is minor or insignificant and the value of the parts or components is a significant share of the total value of the merchandise.

imported from a third country where it was assembled or completed from parts or components that are subject to a US antidumping order, may be included in the scope of the antidumping order. Determinations regarding anticircumvention must be made within 10 months after initiation of an anticircumvention investigation.

Subsidies

In addition to the procedural changes to US countervailing duty law listed in Subtitle A of Title II of the implementing bill, Subtitle B amends the existing statute in the following ways: it incorporates the Uruguay Round agreement's definitions of subsidy and specificity, which largely reflect existing US law; it implements the agreement's stricter disciplines on subsidies that, by their nature, are presumed to cause harm to other countries' industries; it implements the agreement's three categories of nonactionable subsidies (those for regional development, research and development, and environmental improvements); it provides for the automatic expiration after five years of the nonactionable subsidies provisions of US countervailing duty law, unless extended by Congress; and it provides a specific opportunity for action under section 301 to address instances where nonactionable subsidies are found to cause "serious adverse effects."

Nonactionable Subsidies

Although the bill adopts the subsidies agreement's definitions of nonactionable subsidies, the SAA provides that the term "pre-competitive development activity" in the R&D provision will be construed narrowly (e.g., to make it clear that, as a general rule, a prototype must undergo substantial modification in order to be capable of any commercial use), to ensure that it is not applied so as to permit subsidies for production or export to be nonactionable. Terms in the environmental provision (such as "one-time nonrecurring measure") are understood to prevent the repeated use of nonactionable subsidies to offset the costs of individual new environmental requirements. Subsidies will be treated as nonactionable only when they are limited to one subsidy per "new environmental requirement" and per facility,[18] and when provided to facilities that have been in operation for at least two years when the new requirements are imposed.

The nonactionable subsidies provisions of the Uruguay Round subsidies agreement expire five years after the WTO enters into force, unless there is an agreement to extend them. The implementing bill provides that the

---

18. This is done to ensure that slightly different environmental requirements do not permit repeated subsidization of the same facility.

US trade representative, after consulting with the appropriate congressional committees and other interested parties, may agree to extend the application of the nonactionable subsidies provisions beyond the five-year period. The trade representative must submit legislation to implement the agreed extension, which would be eligible for consideration under fast-track procedures.

Repeal of and Outstanding Orders under Section 303

The implementing bill repeals section 303, which currently applies to countries that are not signatories to the Tokyo Round subsidies code, does not require an injury test in cases involving such countries, and includes its own definition of subsidy. Instead, US law is amended to provide that the injury test will only be applied to products of countries that are WTO members (and thus subject to the new subsidies agreement). For outstanding orders issued under section 303, the injury test will only be applied when the country becomes a member of the WTO.

Safeguards

Current US law and practice are already largely consistent with the Uruguay Round safeguards agreement. The implementing bill codifies much of what was already US practice, but amends the safeguards provisions of US law to provide more rapid and effective relief to an industry under certain "critical circumstances."[19] Under this provision the ITC is required to make a determination on the applicability of "critical circumstances" within 60 days after a petition is filed, and the president is allowed 30 days to decide what action, if any, to take. Provisional relief could thus be provided within 90 days. The bill also revises the period of relief available to an initial four years, with a possible extension of another four years.[20]

The implementing bill changes all references in section 203 to "orderly marketing agreements" to "agreements described in subsection (a)(3)(E) of section 203." The agreements covered in this subsection fit the description of orderly marketing agreements, although the words "orderly marketing" have been stricken from the statute. Section 203 thus seems to violate the Uruguay Round agreement, which expressly prohibits orderly marketing agreements "or any other similar measures" (Article 11:1b).

New Issues

Services

Implementing the General Agreement on Trade in Services requires no changes in US laws. Nonetheless, the implementing bill sets forth the

---

19. This provision is not per se required by the safeguards agreement.

20. Under current law the period of relief is also limited to eight years, but the initial period of relief may be greater than the four years set by the agreement.

United States' objectives in ongoing negotiations on trade in financial services, basic telecommunications, and civil aircraft. For example, the United States seeks "commitments, from a wide range of commercially important developed and developing countries, to reduce or eliminate barriers to the supply of financial services, including barriers that deny national treatment or market access by restricting the establishment or operation of financial services providers" as a condition for access to its financial services markets. In basic telecommunications the main negotiating objective is "to obtain the opening on nondiscriminatory terms and conditions of foreign markets for basic telecommunications services through facilities-based competition or through the resale of services on existing networks." The SAA elaborates on these negotiating goals and sets forth the goals to be achieved in the negotiations on maritime transport services, which are to be concluded by 30 June 1996. Generally, if the administration is not satisfied with the results of the extended negotiations, it may take or maintain a most-favored-nation (MFN) exemption with regard to the sector(s) in question, after consulting with Congress and the affected industries.

Investment

Although no changes in US law were necessary to implement the Uruguay Round TRIMs agreement, in the SAA the administration commits itself to conducting an annual review of the implementation of the TRIMs agreement as part of its annual report on the Trade Agreements Program and the National Trade Policy Agenda, starting with the 1996 report. The review should address investment measures covered by the TRIMs agreement as well as measures outside the scope of the agreement.

Intellectual Property

Presently, section 337 of the 1930 Tariff Act, as amended, allows the ITC to act against imports of goods that violate US patents or copyrights. A 1988 GATT panel ruling found that some aspects of section 337 were inconsistent with the GATT national treatment obligation; specifically, infringement actions brought in federal district courts involving domestic goods differed from ITC procedures involving imported goods.[21]

Subtitle C of Title III of the Uruguay Round Agreements Act, brings section 337 into compliance with the GATT panel finding by conforming

---

21. Moreover, whereas relief against domestic goods may only be sought in US district courts, holders of intellectual property rights may seek relief against imported goods both there and from the ITC. Thus actions could be maintained against imported goods, but not domestic goods, in two separate fora simultaneously.

ITC procedures to those followed by federal district courts in intellectual property infringement suits. It eliminates the 12-month deadline under current law (18 months in more complicated cases) by which the ITC must make its determinations and instead requires the ITC to conclude its investigation by the earliest practicable time. A target date for its final determination must be established within 45 days of initiation of the investigation.

In addition, Title V of the implementing bill, which implements the new provisions on intellectual property, contains changes in federal laws with respect to copyrights, trademarks, and patents; other areas of US intellectual property law are unaffected by the agreement on trade-related intellectual property rights (TRIPs).

The bill changes the length of patent terms, from 17 years from the date the patent is granted to 20 years from the date the patent is filed. This change should solve the problem of "submarine patents"—patents whose applications remain secret as a result of delays caused by their inventors' filing continuance applications, only to surface and knock out patent protection that may already have been granted. To ease the potentially adverse impacts of the patent term change, the bill provides for limited extensions of the patent term (of up to five years) if there are delays resulting from successful federal court appeals or from internal Patent and Trademark Office (PTO) appeals, or other technical delays resulting from requests by the PTO to patent applicants.

The trademark provisions of the implementing bill extend the period of nonuse of a trademark that constitutes prima facie evidence of its abandonment—from the current two years to three—as required under the TRIPs agreement. In addition, the implementing bill prohibits registration of a misleading geographical indication identifying wines or spirits.

The copyright provisions of the implementing bill eliminate the sunset provision on rental rights in computer programs, protect against bootlegging of sound recordings or music videos of a live performance, and restore copyright protection to works already in the public domain in the United States but still under protection in a WTO member that is the source of the work.

Institutional Reforms

Dispute Settlement

Presently, sections 301–309 of the 1974 trade act, as amended, allow the US trade representative to enforce US rights under international trade agreements, including the Uruguay Round agreements, and to respond to certain unfair foreign trade practices. They require the trade representative to make determinations within 18 months after the investigation is initiated (or within 30 days after the conclusion of the GATT dispute settlement process, whichever is earlier) for investigations involving trade agreements other than the Tokyo Round subsidies code. For the subsidies code, and in all other cases, a determination of actionability has to be made within 12 months after the investigation is initiated. The so-called special 301 provision requires identification of countries that deny intellectual property rights protection or access, for possible action under section 301. Presently, the US trade representative is required to make a determination within six months (nine months in complex cases or if the country under investigation is making substantial progress) after the investigation is initiated.

Very few changes were needed to bring section 301 into conformity with the new WTO dispute settlement procedures. The implementing bill extends the existing 18-month time limit to cases involving the new subsidies agreement, but retains the 12-month time limit for all cases that do not involve a violation of a Uruguay Round agreement (nonagreement cases) and for special 301 investigations that do not involve a violation of the TRIPs agreement or another trade agreement.

The implementing bill further clarifies that "unreasonable" acts by a foreign country under section 301 include inadequate intellectual property protection, even if the country has implemented the TRIPs agreement, as well as restrictions on market access affecting intellectual property rights in protected works. In identifying foreign countries' practices as "unreasonable" under special 301, the history of a country's intellectual property protection and its prior treatment under special 301 are to be considered. In addition, the list of intellectual property rights to be addressed is updated to include, for example, related rights (see the chapter on intellectual property in this volume), trademarks, and trade secrets.

Rulings issued by WTO dispute panels or the WTO Appellate Body have no binding effect under US law. If a report recommends that the United States change laws that are ruled to be inconsistent with a Uruguay Round agreement, it is up to Congress to decide whether to make such a change. Likewise, rulings have no binding effect on the practices, regulations, or enforcement procedures of federal agencies or state governments. As noted in the chapter on dispute settlement in this volume, the DSU provides for alternative means of resolving a dispute, including trade compensation, other types of negotiated settlements, or, ultimately, the suspension of trade concessions benefiting the offending country. In addition, when a country's laws or practice have been ruled inconsistent with its obligations under a Uruguay Round agreement, the DSU leaves the question of how to implement the required changes up to the offending country's discretion—it may, for example adopt new legislation, issue changes in regulations, or take judicial action.

To ensure greater transparency in WTO dispute settlement procedures, the implementing bill further requires the US trade representative to maintain a file, accessible to the public, on each dispute settlement proceeding to which the United States is a party. In addition, all US written submissions as well as panel and Appellate Body reports must be made available to the public promptly after their submission to the panel or Appellate Body or circulation to WTO members. The trade representative is further required to request that other WTO members that are parties to a dispute involving the United States permit the release of their written submissions to the public, or nonconfidential summaries thereof.

In addition, the implementing bill codifies the executive order currently in effect that extends so-called Super 301 authority through 1995. The bill also preserves the language of the executive order that changed the deadline for designation from one month (as originally established in the 1988 trade act) to six months after publication of the National Trade Estimates, and called for the identification of priority foreign practices, not priority countries.

World Trade Organization

In section 101(a) of the implementing bill Congress approves the Uruguay Round agreements comprising the WTO Agreement, annexes 1 and 2 of the WTO Agreement (e.g., on safeguards, antidumping, textiles and apparel, TRIPs, and trade in services), and two of the four plurilateral agreements (on government procurement and bovine meat).[22]

To assuage concerns about the implications of the WTO for US sovereignty, the implementing bill includes a "special legislative procedure" that allows both the House and the Senate to vote after five years on continued US participation in the WTO. This measure mirrors the resolution of disapproval used in ending tariff concessions for countries under the Jackson-Vanik provisions (section 402 of the 1974 trade act).[23] It also includes provisions that require the US trade representative to report extensively, in an annual report to Congress, on WTO actions and activities before Congress approves WTO appropriations.

The implementing bill states explicitly that those US federal laws not addressed in the bill are left unchanged. The Statement of Administrative Action that accompanies the bill includes an illustrative list of federal environmental and health safety laws that are not amended by the bill.

Some provisions in the Uruguay Round agreements directly or implicitly affect state and local laws and regulations. However, each WTO member decides for itself *how* to conform national and subnational laws

---

22. The United States is currently not a signatory to the plurilateral agreement governing dairy trade, and the civil aircraft agreement has not been changed since Congress approved it in 1979. Annex 3 to the WTO Agreement (on the trade policy review mechanism) does not require congressional action.

23. *Inside US Trade,* 19 August 1994, p. 13.

and regulations with its obligations under the agreements. To that effect, and to reassure state officials that the WTO will not infringe on their sovereignty, the implementing bill establishes a detailed mechanism of state-federal consultation and cooperation aimed at conforming state laws and practices with the Uruguay Round agreements and addressing issues relating to the agreements that could have an impact on states.

The implementing bill provides that "no state law, or the application of such a state law, may be declared invalid . . . on the ground that the provision or application is inconsistent with any of the Uruguay Round agreements, except in an action brought by the United States for the purpose of declaring such law or application invalid." The Uruguay Round agreements do not invalidate state laws that do not conform to the rules set out in those agreements—even if a dispute settlement panel finds a state measure inconsistent with such an agreement. However, if federal-state consultations fail to resolve the matter so that the measure is brought into conformity with US international obligations, and if the federal government feels the need to act to overcome such inconsistency, it can institute action in the relevant federal district court against the state in question.

However, the federal government has never taken such action in the history of the GATT, and is unlikely to do so in the future. Moreover, the SAA expressly states that the "authority conferred to the United States under this paragraph is intended to be used only as a "last resort," in the unlikely event that efforts to achieve consistency through the cooperative approach . . . have not succeeded."

In case such action is instituted, the federal government has the "burden of proving that the law that is the subject of the action . . . is inconsistent with the agreement in question," and the court will reach its own, independent interpretation of the relevant provisions of the agreement.[24] In these proceedings, WTO dispute panel or appellate body reports "shall not be considered as binding or otherwise accorded deference" (section 102.2.B(i)) but may be introduced for consideration by the court.

Fast-Track Authority, GSP Extension, and CBI Parity

Early drafts of the US implementing bill included a proposal to renew the administration's fast-track negotiating authority for trade agreements. The Clinton administration was anxious to secure this renewal, hoping

---

24. The SAA makes this point clearly: "Although ultimately the federal government, through its Constitutional authority and the implementing bill, retains the authority to overrule inconsistent state law through legislation or civil suit, use of this authority has not been necessary in the nearly half-century that the GATT has been in effect" (SAA, p. 18).

to proceed with bilateral trade negotiations with Chile and other Latin American and Asian countries. However, the proposal was dropped from the bill, mainly because of the controversial inclusion of labor and environmental negotiating objectives. So, at present, the administration has no authority to negotiate new trade agreements under fast-track procedures.

The implementing bill includes a provision that extends the existing Generalized System of Preferences (GSP) for 10 months beyond its original expiration date, until 31 July 1995. The duty preferences will be retroactive to 30 September 1994. However, importers will have to pay MFN-rate duties on GSP products from 1 October until the implementing bill is passed by Congress. Those duties will be refunded after the bill is passed and GSP is renewed. None of the changes in the GSP program that the administration originally proposed as part of the implementing legislation were included in the final bill; hence they will have to be taken up again in future trade legislation. Another provision that was dropped from the implementing bill in the last stages of the markup process related to proposals to extend NAFTA market access benefits to the countries of the Caribbean Basin Initiative (the so-called CBI parity provision).

Appendix B:
Computable General Equilibrium Models and the Uruguay Round

This appendix discusses multicountry computable general equilibrium (CGE) models that have been used to project the economic effects of the Uruguay Round.[1] The CGE models discussed in this appendix and summarized in table B.1 have evolved from a number of different sources. Most of the models are limited to a static analysis of the effects of tariff reductions and assume perfect competition and constant returns to scale in all markets.[2] These assumptions reflect their origins: most models have their roots in efforts to estimate the effects of agricultural trade reform on developing countries, and were later extended to cover other sectors as well as other countries. Consequently, several of the models tend to understate the gains from trade liberalization in nonagricultural sectors such as manufacturing and services.

In addition, static models do not capture the impact of trade liberalization on economic growth resulting from such factors as scale economies, imperfect competition, innovation, and endogenous growth processes. These are likely to increase the actual net gains substantially; in fact, the dynamic gains from multilateral trade liberalization should in the medium and long run turn out to be far more important than the static and short-run gains (see, e.g., Baldwin 1992, 100:162–174). Therefore, current academic research is focused on CGE models that incorporate imperfect competition, scale economies, and dynamic effects; several models attempting to incorporate these effects have already been applied to an analysis of the North American Free Trade Agreement.

---

1. This appendix benefited substantially from comments by J. David Richardson.

2. However, Francois et al. (1994) also incorporate assumptions relating to imperfect competition and economies of scale into their base model.

The CGE studies differ among themselves mainly in the way in which they divide the world up into sectors and regions, and in how closely their liberalization scenarios approximate the negotiated outcome of the Uruguay Round. However, none of the studies precisely reflect the actual results of the Round; instead they are based on estimates for broad product categories as to what the exact reductions in tariffs and other barriers to trade would be. More important, the studies leave out important aspects of the final results, because most of what was negotiated is not easily susceptible to quantitative analysis—for example, changes to rules governing trade in services,[3] investment, and intellectual property. The studies therefore limit their scope to estimates of the economic effects of the market access aspects of the Round—tariff reductions, reform of agricultural trade, and reform of the textiles and apparel trading regime—while ignoring the effects of a strengthened and extended set of trade rules as well as of institutional improvements.

The models have rather limited sectoral disaggregation within manufacturing, let alone services. Current tariff levels in manufacturing are low in comparison with those in agriculture, but in industrial countries the manufacturing sector constitutes a much larger share of GDP than does agriculture. Accordingly, insufficient disaggregation of manufacturing may substantially understate the gains from trade liberalization in the Uruguay Round.[4]

Many developing countries should benefit substantially from the Uruguay Round reforms, particularly the phased removal of quantitative restrictions on textiles and apparel exports to industrialized economies. However, some net food-importing developing countries may be adversely affected by increases in world agricultural prices due to reduced agricultural subsidies, especially in the grains sector.[5]

On the other hand, some developing countries may be able to revive domestic agricultural production that was destroyed by the subsidized

---

3. A notable exception is Nguyen et al. (1993), which modeled a 40 percent cut in the tariff equivalent of nontariff barriers to trade in services; however, the study acknowledges the limitations inherent in estimating and modeling such barriers to services trade.

4. For example, in the model employed by Francois et al. (1994), 43 percent of US manufacturing exports are represented in only 1 of the 15 commodity groups used ("other manufactures"), whereas mining, forestry, and fishery products—accounting for 2.1 percent, 0.6 percent, and 0.5 percent of US merchandise exports, respectively—each are represented in separate commodity groups. As a result, significant understatement of the income gains to the United States is to be expected, and not mere inaccuracy, because aggregation averages high barriers that cause increasingly sizeable losses as they rise (losses increase with the square of a tariff rate) with low barriers that cause minor losses.

5. In recognition of these potential adverse effects, the Uruguay Round agreement includes a ministerial decision ("decision on measures concerning the possible legislative effects of the reform programme on least-developed and net-food importing developing countries") that sets out objectives for food and agricultural development assistance.

dumping of farm products by the European Union and the United States. Higher world grain prices could promote renewed production in countries that became net food importers because of these practices—and thus relieve somewhat their balance of payments pressures. This effect is also not captured by CGE models because CGE computations always need to assume some production in a sector to calculate the effects of trade liberalization.

CGE Model Results

The studies summarized in table B.1 all conclude that the Uruguay Round agreements will result in net aggregate gains for most countries.[6] Estimates of the annual increase in global income from full implementation of the Uruguay Round range (in 1992 dollars) from a modest $60 billion (Yang 1994; this estimate includes static gains only) to a whopping $512 billion (Francois et al 1994; their estimate includes certain quasi-dynamic effects) by 2005. For the industrial countries the studies generally suggest that larger gains will accrue to the European Union, where the initial distortions in agriculture are particularly severe. Again, this result is due to the heavy agricultural bias of the models. Estimated gains for the United States, in 1992 dollars, range from $15 billion (by 2002, static gains only; Goldin et al. 1993) to $126 billion (by 2005, including quasi-dynamic gains; Francois et al. 1994).

The first three studies in table B.1 (which are the most recent) base their calculations on a model originally developed by Hertel and Tsigas (1993), the Global Trade Analysis Project (GTAP) model. In general, the GTAP model is heavily skewed toward natural resources sectors, with separate commodity groups for mining and for iron and steel products; the manufacturing sector is analyzed at a far more aggregated level. This means that the gains calculated for countries whose economies are less rooted in the natural resources sector are significantly understated (see note 4 above).

Yang (1994) tries to incorporate one type of dynamic gain into the GTAP framework. In essence, the study attempts to capture the externalities generated by export growth following trade liberalization (modeled very

---

6. Several other studies provide estimates of the likely effects of multilateral trade liberalization; these include Deardorff and Stern (1990), Stoeckel et al. (1990), and Trela and Whalley (1990). Results from these studies are not discussed in this appendix because the trade liberalization scenarios on which they are based do not approximate the final Uruguay Round agreement closely enough. In addition, the study by Brandão and Martin (1993) is not included because it incorporates only the agriculture portion of the agreement; DRI/McGraw-Hill (1993) is excluded because it uses a linked macroeconomic model, not a CGE model; and US Trade Representative (1990) based its projection of static and dynamic gains on estimates of static gains by Stoeckel et al. (1990).

Table B.1 Comparison of CGE models assessing the macroeconomic effects of Uruguay Round trade liberalization

Study	Model characteristics	Trade liberalization scenario	Welfare effects	Increase in real exports (percentages)
Francois et al. (1994)	GTAP (Global Trade Analysis Project) incorporating scale economies and imperfect competition Static gains (also dynamic investment-income linkages) Scale economies Imperfect competition 9 countries and regions 15 commodity groups Base year is 1990 Calculates 1990 counterfactual and projections for 2005	Scenario I: Tariff reductions per Final Act Elimination of QRs (mainly MFA) "Liberal" agricultural reform per Final Act Scenario II: Tariff reductions per Final Act Elimination of QRs (mainly MFA) "Moderate" agricultural reform per Final Act	By 2005, in billions of 1992 dollars: Scenario I:[b] World: 317.3 United States: 80.0 Canada: 8.2 European Union: 102.8 Japan: 21.0 Scenario II:[c] World: 293.1 United States: 76.2 Canada: 8.2 European Union: 94.0 Japan: 12.6	Scenario I:[a] World: 15.4 United States: 17.3 Canada: 12.7 European Union: 18.3 Japan: 5.4 Scenario II: World: 14.8 United States: 17.1 Canada: 12.5 European Union: 17.4 Japan: 4.7
Yang (1994)	GTAP model incorporating export externalities Static effects only Constant returns to scale in production Perfect competition 10 countries and regions 10 commodity groups	20 percent cut in agricultural production subsidies; 36 percent cut in agricultural export subsidies Phaseout of the MFA Tariff reductions per Final Act	Without export externalities (billions of dollars): World: 59.6 United States and Canada: 17.2 European Union: 21.8 Japan: 16.1 With export externalities: World: 116.4 United States and Canada: 26.9 European Union: 26.2 Japan: 10.3	Not calculated or not reported
GATT (1993)	GTAP model Static effects only Constant returns to scale in production Perfect competition Imperfect substitution between	Market access offers as of 19 November 1993 MFA quota liberalization 20 percent cut in agricultural production subsidies; 36 percent cut in agricultural export	By 2005, in billions of 1992 dollars: World: 230 United States and Canada: 67 European Union: 98	By 2005, in 1992 dollars: World: $745 billion (12.4 percent) United States and Canada: 8 percent

Study	Model and assumptions	Policy experiment	Welfare gains	
	imports and domestic products in consumption 10 product categories 7 regions Base year is 1990 Timeline: 1990–2005 10-year implementation (1995–2005)	subsidies and import protection measures		European Union: 10.3 percent
OECD (1993)	RUNS model Constant returns to scale in production Perfect competion Static gains only Imperfect substitution between imports and domestic products in consumption 7 countries and regions 4 commodity groups Base year is 1992 Timeline: 1992–2002 Cuts are phased in over a 10-year period (1993–2002)	36 percent reduction in all tariffs and nontariff barriers (both manufacturing and agricultural)	By 2002, in billions of 1991 dollars: World: 274 United States: 27.6 European Union: 71.3 Japan: 42.0 Canada: 6.6	Not calculated or not reported
Goldin et al. (1993)	RUNS model Constant returns to scale in production Perfect competition Imperfect substitution between imports and domestic manufacturing products in consumption Static gains only 22 regions (6 in OECD) 20 commodities (15 agricultural) Base period is 1985–90 Timeline: 1990–2002	30 percent reduction in nonagricultural tariffs, and a 30 percent reduction in agricultural input subsidies and supports	By 2002, in billions of 1992 dollars: World: 213 United States: 14.8 (0.2 percent of GDP)	Not calculated or not reported
Nguyen et al. (1991–93)	SALTER model Constant returns to scale in production Perfect competition	Agriculture: 30 percent reduction in all producer-subsidy equivalents; 40 percent reduction in all border measures (20	In billions of 1986 dollars: World: 212.2 (1.1 percent of GDP)	World: 20.2 percent

continued next page

Table B.1 Comparison of CGE models assessing the macroeconomic effects of Uruguay Round trade liberalization (continued)

Study	Model characteristics	Trade liberalization scenario	Welfare effects	Increase in real exports (percentages)
	Imperfect substitution between imports and domestic products in consumption Static gains only 10 countries and regions 9 commodity groups	for low-income regions) Elimination of MFA quotas Manufactures: 30 percent cut in tariffs; 40 percent reduction in nontariff barriers (for basic intermediates and high-technology goods, deeper cuts assumed) Services: 40 percent reduction in nontariff barriers	United States: 36.4 (0.8 percent of GDP)	Not calculated or not reported
Hufbauer and Elliott (1994)	Partial equilibrium model	Phaseout of MFA quotas and 12 percent reduction in tariffs Expiration of machine tool VRA Tariffication of agricultural quotas; tariff cuts assumed to be zero 5 percent tariff cut on frozen concentrated orange juice 34 percent tariff cut in 12 peak tariff sectors 34 percent tariff cut in all other manufacturing sectors	Assuming immediate implementation, in billions of 1990 dollars: United States: 32.8	

QRs = quantitative restrictions; MFA = Multi-Fiber Arrangement; VRA = voluntary restraint agreement

a. Results are reported for the version of the model that incorporates the investment-income linkage.
b. Incorporating the investment-income linkage, the national income effects are $512.1 billion for the world, $125.9 billion for the United States, $13.8 billion for Canada, $162.0 billion for the European Union, and $30.7 billion for Japan.
c. Incorporating the investment-income linkage, the national income effects are $477.2 billion for the world, $120.7 billion for the United States, $13.3 billion for Canada, $154.8 billion for the European Union, and $23.9 billion for Japan.

simply as technological change occurring in the industry driven by export expansion)—albeit in a comparative static framework. Hence it does not capture any dynamic growth effects of trade liberalization; rather, it captures only a one-time increase in exports and the resulting one-off externalities. The trade liberalization scenario is based on a 20 percent cut in agricultural production subsidies, a 36 percent cut in agricultural export subsidies, a phaseout of Multi-Fiber Arrangement (MFA) quotas on textiles and apparel, and tariff reductions that closely approximate those agreed upon in the Final Act of the Uruguay Round. Yang (1994) estimates that the world would gain about $116 billion annually in income by 2005 (in 1992 dollars), with $27 billion accruing to the United States and Canada.

However, the income gains to the world, and in particular to the United States, are likely to be understated. First, the commodity categories in the model are intended to represent the commodities that are of major interest to the East Asian economies: agriculture, mining, processed foods, textiles, clothing, iron and steel, transport equipment, machinery and equipment, other manufactures, and services. Moreover, since export expansion of more sophisticated manufactures presumably generates greater externalities, and since more open economies reap externalities more broadly, the United States should be expected to gain more than Yang projects. In addition, whereas Yang measures the effects of export externalities, he ignores similar externalities on the import side (e.g., increased competition of imported goods forcing domestic firms to improve their efficiency), as well as any cross-sectoral effects of export externalities.

One of the more widely quoted estimates of the likely gains from the Uruguay Round is a study published by the GATT (1993), which is also based on the GTAP model. It models trade liberalization resulting from the Uruguay Round as a 20 percent cut in agricultural production subsidies, a 36 percent cut in agricultural export subsidies and import protection measures, phaseout of the MFA quotas, and tariff reductions that reflect the market access offers as of 19 November 1993. The static gains to world income are projected to amount to $230 billion annually by 2005 (in 1992 dollars), with $67 billion accruing to the United States and Canada. The GATT study also projects that world merchandise trade would grow by 12.4 percent (or $745 billion, in 1992 dollars) by 2005 beyond what would occur without liberalization; for the United States and Canada, exports are estimated to grow by 8 percent.

Again, these results may understate the actual gains to be achieved as a result of Uruguay Round–mandated trade reform, given the high level of aggregation and a strong bias toward natural resource sectors. The 10 commodity categories used in the study are agriculture; mining; processed foods; textiles; clothing, footwear, and luggage; wood products; fuels and chemicals; metals; other manufactures; and services.

The study by Francois et al. (1994) is among the first to try to extend the analysis to include assumptions of imperfect competition and economies of scale, as well as a quasi-dynamic linkage between higher saving and investment induced by static efficiency gains (the investment-income linkage), in an effort to incorporate some measure of dynamic effects of trade liberalization into the GTAP model. The study assumes tariff reductions for industrial goods along the lines of the Uruguay Round Final Act, and elimination of the MFA quotas as well as of European automobile import restraints. In addition, it models two different scenarios for agricultural reforms, depending on whether countries try to minimize the impact on agriculture (the "moderate" scenario) or live up more fully to the spirit of the Uruguay Round agreements on agriculture (the "liberal" scenario).

As a result, the annual gain to world income is projected to amount to between $100 billion (with "moderate" agricultural effects) and $122.2 billion (with "liberal" agricultural effects) by 2005 (in 1992 dollars). When the assumptions of imperfect competition and scale economies and the investment-income linkage are incorporated, the projected annual gain to world income in 2005 is between $477 billion and $512 billion, respectively. For the United States, annual gains in 2005 would be $31 billion in an analysis assuming perfect competition, constant returns to scale, and "moderate" agricultural effects, and $126 billion in an analysis assuming imperfect competition, economies of scale, investment-income linkage, and "liberal" agricultural effects.

Although this study calculates the effects for 15 commodity groups, the composition of these groups is still strongly biased toward natural resources.[7] Moreover, the model only approximates the dynamic growth effects of trade liberalization by applying a rough multiplier to the static income gain (similar to Baldwin 1992) to derive the induced dynamic gains over the medium run. In other words, it does not project permanent changes in growth rates, but relates instead to changes in steady-state levels of income induced by extra saving.

A second group of studies derives from ongoing research at the World Bank and the OECD Development Centre, which jointly developed the Rural-Urban/North-South (RUNS) model. This model was originally developed to estimate the effects on the developing world of agricultural trade reform in the industrialized countries. Although the sectoral coverage was eventually expanded to include manufacturing sectors, the model is still heavily biased toward developing countries and the agricultural sector.

Goldin et al. (1993) used the RUNS model to measure the effects of a 30 percent tariff reduction, both for agriculture and for other merchandise

---

7. Product categories are other agriculture; mining, crudes, and minerals; manufactures, processed foods, and beverages; trade and transport services; other services; forestry products; fishery products; grains; textiles; clothing; chemicals and rubber; primary iron and steel; other primary metals; fabricated metal products; and transport equipment.

trade sectors, as well as a 30 percent reduction in agricultural input subsidies. The study calculated that the annual gain to world GDP would be $213 billion by 2002 (in 1992 dollars), while income gains to the United States would amount to about $15 billion—an increase in GDP of 0.2 percent over what would otherwise occur. However, the agricultural reforms it postulates—30 percent reductions in all agricultural tariffs and input subsidies—exceed by a substantial amount what the Uruguay Round actually achieved (for reasons detailed in the chapter on agriculture in this book).

Goldin et al. (1993) is an analysis mainly of the effects of liberalization in the agricultural sector; of the 22 sectors included, only 3 are industrial, one of which is fertilizers. In addition, the study does not attempt to calculate the effects of reductions in the level of nontariff barriers, which means that it excludes the elimination of textiles and apparel quotas under the MFA. The level of aggregation of the nonagricultural sectors, combined with the exclusion of nontariff barriers, means that the estimates of the gains from nonagricultural liberalization are almost certainly understated.[8]

Among the most widely quoted estimates of the gains from the Uruguay Round is a study by the OECD (1993a) that attempts to incorporate the gains from liberalization of nontariff barriers into the RUNS model. The study models a 36 percent reduction in all tariff and nontariff barriers for merchandise trade sectors, as well as a 36 percent reduction in agricultural tariffs and input subsidies. It calculates that the annual gain to world income would be $274 billion by 2002 (in 1992 dollars), of which $28 billion would accrue to the United States. This study generally suffers from the same limitations as Goldin et al. (1993), but it further understates the gains to be expected from the Uruguay Round because of its even higher level of aggregation: its model consists of only four broad commodity groups and seven countries and regions.

Nguyen et al. (1993) is the only study that does not seem to suffer from the same agricultural focus, although it still calculates gains at a very high level of aggregation.[9] Nguyen et al. analyze the liberalizations proposed in the draft agreement offered by GATT Director General Arthur Dunkel in December 1991; the authors use a computable equilibrium model that they first presented that same year. The draft agreement is represented

---

8. For example, Hufbauer and Elliott (1994) estimate that the consumer gains from immediate removal of all US textile and apparel quotas would be about $16 billion.

9. Its nine commodity groups are agriculture and food; basic intermediates (primary metals, textiles, wood products, chemicals); mining and resource extraction; light industries (apparel, furniture); forestry and fishing; automobiles and parts, and machinery and equipment; high-technology manufactures (pharmaceuticals, instruments, electrical machinery); intermediate manufactures (fixtures, electrical equipment, office supplies, printing and publishing); and nonfactor services.

in the model as a set of reductions in tariffs and tariff equivalents of nontariff barriers for all traded goods; for basic intermediates this reduction is assumed to be 50 percent; all other manufactures benefit from a 30 percent cut in tariffs and a 40 percent reduction in nontariff barriers. For agriculture and textile import quotas, reductions in producer subsidy equivalents are modeled. In the case of services, a rough estimate is made of the tariff equivalent of the nonborder barriers, and this is then reduced by 40 percent. As a result, world income is expected to rise by 1.1 percent, or $212 billion (in 1986 dollars) annually, while the United States gains about $36 billion, or 0.8 percent. In addition, world trade is projected to increase by 20 percent. The study generally goes beyond the level of trade reforms actually achieved and is based on a highly aggregated commodity composition—somewhat skewed toward natural resource–based economies—thereby understating the gains for most industrialized countries by a substantial amount. The volume of world trade is expected to increase by 20 percent.[10]

Partial Equilibrium Model Results

The results of CGE modeling contrast with those from the limited, but more detailed, partial equilibrium (PE) analysis of the impact of liberalization. PE modeling offers the advantage of being both relatively simple and transparent, and easily applicable to very detailed data. Its main shortcoming is that it does not take into account interactions between different sectors and markets and thereby misses critical economywide aspects of the Uruguay Round reforms.

Gary Clyde Hufbauer and Kimberly Ann Elliott, in an Institute for International Economics press release dated 11 January 1994, estimated the effects of trade liberalization under the Uruguay Round using a PE model that was originally developed to measure the cost of protection for 21 sectors in the United States that were highly protected in 1990. They concluded that immediate implementation of liberalization agreed to in the Uruguay Round would result in gains of about $32.8 billion for US consumers, reducing the consumer costs of current US protection by almost one-half, from $70.3 billion (in 1990 dollars).

---

10. In an unpublished revision of their results, Nguyen et al. substantially lowered their estimates of the outcome in the agriculture and textile sections, and reported a large drop in the global welfare effects of the Uruguay Round accords from $212 billion to $70 billion.

References

Acheson, Keith, and Christopher Maule. Forthcoming. "Copyrights and Related Rights: The International Dimension." *Canadian Journal of Communications.*

Baldwin, Richard. 1992. "Measurable Dynamic Gains from Trade." *Journal of Political Economy* 100, no. 1: 162–74.

Bayard, Thomas O., and Kimberly Ann Elliott. 1994. *Reciprocity and Retaliation in U.S. Trade Policy.* Washington: Institute for International Economics.

Bergsten, C. Fred, and Edward M. Graham. Forthcoming. *The Globalization of Industry and National Governments.* Washington: Institute for International Economics.

Brandão, A., and W. Martin. 1993. *Implications of Agricultural Trade Liberalization for the Developing Countries.* World Bank Working Papers WPS 1116. Washington: World Bank.

Cline, William R. 1990. *The Future of World Trade in Textiles and Apparel,* rev. ed. Washington: Institute for International Economics.

Cline, William R. 1993. "Impact of the Uruguay Round on Textiles and Apparel." Washington: Institute for International Economics (processed).

Deardorff, Alan V., and Robert M. Stern. 1990. *Computational Analysis of Global Trading Arrangements.* Ann Arbor: University of Michigan Press.

Deloitte Touche Tohmatsu International. 1994. *Study of Public Procurement Opportunities: European Union–Government of the United States.* Houston: Deloitte & Touche (22 March).

Destler, I. M. Forthcoming. *American Trade Politics,* 3rd ed. Washington: Institute for International Economics.

DRI/McGraw-Hill. 1993. *Impacts of Trade Liberalization Under the Uruguay Round.* Washington: DRI/McGraw-Hill.

Finger, J. Michael, and K. C. Fung. 1993. *Will GATT Enforcement Control Antidumping?* Policy Research Working Papers 1232. Washington: World Bank.

Francois, Joseph F., Bradley McDonald, and Håkan Nordström. 1994. *The Uruguay Round: A Global General Equilibrium Assessment.* Geneva: GATT Secretariat (12 July).

General Agreement on Tariffs and Trade. 1993a. *International Trade and the Trading System: Report by the Director General, 1992–1993.* Geneva: GATT Secretariat (July).

General Agreement on Tariffs and Trade. 1993b. *International Trade Statistics.* Geneva: GATT Secretariat.

General Agreement on Tariffs and Trade. 1993c. *Economy-wide Effects of the Uruguay Round.* GATT Background Papers. Geneva: GATT Secretariat (3 December).

General Agreement on Tariffs and Trade. 1994. "Annexes to Appendix 1 of the Agreement on Government Procurement." Geneva: GATT Secretariat (6 January).

Goldin, Ian, and Dominique van der Mensbrugghe. 1992. *Trade Liberalization: What's At Stake?* OECD Development Centre Policy Briefs 5. Paris: Organization for Economic Cooperation and Development.

Goldin, Ian, Odin Knudsen, and Dominique van der Mensbrugghe. 1993. *Trade Liberalization: Global Economic Implications.* Paris: OECD Development Centre and World Bank.

Goldin, Ian, Odin Knudsen, and Antonio S. Brandão. 1994. *Modelling Economy-wide Reforms.* Paris: OECD Development Centre.

Hertel, T., and M. Tsigas. 1993. "GTAP Model Documentation." In *Shortcourse in Global Trade Analysis.* West Lafayette, IN: Purdue University (processed).

Hoda, A. 1994. "Trade Liberalization Results of the Uruguay Round." Paper presented at the OECD Workshop on the New World Trading System, Paris (25–26 April).

Hudec, Robert E. 1994. "Dispute Settlement." Paper presented at the OECD Workshop on the New World Trading System, Paris (25–26 April).

Hufbauer, Gary Clyde, and Kimberly Ann Elliott. 1994. *Measuring the Costs of Protection in the United States.* Washington: Institute for International Economics.

Hufbauer, Gary Clyde, and Joanna Shelton Erb. 1984. *Subsidies in International Trade.* Washington: Institute for International Economics.

Hufbauer, Gary Clyde, and Jeffrey J. Schott. 1993. *NAFTA: An Assessment,* rev. ed. Washington: Institute for International Economics.

Industry Sector Advisory Committee on Services for Trade Policy Matters (ISAC-13). 1994. *Report of the Industry Sector Advisory Committee on Services for Trade Policy Matters (ISAC 13) on the Uruguay Round Multilateral Trade Agreements* (15 January).

Jackson, John H. 1990. *Restructuring the GATT System.* New York: Council on Foreign Relations Press.

Jackson, John H. 1994. "Managing the Trading System: The World Trade Organization and the Post–Uruguay Round GATT Agenda." In Peter B. Kenen ed., *Managing the World Economy: Fifty Years after Bretton Woods.* Washington: Institute for International Economics.

Josling, Tim E., et al. 1994. *The Uruguay Round Agreement on Agriculture: An Evaluation.* International Agricultural Trade Research Consortium Papers 9 (July, processed).

Kenen, Peter B., ed. 1994. *Managing the World Economy: Fifty Years after Bretton Woods.* Washington: Institute for International Economics.

Leutwiler, Fritz, et al. 1985. *Trade Policies for a Better Future: Proposals for Action.* Geneva: GATT.

Messerlin, Patrick A. 1990. *Antidumping Regulation or Procartel Law?* PRE Working Papers 397. Washington: World Bank (April).

Nguyen, Trien T., Carlo Perroni, and Randall M. Wigle. 1993. *An Evaluation of the Draft Final Act of the Uruguay Round.* Working Paper. Wilfrid Laurier University (May).

Organization for Economic Cooperation and Development. 1993a. *Assessing the Effects of the Uruguay Round.* Paris: Organization for Economic Cooperation and Development.

Organization for Economic Cooperation and Development. 1993b. *Main Developments in Trade 1993.* Paris: Organization for Economic Cooperation and Development.

Sanderson, Fred H. 1994. *The GATT Agreement on Agriculture.* Discussion Paper Series. Washington: National Center for Food and Agricultural Policy.

Schott, Jeffrey J., ed. 1990. *Completing the Uruguay Round: A Results-Oriented Approach to the GATT Trade Negotiations.* Washington: Institute for International Economics.

Stoeckel, Andrew, David Pierce, and Gary Banks. 1990. *Western Trade Blocs: Game, Set or Match for Asia-Pacific and the World Economy?* Canberra: Centre for International Economics.

Trela, I., and J. Whalley. 1990. "Unravelling the Threads of the MFA." In C. B. Hamilton, *The Uruguay Round Textiles, Trade and the Developing Countries.* Washington: World Bank.

US Department of Commerce, International Trade Administration. 1994. "Uruguay Round: Opportunities for U.S. Industries." Washington: International Trade Administration (June, processed).

US Department of Commerce. 1994. *US Jobs Supported by Merchandise Exports*. Washington: US Department of Commerce (forthcoming).

US Department of State. 1994. "Fact Sheet: US-EU Procurement Agreement." Washington: US Department of Commerce (April, processed).

US Department of the Treasury, Office of Tax Analysis. 1983. *1981 DISC Annual Report*. Washington: US Department of the Treasury.

US House of Representatives. 1994. *Uruguay Round Trade Agreements, Texts of Agreements Implementing Bill, Statement of Administrative Action, and Required Supporting Statements*. House Document 103-316, vols. 1 and 2. Washington: Government Printing Office (27 September).

US International Trade Commission. 1994. *Potential Impact on the US Economy and Industries of the GATT Uruguay Round Agreements*. Publication no. 2790. Washington: US International Trade Commission.

US Trade Representative. 1990. "USTR/CEA Estimate of Possible Ten-Year Gains (1991–2000) to US GNP From a One-Third Cut in Global Tariff and Nontariff Barriers." Memorandum. Washington: Office of the US Trade Representative (October).

Yang, Y. 1994. "Trade Liberalization with Externalities: A General Equilibrium Assessment of the Uruguay Round." Paper presented at a conference on Challenges and Opportunities for East Asian Trade, Australian National University, Canberra (13–14 July).

Index

Peak tariffs, 58, 60, 62, 152
Peanuts, 52
Performance requirements, 113
Performances, provisions in TRIPs agreement for, 116, 168
Permanent Group of Experts (PGE), 88, 158
Pharmaceuticals, 62, 118, 120, 168
Phytosanitary measures, 34, 52–53, 111, 181
Plastics, 30
Plurilateral agreements, 66, 134, 173
Pollution control subsidies, 90, 159
Poultry, 48
Price averaging in antidumping procedures, 80, 155, 188
Price undertakings, 83, 93, 156, 189
Professional and scientific instruments, 30
Professional services, 102, 108
"Protection balance sheet," 142
Provisional application of GATT, 136
Public utilities, 66, 68–71, 74, 75, 154
Punta del Este Declaration, 3, 5, 9, 44, 112

Quad group, 7, 62, 139
Quotas
    in agriculture, 51–52
    minimum access, 46, 51–52, 148
    tariff-rate, 51, 52, 58, 180
    in textiles, 55–56, 150–51

Regional subsidies, 90, 159
Regional trading arrangements, 5, 20, 103, 139
Rental rights, 116, 168
Research and development (R&D) subsidies, 89–90, 158
Retaliation
    country rights under WTO to, 15
    cross-sector, 109–11, 171
    under DSU, 128–31, 171
    under safeguards agreement, 97
    under Section 301, 14, 130–31
Rice, 48, 49, 50, 51–52, 148
Rome Convention, 116, 117
Rules of origin, 183
Rural-Urban/North-South (RUNS) model, 206–07
Russia, 139

Safeguards
    in agriculture agreement, 50–51, 148
    Article XVIII (balance of payments), 94, 103, 163
    EU and US use of, 94, 95, 98
    in GATS, 103, 110
    in subsidies agreement, 91
    in textiles agreement, 57–58, 150–51
    use by and against developing countries of, 94, 96, 97, 163
Safeguards, Uruguay Round agreement on
    assessment of, 12, 98, 163
    conditions of use in, 95

emergency safeguards in, 103
MFN application in, 95, 162
requirements for domestic industry adjustment in, 97
retaliation and compensation rights in, 97
"serious injury" defined in, 96, 162
time limits in, 96–97, 162
transparency in, 103
US legislation implementing, 192
VERs in, 94, 96, 162
Sales-below-cost test, 81, 155, 188
Sanitary and phytosanitary measures, 34, 52–53, 111, 181
Schott, Jeffrey J., 4, 8
Scientific instruments, 30
Scorecard on Uruguay Round results, 8
Secretariat of WTO, 137, 173
Section 301, 14, 130–31, 195
Section 303, 192
Semiconductors, 119
"Serious injury," 96, 162
"Serious prejudice," 89, 92
Service marks, 118
Services
    future negotiations on, 99, 100, 109–10
    in GPA, 67, 154
    growth of global and US trade in, 99
    in NAFTA, 101, 102
    See also names of services
Services, Uruguay Round agreement on. See General Agreement on Trade in Services (GATS)
Set-asides, minority and small business, 74, 75, 183
"Single undertaking" in WTO Agreement, 15, 133–34
Snape, Richard, 102
"Social dumping," 37
Software, 116, 168
Sound recordings, 116, 168
Sovereignty issues, 15–16, 196
Soviet Union, former, 139
Special and differential treatment, 4, 159
Special 301, 195
Staffing needs of WTO, 126, 137, 142
Standard of review in antidumping, 34, 83, 156
Standards, 52–53, 102
Standing to file antidumping petitions, 82, 155, 188–89
Standstill provisions in GATS, 100
State and local governments. See Subcentral governments
Statement of Administrative Action, 179, 184, 193, 196
Startup costs, accounting in antidumping procedures for, 81, 155, 187–88
Steel, 62
Subcentral governments, 66–68, 69, 71, 74–75, 154, 196–97

Subsidies, Uruguay Round agreement on
actionable subsidies under, 88–89, 158–59
assessment of, 12, 93, 160–61
continuing negotiations on, 34
countervailing measures in, 92–93, 160
definition of subsidy in, 86–87, 158
de minimis rule in, 92
dispute settlement in, 88
GATS and, 104, 110
green box (green-light) subsidies in, 46, 49,
53, 147, 191–92
improvements on Tokyo Round code in, 86
monitoring of eligible subsidies in, 91
nonactionable subsidies under, 89–91
price undertakings in, 93
prohibited subsidies under, 87–88, 158
provisions for developing countries and
economies in transition in, 12, 91–92,
159–60
"serious prejudice" in, 92
specificity test in, 87
sunset provision in, 93, 160
US legislation implementing, 191–92
See also names of subsidies
Sugar, 52
Sunset provisions, 83, 93, 156, 160, 189–90
Super 301, 196
Suspension agreements, 93, 189
Sutherland, Peter, 7

Taiwan, 58
Tariff-rate quotas, 51, 52, 58, 180
Tariffs
in agriculture agreement, 44, 49, 148
lost revenue from cuts in, 32
in textiles agreement, 58, 61
Tariffs, Uruguay Round agreement on
ad hoc approach in negotiation of, 60
assessment of, 11, 65–65, 153
average tariff cuts in, 11, 25, 61–62
duty-free trade in, 63, 152
harmonization of tariffs in, 63–65, 152, 185
implications for US trade of, 19–33, 61–63,
152–53, 201–08
peak, 62, 152
provisions against escalation in, 63, 152
tariff bindings in, 11, 50, 62–64, 152
US legislation implementing, 184–85
zero-for-zero commitments in, 61–62, 152
See also names of products
Tariff bindings, 11, 50, 62–64, 152
Tariffication, 10, 45, 49–50, 148
Telecommunications, 73–75, 101, 105–06, 108,
110, 165, 193
Textiles and apparel, Uruguay Round
agreement on
assessment of, 11, 59, 151
average cuts in tariffs under, 58, 61
estimates of effects of, 32
implications for United States of, 58–59

peak tariffs in, 58
phaseout of MFA quotas in, 55–56, 150–51
safeguards in, 57–58
transition period in, 11, 55–59, 150
treatment of developing countries in, 56, 58
US legislation implementing, 183
Textiles Monitoring Body, 57, 150, 182
Tobacco, 63, 180
Tokyo Round, 4, 60, 86, 91, 94
Tourism, 109, 110
Toys, 62
Trade Agreements Act of 1979, 183, 184
Trademarks, 118, 122, 169 , 194
Trade policy review mechanism, 16, 96, 137,
141–43, 175
Trade-related aspects of intellectual property
rights (TRIPs), Uruguay Round agreement
on
assessment of, 13, 122–23, 170
compulsory licensing in, 118, 169
developing countries' position on, 115
dispute settlement in, 121
provisions for developing and transition
economies in, 120, 170
transition periods in, 116, 118, 120, 122
US legislation implementing, 193–94
See also names of intellectual property types
Trade-related investment measures (TRIMs),
Uruguay Round agreement on
assessment of, 14, 167
developing countries' opposition to, 112
dispute settlement in, 113
compared with NAFTA, 101, 112
national treatment in, 112, 113
rules on quantitative restrictions in, 113
transition period for developing countries in,
113
US legislation implementing, 193
See also names of investment measures
Trade secrets, 120, 169
Transition orders, 190
Transition periods
for developing countries, 113, 120
in textiles agreement, 11, 55–59, 150, 182
in TRIMs agreement, 113
in TRIPs agreement, 116, 118, 120, 122
Transparency, 76, 103, 141, 195–96
Transport equipment, 61
Transport services, 105, 106, 110, 165
Travel and tourism, 109, 110
Treaty on Intellectual Property in Respect of
Integrated Circuits, 116
TRIPs Council (Council for Trade-Related
Aspects of Intellectual Property Rights),
119, 121
Tsigas, M., 201

Understanding on Financial Services, 108
Unions, 82

Other Publications from the
Institute for International Economics

POLICY ANALYSES IN INTERNATIONAL ECONOMICS Series

1 The Lending Policies of the International Monetary Fund
   John Williamson/*August 1982*
                   ISBN paper 0-88132-000-5   72 pp.

2 "Reciprocity": A New Approach to World Trade Policy?
   William R. Cline/*September 1982*
                   ISBN paper 0-88132-001-3   41 pp.

3 Trade Policy in the 1980s
   C. Fred Bergsten and William R. Cline/*November 1982*
   (out of print)   ISBN paper 0-88132-002-1   84 pp.
   Partially reproduced in the book *Trade Policy in the 1980s.*

4 International Debt and the Stability of the World Economy
   William R. Cline/*September 1983*
                   ISBN paper 0-88132-010-2   134 pp.

5 The Exchange Rate System, Second Edition
   John Williamson/*September 1983, rev. June 1985*
   (out of print)   ISBN paper 0-88132-034-X   61 pp.

6 Economic Sanctions in Support of Foreign Policy Goals
   Gary Clyde Hufbauer and Jeffrey J. Schott/*October 1983*
                   ISBN paper 0-88132-014-5   109 pp.

7 A New SDR Allocation?
   John Williamson/*March 1984*
                   ISBN paper 0-88132-028-5   61 pp.

8 An International Standard for Monetary Stabilization
   Ronald I. McKinnon/*March 1984*
                   ISBN paper 0-88132-018-8   108 pp.

9 The Yen/Dollar Agreement: Liberalizing Japanese Capital Markets
   Jeffrey A. Frankel/*December 1984*
                   ISBN paper 0-88132-035-8   86 pp.

10 Bank Lending to Developing Countries: The Policy Alternatives
   C. Fred Bergsten, William R. Cline, and John Williamson/*April 1985*
                   ISBN paper 0-88132-032-3   221 pp.

11 Trading for Growth: The Next Round of Trade Negotiations
   Gary Clyde Hufbauer and Jeffrey J. Schott/*September 1985*
                   ISBN paper 0-88132-033-1   109 pp.

12 Financial Intermediation Beyond the Debt Crisis
   Donald R. Lessard and John Williamson/*September 1985*
                   ISBN paper 0-88132-021-8   130 pp.

13 The United States-Japan Economic Problem
   C. Fred Bergsten and William R. Cline/*October 1985, 2d ed. January 1987*
   (out of print)   ISBN paper 0-88132-060-9   180 pp.

BOOKS

Currencies and Politics in the United States, Germany, and Japan
C. Randall Henning/*September 1994*
                    ISBN paper 0-88132-127-3   432 pp.

Estimating Equilibrium Exchange Rates
John Williamson, editor/*September 1994*
                    ISBN paper 0-88132-076-5   320 pp.

Managing the World Economy: Fifty Years After Bretton Woods
Peter B. Kenen, editor/*September 1994*
                    ISBN paper 0-88132-212-1   448 pp.

Reciprocity and Retaliation in U.S. Trade Policy
Thomas O. Bayard and Kimberly Ann Elliott/*September 1994*
                    ISBN paper 0-88132-084-6   528 pp.

The Uruguay Round: An Assessment
Jeffrey J. Schott, assisted by Johanna W. Buurman/*November 1994*
                    ISBN paper 0-88132-206-7   240 pp.

SPECIAL REPORTS

1 Promoting World Recovery: A Statement on Global Economic Strategy
   by Twenty-six Economists from Fourteen Countries/*December 1982*
   (out of print)   ISBN paper 0-88132-013-7   45 pp.

2 Prospects for Adjustment in Argentina, Brazil, and Mexico:
   Responding to the Debt Crisis
   John Williamson, editor/*June 1983*
   (out of print)   ISBN paper 0-88132-016-1   71 pp.

3 Inflation and Indexation: Argentina, Brazil, and Israel
   John Williamson, editor/*March 1985*
                    ISBN paper 0-88132-037-4   191 pp.

4 Global Economic Imbalances
   C. Fred Bergsten, editor/*March 1986*
                    ISBN cloth 0-88132-038-2   126 pp.
                    ISBN paper 0-88132-042-0   126 pp.

5 African Debt and Financing
   Carol Lancaster and John Williamson, editors/*May 1986*
   (out of print)   ISBN paper 0-88132-044-7   229 pp.

6 Resolving the Global Economic Crisis: After Wall Street
   Thirty-three Economists from Thirteen Countries/*December 1987*
                    ISBN paper 0-88132-070-6   30 pp.

7 World Economic Problems
   Kimberly Ann Elliott and John Williamson, editors/*April 1988*
                    ISBN paper 0-88132-055-2   298 pp.

   Reforming World Agricultural Trade
   Twenty-nine Professionals from Seventeen Countries/*1988*
                    ISBN paper 0-88132-088-9   42 pp.

8 Economic Relations Between the United States and Korea:
   Conflict or Cooperation?
   Thomas O. Bayard and Soo-Gil Young, editors/*January 1989*
                    ISBN paper 0-88132-068-4   192 pp.

FORTHCOMING

The Globalization of Industry and National Governments
C. Fred Bergsten and Edward M. Graham

The Political Economy of Korea–United States Cooperation
C. Fred Bergsten and Il SaKong, editors

International Debt Reexamined
William R. Cline

Trade, Jobs, and Income Distribution
William R. Cline

Overseeing Global Capital Markets
Morris Goldstein and Peter Garber

Foreign Direct Investment in the United States, Third Edition
Edward M. Graham and Paul R. Krugman

Global Competition Policy
Edward M. Graham and J. David Richardson

Toward a Pacific Economic Community?
Gary Clyde Hufbauer and Jeffrey J. Schott

Measuring the Costs of Protection in Japan
Yoko Sazanami, Shujiro Urata, and Hiroki Kawai

The Case for Trade: A Modern Reconsideration
J. David Richardson

The Future of the World Trading System
John Whalley, in collaboration with Colleen Hamilton

For orders outside the US and Canada please contact:

Longman Group UK Ltd.
PO Box 88
Fourth Avenue
Harlow, Essex CM 19 5SR
UK

Telephone Orders: 0279 623923
Fax: 0279 453450
Telex: 81259

Canadian customers can order from the Institute or from either:

RENOUF BOOKSTORE
1294 Algoma Road
Ottawa, Ontario K1B 3W8
Telephone: (613) 741-4333
Fax: (613) 741-5439

LA LIBERTÉ
3020 chemin Sainte-Foy
Quebec G1X 3V6
Telephone: (418) 658-3763
Fax: (800) 567-5449